D1496407

Bossism and Reform in a Southern City

Bossism and

Reform in a Southern City

Lexington, Kentucky
1880–1940

James Duane Bolin

THE UNIVERSITY PRESS OF KENTUCKY

Publication of this volume was made possible in part
by a grant from the National Endowment for the Humanities.

Scholarly publisher for the Commonwealth,
serving Bellarmine College, Berea College, Centre
College of Kentucky, Eastern Kentucky University,
The Filson Club Historical Society, Georgetown College,
Kentucky Historical Society, Kentucky State University,
Morehead State University, Murray State University,
Northern Kentucky University, Transylvania University,
University of Kentucky, University of Louisville,
and Western Kentucky University.
All rights reserved.

Editorial and Sales Offices: The University Press of Kentucky
663 South Limestone Street, Lexington, Kentucky 40508–4008

04 03 02 01 00   5 4 3 2 1

Frontispiece: Photo of Lexington, Kentucky's Main Street in 1915,
with pedestrians, electric streetcars, and motorized vehicles vying for
room. (UK Special Collections)

Library of Congress Cataloging-in-Publication Data

Bolin, James Duane, 1955-
    Bossism and reform in a southern city : Lexington, Kentucky,
  1880-1940 / James Duane Bolin
       p.   cm.
    Includes bibliographical references (p.) and index.
    ISBN 0-8131-2150-7 (cloth : alk. paper)
    1. Lexington (Ky.)—Politics and government.   2. Political cor-
  ruption—Kentucky—Lexington—History.   I. Title.
  F459.L6 B65 2000
  976.9'47—dc21   99-049405

This book is printed on acid-free recycled paper
meeting the requirements of the American National Standard
for Permanence of Paper for Printed Library Materials.

∞ ✿

Manufactured in the United States of America

For Evelyn Seaton Bolin

Contents

Illustrations follow page 110

Acknowledgments

This work on bossism and reform in a southern city would never have been completed without a personal cadre of bosses (family members, mentors, editors, outside readers, colleagues, and friends), ward lieutenants (librarians, archivists, and graduate students), precinct captains (students, secretaries, and passers-by patient enough to listen to my fascination with the topic), and reformers (family members, mentors, editors, outside readers, colleagues, and friends).

It was my mentor, Humbert S. Nelli, who first told me—in his Urban History course—about a Lexington character named Billy Klair. In the years since that introduction Dr. Nelli has served as my teacher, mentor, and friend. Even before Dr. Nelli, I had the good fortune of having a high school teacher, Hugh Ridenour, whose love for the discipline of history was contagious. My friend, mentor, and colleague Kenneth M. Startup provided constant scholarly and spiritual inspiration and support. My chair and deans at the Department of History and the College of Humanistic Studies at Murray State University—James W. Hammack, Joseph Cartwright, and Ken Wolf—afforded a trinity of encouragement and support. Other Department of History colleagues—B. Anthony Gannon, Charlotte Beahan, Bill Mulligan, T. Wayne Beasley, Ted Franklin Belue, Joseph Fuhrmann, Terry Strieter, Bill Schell, Abbanik Hino, Marcia Vaughan, Stephanie Carpenter, James Galt-Brown, Lesley Gordon, and our department secretary, Kay Hays—inspired and encouraged me, and provided a pleasant, collegial environment in which to work. I would also like to thank John Rall for his encouragement and support. Colleagues at other institutions, like Judith Rhoads, Brenda Saunders, and Jerry Gibbens, did the same. Murray State University, as a member of the consortium that makes up the University Press of Kentucky, supported the project. I am grateful to administrative leaders—Kern Alexander, the president, and Gary Brockway, the provost—at Murray State for their support.

My friend Thomas H. Appleton Jr. provided a model of professional and friendly support. Paul Fuller, Roger Lotchin, and John D. Wright Jr. encouraged me in the early and later stages of the project and offered invaluable suggestions that improved the work.

I would like to thank Lisa Carter at Special Collections, University of Kentucky, Robin Rader, and Leah Thomas at the Lexington-Fayette County Public Library, Mary Winter at the Kentucky Historical Society, Ron Garrison at the *Lexington Herald-Leader*, B.J. Gooch at Special Collections, Transylvania University, Marjorie R. Scott, and Wynelle Deese for help in securing appropriate photographs. My friend Chuck Perry is responsible for the author's photograph on the book's jacket.

My students at Madisonville Community College, Williams Baptist College, and Murray State University must be commended for their endurance in listening to stories about a boss and a political machine not found in the indices of their textbooks.

Friends like Janice and Phil Gibson and Jill and Bill Shoulta gave moral support and perspective. Finally, and especially, I want to thank my family— James Wesley and Cammie Mann Bolin, my dear father and mother, who endured for years talk of an exotic character in a central Kentucky city; a brother and his family, whose love was evident; and a group of in-laws who made life a joy. My precious children, Wesley and Cammie Jo, sacrificed reading and family playtime because their daddy was "working on Billy Klair." And then there is Evelyn, who did everything else. For this, the book—for better or worse—is dedicated to her.

Prologue

The diminutive, bespectacled, balding figure emerged from the side entrance of his substantial two-story, brick home on the corner of Georgetown and Short Streets on Lexington's west side. The house bespoke solidity and was not unlike other stately residences in the tradition-rich inner-Bluegrass city.

It was a Sunday morning in the spring of 1926, and the aging, but still sprightly, political boss could not help noticing the changes that had come to the city since his childhood. He looked across Georgetown Street toward the Henry Clay memorial in Lexington Cemetery and toward the adjacent Calvary Cemetery, where many of his Catholic relatives and friends rested. Nearby were the rows of "shotgun" houses that had once been home to large numbers of Lexington's Irish population. William Frederick Klair was at home.

Georgetown Street itself—running north past the Klair residence toward the Eastern Kentucky Hospital for the Insane, an institution that had benefitted from Congressman Klair's influence and support—had been laden for a decade with streetcar tracks. It had become increasingly crowded of late with pedestrians, electric streetcars, and more recently with motor cars and busses. Now, on this Sunday morning, it would be a few more hours before most of the Lexington faithful would make their ways to their respective houses of worship. Klair appreciated this rare daylit moment when the street was silent.

The boss reflected for only a moment, then adjusted his bow tie, lit his morning cigar, ambled toward the corner to Short Street, turned right, and then walked briskly toward the city's core. Klair's quick pace was familiar to Lexington's residents. Indeed, elderly Lexingtonians remembered a seven-year-old Klair outrunning his newsboy competitors to reach paying customers on the city's more lucrative street corners. Now the older Klair hurried still—toward his office for the meeting of his "Sunday School," a weekly gathering with members of the police force, political cronies, and ward-heelers.

Not wishing to neglect his religious duties, Klair crossed Short at Jefferson Street, discarded his cigar, proceeded across the Jefferson Street electric tracks to the opposite corner, and then on a few steps more to St. Paul's Catholic Church. As he entered the church for early mass, he glanced at the impressive church clock, the city's only "turret clock," embedded in the tower high above the center double doors at the front of the formidable structure.

St. Paul's was important to Klair. He had attended its parochial school as a boy, and as a young, upstart politician he had leaned on its German and Irish congregation for political support. Although no longer as dependent on the church's ethnic membership for his political base, he was nonetheless cognizant of the spiritual sustenance that only the church could provide. Within the walls of St. Paul's, Klair was at home. For the young Klair, St. Paul's had been in the eye of his political storms; now the mature Klair was thankful for the haven that it provided.

After mass, Klair followed other communicants outside. He smiled and acknowledged greetings of "Mornin', Billy," and "Good to see you, Billy." Despite his political prominence, or perhaps because of it, Klair had encouraged friends and acquaintances to "just call me Billy." It was his identification with his constituents, along with his provision of services for them, that proved to be the source of his appeal, the bedrock of his power.

Klair now continued his journey eastward along Short Street. The massive, Richardsonian Romanesque courthouse loomed ahead, but that was not the boss's destination. Instead, he ducked into the Security Trust Building, completed in 1905 as the city's first skyscraper, and took the elevator to his sixth-floor office. Klair shed his jacket, lit a fresh cigar, positioned himself behind his desk, glanced at some papers on the cluttered desktop, and waited for "the boys" to arrive.

There were plans to make, assignments to distribute, deals to cut, jobs to give, votes to secure. Undaunted at the work to be done, Billy Klair smiled to himself. He was at home.

This apocryphal "morning in the life of Billy Klair" was written after years of trying to understand Klair and his political success in a southern city. The goal was to try to highlight Klair's political base and to emphasize his "good old boy" relationships with those that insured his longevity in Lexington politics.

The portrait is based on research in Lexington newspapers, in the paper collections of local and state politicians, and on interviews with those Lexingtonians and Kentuckians who remembered Klair and his storied political machine.

Yet this attempt at historical fiction came crashing down with a conversation in 1995 with Joe Scott, the son of Klair's insurance partner, Thomas Scott. I offhandedly asked about Klair's walk down Short Street to his office each morning. Scott replied: "Oh, a car always came for Billy. He didn't walk to work."[1] The car, a dark green Lincoln, picked the boss up at his Georgetown Street residence and delivered him to the front door of the Security Trust Building.

Still, I continue to believe that truth remains in this flight of fancy into historical fiction. Klair had a way with poor Lexingtonians. He also had a way with the middle class and with wealthy members of the Bluegrass elite. His encouragement for others to "just call me Billy" was coupled with morning limousine rides to a downtown office. The combination of Klair's appeal to poor and wealthy alike was the secret to his success and long-held place in politics, a combination that also holds the key to an understanding of southern urban bossism and reform.

The life of William Frederick "Billy" Klair spanned a period of dynamic growth and change for the southern city of Lexington, Kentucky. In the years between Klair's birth in 1875 and death in 1937, Lexington grew from a sleepy market town with a population of 16,656—according to the 1880 census—into a bustling, thriving city; the first census after Klair's death—the 1940 count—fixed the city's population at 49,304. As the city was tripling in population, Klair witnessed a multiplicity of other changes as well, profound changes that transformed not only Lexington, but the nation and the world: urbanization, industrialization, immigration; attempts by progressive reformers to deal with the changes wrought by such movements; America's involvement in a world war "to make the world safe for democracy"; the "roaring twenties"; the Great Depression. Klair witnessed these events firsthand.

Klair, however, was more than a witness to the city's transformation. He transformed it himself. As a political boss, as a practitioner of what George Washington Plunkitt referred to as "honest graft," as a behind-the-scenes organizer and political leader, Klair applied lessons from the machine age, lessons of organization, innovation, manipulation, power, and control, to transform diverse groups of Lexingtonians and Kentuckians into supporters—albeit often reluctant or unaware supporters—of a powerful political machine.[2]

Symbolic of the plethora of changes in Lexington during the last two decades of the nineteenth century and the first four decades of the twentieth were the various innovations in the city's transportation system. In this, as in other changes that came to Lexington, Klair was a central figure, serving as president of the Yellow Cab & Transfer Company and as a member on the board of the Home Construction Company, the concern that paved most of the city's streets. But as the horse and wagon gave way to a succession of mule cars, electric streetcars, and eventually motor cars and busses, and as the city's population, aided by these transportation innovations, spread out amoeba-like from the core of the old walking city, one characteristic of Billy Klair's Lexington did not change. Throughout this period local government and the city's politics were influenced—more often than not, dominated—by machine rule. Just as the city's infrastructure of tracks and streets held the physical city together, Klair's machine brought order of a kind. And just as Lexington's transit system provided a needed service for Lexingtonians, so did Billy Klair. The influence and significance of Lexington's Democratic machine during Klair's lifetime was unchanging in a city of change.

This is not to say that Lexington's local government structure remained the same. From a mayor-council system in the early 1800s, Lexington's charter was changed to a complicated mayor-council-aldermen setup that lasted from the late 1880s to 1912. In 1912 the city's electorate adopted a commission plan of city government, only to discard that form for a city manager format in 1931. But just as the changes from mules to motors in the city's transportation system continued to follow well-worn paths from the city's center, Lexington's government, while changing in form, rarely strayed from the domineering manipulations of a powerful political boss. Changing government structures were coupled with unchanging political realities.

Throughout Kentucky, powerful organizations and political machines dominated the political landscape. Machines flourished in the state's three largest cities—Louisville, Covington, and Lexington—and in Frankfort, the state's capital. These operations and the individuals who led them have been neglected by historians. In Louisville, after John and James Whallen had established the "green room" of the Buckingham Theater as "the hub of local Democratic politics," Michael Joseph "Mickey" Brennan—himself "coached" by the Whallen brothers—soon became "the unchallenged leader of the Democratic party" in that city. In Covington, Republican Maurice L. Galvin, not reluctant to work with Democrats in the state, used his organizational skills to "become one of the chief political bosses in the state bipartisan combine."

Percy Haly, a Democrat, fashioned from his base in Frankfort a statewide political machine of his own that often dominated Kentucky politics.[3] After referring to politics as "the most primal force in Kentucky" in his book *Hard Times and New Deal in Kentucky, 1929–1939*, George T. Blakey failed to discuss local politics at all, although powerful local politicians often determined state actions.[4]

Indeed, little has been written about Kentucky's best example of what Plunkitt of Tammany Hall would consider to be a "true" boss. From his base in Lexington, Billy Klair was recognized as the "undisputed czar" of Lexington politics and eventually established statewide power and influence. Boss Klair became King Klair, and this book is about him.

This book is also about Klair's Lexington, a city that has been ignored by historians.[5] Except for John D. Wright Jr.'s *Lexington: Heart of the Bluegrass*, a handsome pictorial study, this important western and southern city has been neglected. Such negligence is owing perhaps to the desire to perpetuate the "myth" of Lexington, that Lexington's prosperity and continued growth in size and reputation are a continuation of its glorious past as the Athens of the West and as the Queen City of the Bluegrass. Accounts of the popular view of Lexington's continuous progress have perpetuated the myth and failed to recognize the underside of Lexington's past. A serious study of Lexington politics undermines this popular myth, revealing a side of Lexington that has been neglected—perhaps purposefully—in the past. The picture postcard view of elegant mansions, of well-bred horses prancing on beautiful Bluegrass farms owned by well-heeled Lexingtonians, must be balanced with a reckoning with the city's well-known vice district, housing problems, racial tensions, and corrupt politics.

Dennis Mulligan, an Irish grocer and politician, introduced Lexingtonians to machine politics—at least on the ward level—in the period following the Civil War. As his influence waned in the last two decades of the century, another more adept politician took his place. Billy Klair's influence as the head of the city's Democratic organization was legendary. However, the legend is fading, and as the legend of Billy Klair fades, an opportunity to understand southern bossism and reform in the late nineteenth and early twentieth centuries is in danger of being lost.

As an upper South border state, the history of Kentucky and Kentuckians in this period proves just as daunting as the state's antebellum and Civil War past. "A land and a people of contrast," in the words of historian Thomas D. Clark, an understanding of the state and its people is daunting indeed.[6] It is my contention that such an understanding of the state in this period is impossible without understanding something about political bossism and reform. Because the political was and continues to be such an important part of the fabric of the state, Billy Klair's life reveals much about Kentucky. At the same time, a study of Klair proves just as challenging as the attempt to understand the hodgepodge of Kentucky politics during this period.

Unlike the vocal and eccentric Ed Crump of Memphis, Klair was "very, very skittish about getting his name bandied around too much. He didn't want to get in the public eye." Instead, Klair attempted to keep himself "pretty securely out of public sight. He wasn't a man that you saw every time you turned around." Historian Clark, who came to teach at the University of Kentucky at the beginning of the depression years, did not recall Klair "being out in the so-called Lexington society. I think he shunned that. I don't know if he had an entree into it in the first place, but if he did he shunned it." Clark went on to state, "I doubt if Billy Klair were living if you'd get very far interviewing him."[7]

Upon Klair's death in 1937, an editorialist for the *Lexington Herald* reminisced that Klair "wrote little; spoke seldom. 'I am a performer,' he would say, clinging to the theory so well-proved throughout his life that action speaks louder than words." The writer concluded that "because of this no record remains of his observations. The proverbial remarks that he made, quoted from Pikeville to Paducah, are in no printed form." Contemporaries of Klair are no less scarce. Clark despaired: "I've been trying to think of some old lawyer. They're all dead. At one time I could have told you about a lot of people to go see [about Klair], but they're just not around anymore."[8]

Despite Klair's reticence, and despite the scarcity of extant contemporary accounts, Klair's immense influence in local and state politics is well documented in scattered and varied sources. While he wrote little, leaving few personal accounts of his political and private actions, his activities were covered religiously in local and state newspapers. Other sources abound, sources that reveal insights into Klair's methods and actions, insights necessary for an understanding of Lexington and Kentucky politics.

In 1963 a writer for the *Lexington Herald-Leader* stated that starting at the turn of the century and continuing for four decades "the person of Billy Klair cast a significant shadow over Kentucky politics." An earlier edition of the *Herald* declared that it "is doubtful if any man nominated and elected to public office within a quarter of a century has been so large a factor in shaping the turn of events." The story of Klair's life, according to the *Herald*, "would make a novel of unexampled interest." Kentucky politician John Y. Brown Sr.

recalled that at one time Klair was "probably the most powerful man in the state of Kentucky." Naming governors, speakers, congressmen, and mayors, "the little statesman" was remembered for his benevolent use of power.[9] But it was power, nonetheless, and his quest for power motivated his political actions.

While George T. Blakey referred to politics as "the primal force in the state," Clark asserted that a "popular misconception in Kentucky history has been the notion that all citizens of the state have concerned themselves with political matters."[10] Clark's assertion held true for Lexington, for it was the blind following of the machine by the majority of Lexington's residents that allowed bossism to hold sway in the city for so many years. At the same time, the force of politics, whether primal or not, was and continues to be an important part of the lives of individuals in Kentucky and the South. The tale of Lexington's politics is important, and Lexington's political story in the two quarter centuries on both sides of 1900 is largely the story of Billy Klair.

Part I

It is true that our corporate existence is only a living monument to the disgraceful stupidity and shameful Rip Van Winkleism of our community.

Henry T. Duncan

No American city of its age can more justly claim the attention of the tourist than Lexington. It is rich in historic associations, is a complete epitome of Old Kentucky life and manners, and is surrounded by all the attractions of a region which, for pastoral beauty and fertility, is unsurpassed upon the face of the globe. . . . The social and commercial capital of the famous "Blue Grass Region" is situated in what Bancroft styles "the unrivaled valley of Elkhorn creek."

G.W. Ranck

1

It Is a New Lexington!

With contrasting views Henry T. Duncan and George W. Ranck described the community into which Billy Klair was born. While Duncan, a founder and editor of the *Lexington Daily Press,* in 1870 the city's first daily newspaper, bemoaned the lack of civic pride of the community's residents, local historian and promoter Ranck emphasized the city's prospects with glowing superlatives. Duncan was aware of numerous problems in need of reform; Ranck was convinced that Lexington's unique advantages would assure the town's growth into a major manufacturing center. These contrasting views indicated the tensions and possibilities created by the industrial revolution for a small southern city.

Lexington's location in the Bluegrass region of central Kentucky certainly provided unparalleled opportunities for enterprising individuals. In the late 1700s, Lexington businessmen outfitted overland migrants en route to rapidly developing areas in Tennessee and western Kentucky, and prospering farmers in the Bluegrass marketed their surplus through the town. With the establishment of Transylvania University in 1780 and its move to Lexington in 1789, Lexington flourished culturally as well, and in the words of two urban historians, "for several years [it] had more urbanity about it than any other place in the West." By 1800 Lexington's residents numbered two thousand. The population continued to grow, reaching fifty-two hundred by 1820.[1]

Shortly thereafter, however, Lexington experienced a depression along with the rest of the country when the resumption of imports from Britain following the War of 1812 "bankrupted thousands of American manufacturers and the inflation of real estate values reached a point as high as it could go." The depression proved disastrous for Lexington, at the same time that a new force transformed other towns into bustling cities. While the steamboat enhanced the prospects of river cities such as Louisville and Cincinnati, Lexington's inland location became a "serious competitive disadvantage." In the years following the war, Lexington stopped growing as individuals and their businesses sought the river towns.[2]

Early projects to overcome the inland isolation, first by turnpikes and then by railroads, did not reestablish Lexington's preeminent position in the West. A visitor to the town in 1829, aware of its former prosperity, wrote that Lexington "has degenerated beyond measure." He lamented that "where was once the dwelling of gayety and friendship, with every good and noble sentiment, was now a rusty and moss-grown mansion of ill nature and repulsive indifference."[3]

The coming of the first railroad in 1830, built by the Lexington & Ohio Railroad Company, and the incorporation of the town in 1831 promised better days. Two years later, however, the first of two cholera epidemics rocked the unprepared town. From one-third to one-half of the town's residents fled, businesses closed, and more than five hundred of Lexington's six thousand residents—including some of the town's leading citizens—succumbed to the disease. Henry Clay, a survivor of the plague, wrote from Ashland that "the stores and shops are closed, the presses stopt, and no one moving in the streets except those concerned with the dead or the sick."[4] Images of bodies "piled in heaps at the cemetery gates," and of workmen digging "long trenches . . . to receive the many corpses," presented a stark contrast to the claims of town fathers of healthfulness and serenity. Lexington historian John D. Wright Jr. concluded, "Now that image was shattered. Lexingtonians showed remarkable resilience in recovering from the plague, but the scars remained in areas of poverty that had not been there before."[5] A recurrence of the epidemic in 1849, though not as severe as the 1833 visitation, again reminded surviving Lexingtonians of their vulnerability.

The malady of slavery had been with Lexington from the beginning. Wright recorded what an antebellum visitor might have witnessed upon visiting the town:

There were blacks everywhere, engaged in a great variety of tasks. In the morning, many could be seen going to the Market House where, at the various stalls, other blacks were butchering meat or selling vegetables, fruit, and flowers. Early in the morning, many of the male blacks headed for the factories, or to their tasks as bricklayers and masons, blacksmiths and carpenters, or perhaps to work on the building of the Lexington & Ohio Railroad. Others would be driving wagons or carriages, repairing streets, digging sewers, tending to horses and equipment at the livery stables. Others performed the thousand and one menial tasks at the Phoenix Hotel and many other inns and taverns. Domestic servants in hundreds of residences performed innumerable tasks to keep the daily routine operating successfully.[6]

Blacks, both slave and free, populated the town; a black population of 3,080 in 1860 represented one-third of the town's total number. And while Lexingtonians along with other Kentucky slaveholders boasted of the mild and humane manifestation of the peculiar institution in the Bluegrass, slave insurrections did occur, and "in the heart of Lexington itself, punishment of blacks was painfully and publicly exhibited in the frequent floggings at the massive locust whipping-post on the northeast corner of the courthouse yard, and in the increased number of hangings."[7]

Slaves were bought and sold on Cheapside, adjacent to the courthouse, in increasing numbers, especially as the estates of slaveowning victims of the cholera epidemics were settled. The temptation to sell slaves down the river to plantations in the lower Mississippi Valley made the words of Stephen Foster's "My Old Kentucky Home" a reality for hundreds of Lexington slave families. Verse three of Foster's original lyrics reads:

The head must bow and the back will have to bend,
Wherever the darky may go;
A few more days and the trouble all will end,
In the fields where the sugar canes grow;
A few more days for to tote the weary load,
No matter, 'twill never be light;
A few more days till we totter on the road,
Then, my old Kentucky home, good night![8]

At the same time the antislavery activities of Lexington's Cassius Marcellus Clay, a cousin of Henry Clay, illustrated that Lexington was not immune from the deep divisions over slavery affecting the rest of the country.[9]

During the Civil War itself, the fact that the Bodley House on the corner of Market and Second Streets—Union headquarters during much of the war—sat on an adjacent corner from Hopemont, the home of Confederate cavalry leader John Hunt Morgan, provided a vivid reminder of the war's wrenching effect. Perhaps no other town in the divided nation was as divided as Lexington during the conflict.

Physically, although "Lexington had suffered some property damage from

Union military occupation, and the occasional forays of Morgan's men, it came through the Civil War relatively unscathed." Wright concludes that the "wounds from the war were more psychological, social, and political," and that the "challenge to Lexington was one of undertaking the necessary municipal improvements, expanding railroad facilities, and promoting energetic and inventive economic enterprise to stimulate the growth and prosperity of the city."[10] Postwar city officials were not up to the challenge; respected but aging mayors such as the seventy-one-year-old physician Dr. Joseph Chinn, elected in 1865, and Jerry T. Frazer, a tailor and dry goods merchant elected in 1867 and again in 1869 in his sixties, were unable or unwilling to provide the dynamic local leadership necessary for postwar recovery.

The most pressing need in post-slavery Lexington, as in other southern communities, involved the problem of race relations, a problem magnified in Lexington by the dramatic increase in the black urban population following the war. Before the war, blacks and whites lived within the confines of the old walking city, "the mile-in-radius circle which defined the city's limits." The dwellings of free blacks were interspersed with white residences throughout the town, and slave blacks "lived under a rigid integration dictated by the system of slavery."[11]

After the war, and with the Thirteenth Amendment, this system of forced integration was soon replaced with a rigid system of segregated housing patterns as white Lexingtonians followed the Jim Crow standards of the period. From 1865 to 1870, Lexington's black population nearly tripled in size as forty-six hundred freedmen streamed into the town from the Fayette County countryside. By 1870 blacks made up approximately half of Lexington's population.[12]

While Lexington's stately mansions provided an air of prosperity and elegance within the old walking city, newly arrived blacks settled in the town's least desirable areas—in all-black alleys in the interior city, or in outlying areas along railroad tracks, around bridges, stockyards, or cemeteries, or in damp bottomlands. These black residential areas—often little more than hurriedly built shantytowns—were usually named for the developers or owners of the estates on which they were located.

The largest of the black districts was Goodloetown—named after William Cassius Goodloe, the nephew of Cassius Clay—located north of East Main Street between Dewees Street and Midland Avenue. To the north of Goodloetown, George B. Kinkead "developed" Kinkeadtown, and to the west, between Fourth and Fifth, and Broadway and Upper, was Taylortown. Also in Lexington's northern section was Brucetown, named after the noted hemp manufacturer W.W. Bruce. Pralltown was built in the southern part of Lexington by John A. Prall, and stretched from South Limestone to the railroad tracks. Also huddled in the deep valleys in the smoke along the tracks were Lee's Bottom and Davis Bottom. Formerly Irish enclaves, Davis Bottom and Irishtown were occupied increasingly by newly arrived blacks.[13] Although these neighborhoods were originally developed as philanthropic ventures, the disparity in economic opportunities for freedmen mirrored the gap in the quality of black and white residences. In 1880 blacks represented 45 percent of the Lexington population, but only 6 percent of the city's wealth.[14]

While the town's incorporation in 1831 and the establishment of Lexington as a railroad center in the mid-1800s prevented the community from "sinking to the level of a crossroads town" in the prewar years, it was not until the 1880s that recovery from antebellum and wartime ills was noticeable. In 1882 Kentucky's *Richmond Register* proclaimed, "Lexington is waking up and her Rip Van Winkle rest is surely broken."[15] The *Register*'s editor pointed enviously to several developments that had transformed Lexington, seemingly overnight, from a rural hamlet to a thriving city. "Behold what she has done within a year! Built an ice manufactory, a system of street railways, a system of telephone lines and now shows them off to advantage under a brilliant electric light. Other and equally important schemes are being discussed. This is what we like to see. Why should not Lexington be a great place? . . . *It is a new Lexington.*"[16]

The new Lexington of 1882 refused to sever its ties with the past, however. While new avenues for economic growth and prosperity were sought, the community remained a town proud of its traditions. The "economic ligaments of Lexington as a major retail, wholesale, and transportation center" for the Bluegrass continued unchanged.[17] At the same time, the problems of the town's "other side"—blighted neighborhoods, racial tensions, crime—continued apace.

Despite the fact that Lexington had only recently been left behind by the river towns in the race for economic preeminence, astute Lexington businessmen realized the potential of their town's inland location. Echoing the knowing discussions of business entrepreneurs, Ranck asserted that "surrounding the hustle and bustle of Main Street . . . was a magnificent panorama of the nation's finest and most picturesque horse and livestock farms." Lexington's business leaders soon capitalized on this propitious link of town and country. A chamber of commerce, organized on 2 November 1881, immediately began to herald Lexington as the "Queen of the Bluegrass."[18]

In addition to its nascent economic advantages, Lexington remained the cultural center of the Bluegrass. With "ten newspapers, three of which are daily . . . and twenty-three educational institutions, including one university, a new State College, a Commercial College, three large female seminaries, and flourishing public and private schools," 1880s Lexington boasted a remarkable array of cultural and educational opportunities for a community of fewer than twenty thousand residents.[19]

All signs pointed to the development of Lexington into a major metropolitan center. Neglecting the tensions caused by the influx of black freedmen and their families following the war, promoters boasted that Lexington's population had grown from 9,521 in 1860 to 14,801 a decade later. By 1880 the community's population of 16,656 almost doubled its total at the beginning of the Civil War. The economic progress and the building boom of the 1880s, which included a comprehensive system of street railways, insured a continued trend of growth into the new century. The economic, cultural, and numerical growth of Lexington was indeed impressive. While many wealthy members of Bluegrass society continued to cherish traditional southern mores, they also saw the advantage of growth. And in contrast to other areas of Kentucky, described by one journalist as "divided, backward, poor, and largely resentful of culture," Lexington presented a paradox of progress. During the two decades before the turn of the century, Lexington emerged as a thriving urban center; a city of the New South was built on the foundations and traditions of the Old South.[20]

And just as the Old South town was benighted with cholera and slavery, the New South city included a thriving red light district and Goodloetown and Pralltown. In antebellum Lexington, deference was given to the Bluegrass elite in matters of politics and power. In the "new Lexington," however, powerful politicians increasingly depended on the city's underside to gain and maintain control.

Implicit, then, in Lexington's transformation from town to city were developments in the city's system of government. In his *Lexington: Heart of the Bluegrass,* John D. Wright surmised that the modernization and expansion of the city depended on the reform of the structure and operation of the city government. Lexington's experience in the area of government resembled the experience of other cities in the United States.[21]

America's urban centers were often controlled by political bosses in the later years of the nineteenth century. While "factional" or ward organizations were more common, "dominant" or citywide machines developed in some cities as early as the 1890s.[22] While New York City was ruled by the Tammany chiefs, Chicago, Philadelphia, St. Louis, and Kansas City were controlled by a series of astute, and often unscrupulous, machine politicians. Southern cities were no different. Indeed, the South, with its unique past revolving around the peculiar institution, was particularly conducive to the paternalistic aspects of boss rule. Martin Behrman, the leader of the Choctaw Club, ruled New Orleans; the Republican Thomas Kercheval and later the Democrat Hilary Howse orchestrated powerful organizations in Nashville; and as Roger Biles pointed out in *Memphis in the Great Depression*, of "all the twentieth-century urban bosses, none dominated his city as completely for as long as Edward Hull Crump did Memphis, Tennessee." The experience of Lexington illustrates that smaller cities also displayed a penchant for machine rule.[23] If Plunkitt of Tammany Hall could state "that the poor look up to George W. Plunkitt as a father, come to him in trouble—and don't forget him on election day," small southern cities with generations of experience in paternalistic patterns of life and work found such sentiments familiar.[24]

Lexington's first system of government had been established by an act of the Virginia Legislature on 6 May 1782. Under this act "the government of the town's affairs was vested in a board of seven trustees, at the head of which were Colonel John Todd and Col. Robert Patterson." Some 710 acres were assigned to the trustees in fee simple, thus allowing the trustees to grant deeds to the owners of various tracts already allotted. With the formation of Fayette County two years earlier, and the naming of Lexington as the county seat, Lexingtonians found themselves under the authority of a county government that embraced "a goodly portion of Kentucky north and east of the Kentucky River."[25]

Although this large area was reduced through the years by the formation of new counties, on 7 December 1831, almost fifty years after the town's first government was established, Lexingtonians, tired of "feeling hamstrung and ruled by a county government indifferent to urban needs and often dominated by a different political party," persuaded the General Assembly to pass "An Act to Incorporate the City of Lexington." This act replaced the trustees with a mayor and twelve councilmen, granted city taxpayers immunity from county taxes, and gave city officials independence in running the town's affairs. Lexington's first mayor, Charlton Hunt, appointed by the "Board of Councilmen" or "City Council," served not only as the town's chief executive but also as the chief judicial officer. This provision, combining the executive and judicial branches of city government, was declared unconstitutional in 1835, a year after Hunt's death. After 1835 the mayor's responsibilities were limited to those of the chief executive, a separate judge for the city was appointed, and a provision was made for the election of the city council by wards. The city charter remained unchanged until 25 May 1882, when it was amended by the General Assembly to provide for the popular election of the mayor and all city officials. This progressive amendment to the city charter was passed despite the vehement opposition of Councilman Dennis Mulligan—by that time Lexington's most influential political figure—and his supporters.[26] A powerful member of the city council, Mulligan opposed any amendment that would take the power to name the mayor out of the hands of the city council, a body that he had learned to dominate.

In tradition-rich Lexington, it was Mulligan who established the city's long tradition of political bossism, a tradition later built upon by Billy Klair. Mulligan never gained citywide control, remaining a contender for power. Mulligan fits the description of a factional political leader proposed by sociologists Craig Brown and Charles Halaby, who described "a localized network of exchange easily and durably linked [to] neighborhood politicians, who were often already engaged in 'service' occupations (e.g., saloonkeeping), to the needy." In post–Civil War Lexington, the "decentralized nature of representation and power in the city was congenial to the emergence and prosperity of these neighborhood organizations, and equally uncongenial to the consolidation of city-wide control."[27]

The beginning of increased centralization of Lexington's city government, marked by the charter reform of 1882 and considered a threat by Mulligan, actually facilitated the rise of Mulligan's successor. Like other entrepreneurs, Klair found Lexington brimming with possibilities. The town of Klair's birth was becoming the city of Klair's young adulthood, and he found that thriving, growing Lexington—with its wealthy, tradition-conscious elite *and* its new underclass and underside—provided a friendly environment for an aspiring politician. And if Lexington provided an appropriate stage, Dennis Mulligan offered a useful example for the understudy who would eventually become the leading player in the city's political drama.

2

The Mulligan Ring

An affinity for politics was not unusual for "old" immigrants coming to America in the antebellum years. Dennis Mulligan's political aspirations, coupled with a shrewd business acumen, allowed him to survive and prosper in his adopted American home. Born on 12 March 1817 in Claurath, Ireland, Mulligan was left an orphan when both of his parents died in the same month in 1821. The young Mulligan lived with a relative until he was seventeen, when he immigrated to the United States. On arriving in America, Mulligan went immediately to Jamaica, Long Island, where he obtained employment from the mayor of the city, a kindness that paved the way for his continued interest in politics.[1]

By 1835 Mulligan was working with Moses W. Scott, chief engineer of the Long Island Railroad, in surveying railroad lines. It was in this capacity that Mulligan first came to Lexington in 1837. After leaving the employ of the railroad, Mulligan attended a night school at Lexington's Phoenix Hotel, "where he acquired a good practical business education." In the early 1840s, after a two-year stint in the clothing trade, the young entrepreneur went into the grocery business, an enterprise "he carried on . . . with great success."[2]

After establishing himself in this lucrative business, Mulligan married Ellen A. McCoy, a Lexington native, in 1843, and became an "earnest member" of St. Paul's Catholic Church. The Mulligans' only son, James Hillary, was given "a liberal education," studied law, travelled to Paris, and eventually returned to the city as judge of the recorder's court. Because of his "diligence and attention to business," the elder Mulligan soon gained the goodwill and confidence of his fellow citizens, a confidence that won for him a seat on the city council in 1866.[3]

Mulligan's political ambitions were nurtured during his early years in Lexington. James recalled being taken to the Maxwell Springs as a boy to hear the speeches of the great Henry Clay. In 1870 Mulligan built Maxwell Place for James on a fourteen-acre tract fronted on Winslow Street (later Euclid Avenue, and still later the Avenue of Champions) and running along Van Pelt's Lane (later Rose Street). The property boasted three springs that cooled a wooded area long used for political rallies. Clay regarded the area so warmly that he once remarked, "No man can consider himself a gentleman until he has watered his horse at Maxwell Springs."[4]

Although the Great Compromiser certainly made an impression on the enterprising grocer, Mulligan aligned himself with the Lexington Democracy, and his store at the corner of Vine and Limestone soon became the "rallying point" for the city's Democratic Party. Mulligan acquired a reputation for being an "upright, honorable man in all his dealings . . . prominent in every movement for the improvement of the city; not hasty in his decisions, but firm when he has to take a stand; kind and benevolent in disposition." These traits undoubtedly assisted Mulligan in the establishment of a strong Democratic ward machine based on patronage. Dubbed "Mulligan's Ring" by critics, this organization dominated the city's government activities until limited reforms were made in the early 1880s.[5]

Despite Mulligan's reputation for public-mindedness, his bloc of supporters in the city council actually backed "a policy of parsimony in government expenditures, low taxation, and limited indebtedness, regardless of the impact of such policies on the welfare of Lexington."[6] Mulligan's career contradicted the contentions of historians following what Terrence J. McDonald termed the "political cultural theory" in *Parameters of Urban Fiscal Policy: Socioeconomic Change and Political Culture in San Francisco, 1860–1901*. McDonald pointed out that historians like Richard Hofstadter and Oscar Handlin pictured the "free-spending boss" as the hero and the "tightfisted reformer" as the villain. According to Handlin, the boss "expanded the public sector to meet human needs," while reformers rarely considered "the needs and interests of a new citizen."[7] The views of Hofstadter and Handlin were reinforced by sociologist Robert Merton in his classic text, *Social Theory and Social Structure*. For Merton, as for historians following his "functional" framework, "service to the deprived was at the heart of the machine's persistence."[8]

In *The Urbanization of Modern America*, historian Zane Miller argued that the "astonishingly high cost of municipal improvements and services" in developing American cities was the result of "patronage, special favors, and bribery" by political bosses. Miller and other proponents of this political cultural theory "usually regarded the fiscal issue in urban politics as the classic confrontation between free-spending bosses and fiscally conservative reformers." In McDonald's study of San Francisco, however, "Boss" Christopher Buckley consistently "kept the tax rate low and avoided municipal indebtedness."[9] The same was true for Dennis Mulligan in Lexington. Although he had proposed limited expenditures that would benefit or provide favors for trusted political allies, his generally restrictive fiscal policies became increasingly unsuitable for Lexington in the boom years of the 1880s.[10]

Mulligan's obstructionist policies were first challenged in the late 1870s by a group of reform-minded councilmen that included Calvin Morgan, the brother of Lexington's famous Confederate raider, John Hunt Morgan, and Moses Kaufman, Lexington's first German and Jewish councilman. These councilmen challenged the Mulligan bloc in 1880 and succeeded in passing a motion to choose the mayor by popular election. When the election was won by Claudius M. Johnson Jr., the city's reform-minded citizenry found the newly elected mayor to be a kindred spirit.[11]

Johnson, son of the Bluegrass poet Rose Vertner Johnson, was a druggist by trade. He was first elected to the city council in 1878, and his election as mayor in 1880 by a 125–vote majority was followed by victories in 1881, 1882, 1884, and 1886. Described in 1886 in a promotion publication as "one of the most popular Mayors that . . . ever sat in the chair of Chief executive of this city," Johnson "arrayed himself on the side of progress and improvement, . . . placed the finances of the city in a first-class condition and generally conducted the office so as to give satisfaction to all parties."[12]

One party that Johnson and the reformers did not satisfy was Dennis Mulligan. From his seat on the city council, Mulligan opposed almost every measure proposed by the bloc of reformers. From the time the Civil War ended, Mulligan had held almost full sway in the management of the city's affairs, but with the rise of reforming ideas in the late-1870s Mulligan felt his power slipping away. By 1879 Mulligan vigorously opposed measures ranging from what he thought was the extravagant appropriation of $300 to the Lexington Home Guards to innovations in the maintenance of the city's streets.[13]

Mulligan's opposition to a change that would take decisions concerning city street maintenance out of the hands of the mayor and place them under the authority of a paid city engineer was based, according to Mulligan, on the economy of city expenditures. When the city engineer defended the change by stating that "the salary of the Engineer would not increase the expense, because his work would lessen the amount now expended for street repairs," then-councilman Johnson reminded the council of past examples of extravagance by Mulligan and his machine mayors. When the council had discussed improvements on Spring Street between Main and Short Streets, Mulligan had suggested that all of the old rock be removed and replaced with new rock. When Johnson suggested that the boulders already on the street could be broken and used to macadamize the street, Mulligan responded that Johnson's plan would not work because "these rock are sunburnt and are consequently no good." The reformers used what they referred to as the excuse of the "sunburnt rock" to full advantage when it was revealed that the new rock would be hauled by the keeper of the workhouse, Mulligan's friend Martin McLaughlin, at a cost of $226 a day. Mulligan's plan was rejected when the council decided to improve the street by using the old rock at a cost of $36, an improvement that made the street "just as good as any in the city."[14]

Mulligan's plans continued to be thwarted in the late 1870s and early 1880s by Johnson and increasingly by the erudite councilman Moses Kaufman. To curb Kaufman's sometimes lengthy addresses on the reformers' concerns, Mulligan persuaded Jerry T. Frazer, the machine-backed mayor in 1867, and then from 1869 to 1880, to attempt to limit the speeches of the Jewish councilman. Frazer's attempt was not successful, as Kaufman asserted that "he was a member from the First Ward, and as such had as much right to the floor of the Council as Mr. Danahy, who had spoken over a dozen times."[15]

Mulligan's frustration with Kaufman was evident in a 1 July 1880 council meeting when Kaufman rose to address the council and revealed that Mulligan had accused him of making "promises and offers of money to secure my election." Kaufman asserted that Mulligan had also "called me in a contemptuous manner a 'Jew.'" After a lengthy comparison of the respective histories of the Jewish nation with that of Ireland, Kaufman concluded that "my people's defense against all sneers or insults of that character is fully made out in their proud and noble history."[16]

Kaufman continued to press for reforms in the meetings of the city council and also through the pages of the *Lexington Transcript*, a newspaper in operation since 1876. In 1870 the *Lexington Daily Press* was founded by Hart Foster and Henry T. Duncan. Although Duncan eventually joined in the efforts of the reformers, the *Daily Press* was viewed in its early years of operation as the organ of the Mulligan machine. In the "Chimes of Mulligan Guards," a satiric look at the workings of the "Mulligan Ring," the editors of the *Transcript* made clear their concern over the paper's liaison with the hated machine:

"Enter H. T. D. [Henry T. Duncan]"
The editor I am of a Blackguard sheet,
Dennis must be Lord Mayor, Johnson must be beat;
I'm the braggadocio of the Cheapside street!
I'm the chief Muldoon of the Mulligan Guard,
I'm doing dirty work, and I want my reward.
When Dennis was boss of this great citie,
He managed to run it so carefullee,
I got the city printing at favorable prices.
And was left pretty much to my own devices;
My bills—never questioned—were promptly paid,
And thus lots of money under Dennis I made.
But when Johnson got in, I thought I should die,
For he actually said my bills were "too high,"
. . . So I'm for Dennis; Dennis is for me;
And together we'll run this great citie.[17]

Such mundane matters were soon replaced by a battle over a change in the city charter. Immediately after Johnson was sworn in on 11 March 1880, the young mayor presented the following resolution: "*Resolved*, By the Mayor and Council, that the Legislature be requested to so amend the charter of Lexington that there shall be an election by the qualified voters for Mayor on the first Saturday in March, 1881, and every two years thereafter."[18] Although the council succeeded in passing a motion that provided for the popular election of the mayor in 1880, the General Assembly did not amend the city charter until 1882. The delay was due in part to the obstructionist tactics in Frankfort of Rep. James H. Mulligan. Despite the connection between the elder and younger Mulligans, the General Assembly finally amended the Lexington charter, an amendment approved by the Lexington electorate on 25 May 1882.[19] While the Mulligans feared the loss of their political control, the *Transcript* heralded the work of Claudius Johnson and Moses Kaufman in securing the charter change: "It took the 'Children of Israel' forty years to get through the wilderness. It has taken our City Council about twelve years to get through. They have just that much advantage of the children of Israel. It is a remarkable coincidence, however, that Council also had a Moses to lead them."[20]

Although the progressive amendment provided not only for the popular election of the mayor but for all city officials as well, an attached amendment permitting the city government to go into debt to build a city waterworks was not successful. The fight over the waterworks was the most conspicuous of many battles fought between Mulligan and the reformers during the Mulligan years.

Mulligan had sponsored the building of the new market house in 1879, and claimed responsibility for the prosperity of the railroads in Lexington and for the continued location of the state college in the city. The reformers, anxious to downplay any positive publicity for the still influential "boss," asserted that Mulligan's advocacy of the market house came from a purely selfish motive. When members of the machine suggested that their leader was "the leading spirit" in the construction of the market house and the city building, the *Transcript* reported sarcastically that a "prominent local politician elevated his nose and uttered an exclamation more emphatic than religious," and said: "Yes, he was the leading spirit in the market house matter as he is in everything that is to his own interest. He advocated the market house because its erection would increase the value of his property, which is in close proximity. In proof of this he had the market house moved back ten feet, so that people could have a full view of his corner grocery."[21]

As for the railroads, the reformers claimed that when a resolution was passed to donate the market house to the Kentucky Central Railroad for a depot, Mulligan declared that if the resolution was acted upon he would sue the city for "at least $20,000, and for the value of every dollar's worth of property he owned on the south side." Mulligan was even quoted as having said that "stage coaches were much better for the city and country than railroads," an irony considering that Irish railway workers had long served as the bedrock of his support. The *Transcript* reminded its readers that "his opposition to the street railway was so strong while he was in the Council that the enterprise was defeated till the election of a new Council."[22]

Mulligan's advocacy of the State College was also called into question when it was claimed that his lone "nay" was the only dissenting vote when funding to keep the college in Lexington was appropriated. Mulligan was ridiculed derisively as "the stumbling block to the progress of Lexington for years." His opposition to various reforms was spelled out in minute detail: "Mulligan is strongly opposed to all kinds of manufactures. He says Lexington is better off without them, and that she can never have them. He opposed the telephone, because he said it would necessitate too many poles on the street. He opposed bringing the State Capital here. He opposed waterworks, on the ground that Lexington had enough water and that the city pumps were sufficient for every purpose."[23]

Mulligan's opposition to the city's waterworks project provided a fitting climax to his struggles with the reformers. The city's cisterns, wells, and springs were inadequate to support Lexington's growing population, and the close proximity of privies to the wells was responsible for outbreaks of typhoid fever. An ample supply of water was also needed for fire protection. Despite the obvious necessity for a reliable source of water, Mulligan balked when private companies indicated an interest in constructing the waterworks. Using his usual complaint of "too much indebtedness which would require higher taxes," Mulligan also implied, ironically, that the private contractors might profit from the project.[24]

Another severe drought in the fall of 1883 convinced the city government to take action despite Mulligan's objections. A contract was made with the Lexington Hydraulic and Manufacturing Company, and on 30 January 1885 the waterworks began operation with the city's firemen shooting "a column of water as high as the weather vane of the new courthouse."[25]

Thus Mulligan's stubborn refusal to support the needed waterworks, coupled with a glaring political setback in the mayoral election of 1883, made evident the demise of his control in the city. No longer able to name his choice for mayor because of the new city charter of 1882, Mulligan decided to challenge Johnson directly in the popular election, confident that traditional forms of patronage would insure victory. The aging boss's dubious attempt to portray himself as a forward-looking citizen concerned only with the city's progress was met with derision by the reformers.[26]

Johnson and his supporters resurrected the story of the "sunburnt rock" and reviewed a long list of Mulligan objections to progressive measures in the city. The reformers also derided a statement by the chief of the fire department, Paul Conlon, that he could deliver six hundred votes for Mulligan at any time. The *Daily Press* reported that "Paul Conlon's alleged declaration about the ownership of 600 voters has stirred up considerable of a wumpus."[27]

Mulligan's reliance on patronage support from railroad workers, both Irish and African American, and from the police and fire departments, had long been the source of his political success. After all, Mulligan was among the first of hundreds of Irish immigrants who came to the city to work on the large-scale railroad projects. Settling in the less desirable sections of the city such as Irishtown and Davis Bottom, along the railroad tracks and near poor black neighborhoods, many Irish immigrants continued to work on the railroads, while others like Mulligan set up grocery stores and other small businesses.

Mulligan was personally responsible for dispensing patronage positions in the police and fire departments, and some Irishmen like Conlon and Police Chief J.J. Reagan eventually secured the top positions in their departments.[28]

The *Transcript's* "Chimes of Mulligan Guards" recorded Mulligan's election strategy:

> Glorious victory will surely come if all our railroad boys are ready
> To vote early, often and all day steady,
> Just watch and keep them well in hand, for the honor of ould Ireland.
> . . . My pockets are deep, in them I hold Six hundred votes, if all were told.
> They'll do my bid; on this I'll bet—When you are Mayor, this don't forget.
> . . . Indeed I won't, on that depend, I never yet forgot a friend.
> Then if you can't get in fairly, you know,
> We have money and whisky, bully and blow,
> And if we can't make it with railroad diggers,
> We'll come to the breach with Jim; [his] pet niggers.[29]

In Lexington, as in other southern cities, relations between the races were tense and increasingly problematic for Democratic politicians. The dramatic increase in the city's black population following the Civil War—African Americans made up half of Lexington's population by 1870—intensified the problem.[30] As growing numbers of blacks moved into Lexington, and with the ratification of the Fifteenth Amendment, white Lexingtonians feared that black enfranchisement would lead to black control of the city government. Despite a provision for a poll tax in city elections that drastically curbed the number of black voters, Dennis Mulligan understood the practicality of using black "repeaters" in a crisis. Undoubtedly, some black voters, resentful of Radical Republican attempts to monopolize the black vote, joined the Democratic Party willingly. Mulligan convinced others to vote for his candidates through offerings of poll tax payments, whiskey, and other political favors. Also, many Irish voters, living in close proximity to the black neighborhoods, and often serving them through their grocery stores and other businesses, wielded valuable political influence for Mulligan around election time.[31]

For years, Mulligan's reliance on the Irish and blacks, on railroad workers and police and fire departments, to deliver the votes had served him well, but by 1883 these traditional sources of political patronage were not enough as changes in the city beyond Mulligan's control had created a new political dynamic.[32] Johnson's comfortable mayoral victory over Mulligan in 1884 indicated the extent to which Mulligan had failed to change with the times.

Mulligan's stubborn refusal to back needed city improvements was un-doubtedly based on his determined effort to keep the status quo. The use of monies for public works was not relevant in his desired maintenance of power. Funding for improvements would only impinge upon his other sources of patronage. In short, Mulligan was caught in Lexington's transformation from town to city, his deep conservatism blinding him to the "new Lexington."[33]

By 1886 Lexington's population had risen to 26,216. *A Review of Lexington, Kentucky: As She Is,* published that year and boasting the lengthy subtitle, *Her Wealth and Industry, Her Wonderful Growth and Admirable Enterprise; Her Great Business Concerns, Her Manufacturing Advantages, and Commercial Resources,* proclaimed that Lexington was "now the great inland emporium of the state."[34] Changes in the city's government appeared to keep pace with the business boom of the 1880s. The city charter was amended once again in 1886, vesting the legislative power in a board of councilmen and a board of aldermen, known jointly as the general council. Theoretically, the board of aldermen, known locally as the "Upper Lords," was to "act as a senior body to check any rash actions by the council." The new charter also admonished the city's police and fire departments to refrain from taking part in any election except "to cast his vote," a direct reference to the patronage source of the Mulligan "Ring."[35]

With the successful elections of other reform-minded mayors and coun-cilmen in the 1890s, and with Dennis Mulligan's death on 22 February 1901, it appeared that the Lexington machine had also died. As Mulligan was bur-ied in the Calvary Cemetery, a burial ground he was instrumental in acquiring for the Catholic Church, Lexington's forward-looking citizens reminisced about the old days of Mulligan and his "Ring," assuring themselves that the future held only progress and prosperity for the "new Lexington."

But Lexington faced critical problems as the new century opened. In 1901 Mayor Henry T. Duncan, the editor of the *Lexington Daily Press* and a one-time Mulligan ally, enumerated the problems faced by Lexingtonians in his report to the city. According to the mayor, Lexington was cursed with disease, high mortality rates, air pollution, poor drinking water, a wasteful taxation system, and an overall disregard for the city charter. Although reforms such as improved methods of fund disbursements and an emphasis on more efficiency in government were instituted in the 1890s under the leadership of the now reform-minded Duncan, the mayor's description of the general malaise of the city made clear that Lexington's past progress was not sufficient.[36]

While expansion, modernization, and government efficiency were the expressed ideals of what George Tindall has styled "business progressivism," entrenched machine politicians in many cities either fought or ignored the intrusion of any significant governmental reforms in the period from 1880 to 1929.[37] Such was certainly the case with Dennis Mulligan in Lexington. Other southern bosses, however, especially after the turn of the century, espoused social reforms to meet the needs of their constituents. In Nashville, for example, longtime mayor Hilary Howse illustrated what Don H. Doyle described as a "tradition of urban liberalism that characterized the ethnic big city bosses of the Northeast." In the South, urban bosses such as Howse also combined "genuine charity and shrewd politics . . . in the face of brutal conditions of poverty, disease, and discrimination in the inner city." Unlike business progressives who stressed government efficiency, Howse illustrated another reform impulse; he was a "social reformer who expanded government liberally to meet the needs of his people and kept government in check when it interfered with the people's private behavior."[38] Urban bosses of Howse's sort anticipated some of the Keynesian ideas of later New Dealers.

In the last two decades of the nineteenth century, however, battle lines were not drawn clearly between bosses and reformers. Rather, individuals and organizations representing different segments of a city's population fought for a particular brand of reform that would meet the needs of their constituents and of their political ambitions. In Kentucky, the lack of significant reforms around the turn of the century, whether business, social, or political in nature, characterized a state long known for an obstinate unwillingness to change. Kentucky's cities, including Lexington, simply put on a show of progressive reform, mere window dressing.[39]

While falling behind in the area of reform, Kentucky and Lexington displayed their own brand of machine politics beginning with the antics of Dennis Mulligan. Although Mulligan was described as a politician ready to give "vigorous and manly aid in any public or social need," his brand of politics was limited to what Nathan Glazer and Daniel Patrick Moynihan later described in *Beyond the Melting Pot* as the classical Irish belief in "a traditional view of formal government as illegitimate and informal government as truly representative of 'the people.'" Mulligan viewed politics not as a way of bringing progress to the city of Lexington but as a means of bettering his own lot. It was his business.[40] In denouncing his corrupt political activities, the satirical rhyme of Lexington reformers in the *Transcript's* "Chimes of Mulligan Guards" was accurate in describing Mulligan's beliefs about the purpose of government and politics:

By watching my chances from the city, you see,
I made enough money for Jimmy and me.
Not a snap do I care for your town or poor trash,
Bother your improvements! what I want is the cash.[41]

Mulligan's view of government was shaped by his Irish past where politics, according to Glazer and Moynihan, were "thoroughly corrupt" and "stealing an election did not seem immoral as it did to Americans."[42] Although the Glazer and Moynihan description of Irish politics is an extreme generalization, undoubtedly Mulligan's election-day activities and use of government for the betterment of society were reduced to an extremely personal level. Mulligan's brand of social reform was limited to his beneficent activities on behalf of Lexington's St. Paul's Catholic Church. Outside of his use of patronage to repay his political friends and allies, Mulligan used politics to provide a better life for himself and his family.[43]

Mulligan's domination of Lexington's city politics came to an end in the decade of the 1880s. Unwilling to change with the times along with former ally Duncan, Mulligan was unable to thwart the reformers' ambitions for city improvements and changes in the city charter. Duncan's election as mayor on a reform platform in 1893, and again in 1899, was the final insult to Mulligan and his old machine tactics. With Duncan's reelection in 1899, progressives in the city were confident that the mayor would continue with his reform agenda.

Lexington was unable to maintain a reform tradition in government in the early years of the new century, however. News of the swearing-in ceremony of Mayor Duncan in the 1 January 1900 issue of the *Lexington Daily Leader* was overshadowed by increasingly disturbing news from Frankfort. The rancorous gubernatorial contest between Republican W.S. Taylor and the Democratic candidate, William Goebel, culminated in the shooting of Goebel on 30 January and his death four days later. Instead of a new era of progress, Goebel's assassination launched "the state into the twentieth century on a wave of anger and bitterness."[44]

Some historians have surmised that the assassination crushed the progressive spirit in the state and that "as a result Kentucky never experienced the reforms of the Progressive Era." But in *Kentucky Politics* Malcolm Jewell and Everett Cunningham asserted that the "Progressive Movement of the early twentieth century had little impact in Kentucky" because of forces other than the tragic death of William Goebel. Railroad, coal-mining, liquor, and racetrack interests who were allied with prosperous Bluegrass farmers and political leaders of both parties held power and retarded progressive reforms.[45]

In his *William Goebel: The Politics of Wrath* James Klotter agreed with Jewell and Cunningham that the Goebel assassination was not the primary reason for Kentucky's backwardness: "Overall . . . the murder . . . did not abort reform. Constructive change did come to the Commonwealth. The fact that it came slowly and with less force than elsewhere owes more to the state's relative poverty, rurality, and continued legacy of violence than to one man's assassination." Instead of a deterrent to reform, Klotter maintained that "reform began in the Democratic rump that ruled following the assassination." According to Klotter the marriage of reform and bossism, a marriage that became a hallmark of southern politics in succeeding years, came not with the death of Goebel but during his brief political career.[46]

For Klotter, Goebel was "the prototype of the twentieth century urban political boss with a reform orientation." While Goebel displayed the "gut-fighting tactics of a political boss," his disgust with the heavy-handed lobbying methods of the Louisville & Nashville Railroad, which resulted in the incorporation of the railroad commission into the otherwise "excessively detailed and rigid" Constitution of 1890, caused one biographer to dub Goebel "the first New Dealer." If regard for Goebel as a forerunner of Franklin Delano Roosevelt's New Deal seems a bit farfetched, neither should he be placed among the populist followers of William Jennings Bryan. Although Goebel advocated such populist reforms as railroad regulation, his programs grew out of a decidedly nonagrarian background.[47]

His advocacy as a state senator for the Goebel Election Law, for instance, was typical of urban progressive reform throughout the nation; in theory such election statutes would end partisan corruption at the polling place. At the same time, his actions varied little from the prevailing southern pattern of political bossism as seen in Howse's Nashville, Crump's Memphis, or in the regime of the "old Regulars" in New Orleans. By the twentieth century, urban political machines, machines that sometimes undermined and sometimes worked with urban reformers, operated throughout the South.[48]

But these were not the machines of politicians like Dennis Mulligan. His time was past, his methods dated. Goebel represented the new model. To his contemporaries, Goebel was not the personification of the new "reform boss" but a controversial paradox. Klotter wrote that "Goebel had either to be a boss or a reformer; he could not be both."[49] For the twentieth-century urban southern boss, however, Goebel provided a useful paradigm. The confusing interplay of bossism and reform was spawned in Kentucky by William Goebel, and the political tradition established by Goebel was carried on in the state's three largest cities in the years following his murder. In Louisville, there was Michael Brennan, in Covington, Maurice Galvin, and in Lexington, William Frederick "Billy" Klair.

3

The Rise of Billy Klair

B illy Klair was born the fifth of seven children to Henry M. and Barbara
Volts Klair on 14 December 1875. Henry, born in Germany, had come to
Versailles, Indiana, as a youth, opened a tailor's shop there, and met Barbara
Volts, also of German parentage. Soon married, the young couple moved to
Lexington, where Henry continued to follow the tailor's trade.[1]

Although the father was described as "a democrat in politics and a man of
many excellent qualities of mind and heart," he left the family seven years
after Billy's birth and went to Louisville, where he struggled with various
business enterprises until his death in 1902. After receiving an elementary
education at St. Paul's parochial school, Billy found it necessary at the age of
seven to begin selling newspapers to help support the family. George B.
Kinkead, a Kentucky representative—and an admirer and early patron of the
energetic boy—recalled these years in more effusive detail: "When a little boy,
bright eyed and full of hope, with a right to expect as his heritage the education that this wonderful country affords to her humblest citizens, conditions
arose that made it imperative that he should forego those hopes, and called
upon him, whilst yet in tender years, to make requisition on his youthful
strength and energy and constitute himself the bread winner of a family."[2]

Like Eugene Gant in Thomas Wolfe's *Look Homeward Angel*, young Klair
sold newspapers on the streets of a town that was fast becoming a city. Kinkead
remembered how seriously he took up his new employment: "In rain and snow,
ill clad, and throughout all seasons, he met and discharged this stern obliga-
tion of duty." Rejecting—"tearfully and regretfully"—the advice and aid offered by Kinkead's father, then the chairman of the board of trustees of the
State College located in Lexington, Klair "suffering no boyish pastime or plea-

sure to interfere . . . presented himself and his paper with scrupulous punctuality daily."[3]

Historian Charles Staples remembered that while other newsboys meticulously counted and organized their daily supply of papers, Billy "hastily grabbed his allotment in good faith, hurried down the street beating the other boys to the customers."[4] Billy remained one step ahead of the other boys for the remainder of his business and political careers.

While Wolfe's Eugene Gant refused to follow his father's dream of a career in the law and politics, Klair used the newspaper business to become acquainted with Lexington's business and professional elite. The *Lexington Herald* suggested that "from babyhood" Klair "found a peculiar interest in politics." Certainly his brand of personal politics that became so familiar to Lexingtonians was first cultivated by the child selling papers on Lexington's street corners. Soon half of the members of the Fayette County bar were buying their morning papers from him.[5]

These new acquaintances proved beneficial. Influential admirers secured for the fifteen-year-old Billy an appointment as page to the Kentucky legislature in Frankfort, where he served from 1889 until 1893. Klair had approached Representative Kinkead about the possibility of a page appointment through Kinkead's kinsman and sergeant-at-arms, Bob Tyler. When Tyler assured Kinkead that he had already "made use of the patronage of the place in a most liberal fashion," Klair, "by no means disheartened," asked "if Mr. Tyler will permit me to act as page without appointment and without compensation." Already at the age of fifteen Klair was more interested in the perquisites of a position, more lucrative and important to him than monetary gain.[6]

He took full advantage of his voluntary post. Other pages, "serving under appointment and regularly on the salaried list, were never too eager to do more than their actual duty required," but Klair "took advantage of this indifference on their part, and whenever a member summoned a page it was he and not the other boy that responded." In two weeks' time it was generally conceded that "little Klair . . . practically did the work of all the pages." When Klair approached Kinkead a second time, this time to propose the appointment of an extra page, he assured the respected legislator that the votes were there and "then named from memory the members upon whom he relied."[7]

With the legitimate position secured, Klair became the "best posted individual on the floor . . . followed every important bill throughout the intricacies of legislation, and could tell at any time from memory its exact status." In the following years Klair was appointed messenger, speaker's page, and sergeant-at-arms, steadily advancing through the ranks and rising in the esteem of the legislators.[8]

These years were exciting and educational for the young Klair. In Frankfort, he became familiar with the process of lawmaking as well as with the lawmakers themselves. At the same time he gained a rudimentary education in the complex world of Kentucky politics. He witnessed the bitter free silver elections—for governor, the senate, and the presidency—of the latter 1890s when a split in the Democratic ranks allowed Republican victories. When the legislature was not in session Klair hurriedly rushed home to Lexington, where he breathlessly recounted to his family and friends the latest news from the state capital. Klair did not forget his hometown. According to Kinkead, Klair even "in the humbler positions he had . . . filled . . . was never unmindful of Lexington, and accomplished more for her people in that subordinate capacity than many members did for their constituents, though equipped with the credentials of their people and enjoying a seat and voice on the floor of the House." In election years Klair was always available and eager to give assistance to the local Democratic organization at the precinct level.[9]

In 1898 Klair observed William Goebel, the president pro tem of the Kentucky Senate from Kenton County, as he introduced a bill entitled "To Further Regulate Elections," legislation that would become the Goebel Election Law. The bill empowered the General Assembly to appoint members to a "Board of Election Commissioners." The board would choose election commissioners for each of the state's counties, who would then select precinct officials, examine returns on election day, and rule on results. Many Democrats hoped the bill would keep Republicans from stealing elections, but the bill was controversial among Republicans and Democrats alike. Although it was introduced by Goebel as a reform measure, members of both parties "viewed it as a self-serving attempt by Goebel to strengthen his political power in the state."[10]

Klair admired the smooth tactics of the Covington senator, identifying instantly with the controversial son of German-born parents. The following year Klair attended the state Democratic convention in Louisville, which became known as the "Music Hall Convention." The convention resulted in a split of the party when some Democrats charged Goebel with trickery and deceit for his maneuverings in wresting the gubernatorial nomination from Parker Watt Hardin and William Johnson Stone. Dissatisfied Democrats later met in Lexington, denounced the Goebel Election Law and the Music Hall Convention, and nominated their own candidate for governor. Meanwhile, Republicans, encouraged by the Democratic split, nominated William S. Taylor.[11]

In 1899, while most of the attention was on the race for governor, Klair completed his rise from newsboy to precinct organizer to legislator when he was elected to represent the Sixty-first Representative District in the state General Assembly. Although strongly opposed by the press and the city's Protestant clergy, Klair garnered support from the city's young Democrats, led by Moses Kaufman, the Lexington reformer and old nemesis of Dennis Mulligan, and from John Whallen, the Louisville boss, who was along with his brother James the owner of the Buckingham Theater, hub of Democratic politics in the Ohio River city. While the Jewish reformer Kaufman rallied the local electorate, the Whallen brothers, aware of Klair's ability and energy, provided valuable financial support for the campaign. In his first election battle Klair realized the compatibility of bossism and reform. Winning by a plurality of some three hundred votes over Col. Roger Williams, the founder of Lexington's Iroquois Hunt Club, Klair benefitted from his years of apprenticeship in Frankfort. Because of his hardworking reputation as a page in the state legislature, and because the General Assembly exercised its new responsibility to choose election officials, Klair certainly "prospered under the Goebel Election Law."[12]

The newsboy's defeat of the "Colonel" was on the surface a shocking reversal of the southern, Bluegrass way, but closer scrutiny makes it a less dramatic shift. The old planter oligarchy, represented by the Colonel and associated so closely with the Bluegrass region of Kentucky, was grounded in an assertive and oppressive paternalism that secured power for the elite. That oligarchic structure, so familiar to southerners, at its heart shared a marked affinity with the developing political acuity of Billy Klair.

The paternalism of the reformers, referred to by John D. Buenker as "genteel activists" or "patricians," has been discussed by more than one historian. In *The Paradox of Southern Progressivism, 1880–1930*, William A. Link argued persuasively that "two fundamental values clashed" in the South during the Progressive Era: "the paternalism of reformers and the localism and community power of traditionalists." Link asserted that paternalism "explains the often erratic behavior of reformers: how they embraced uplift and progress, yet believed in a hierarchy of race and culture; how they were fervent advocates of democracy, yet also endorsed measures of coercion and control."[13] While Link referred to the paternalistic attitudes of reformers in racial reform and in reformers' attitudes toward poor southern mountaineers, paternalism was also related—on several levels—to southern bossism. In Lexington, Klair came to represent protection, security, and control in his benevolent watchcare of the city's German and Irish population, and his patriarchal largesse was extended to other poor, white Lexingtonians. Indeed, Klair's reputation as a friend of the city's less fortunate grew steadily and remains to this day; Father Leonard Nienaber, who in 1934 came to St. Paul's Catholic Church as a young associate pastor, in 1990 still remembered his communicant as "a Christian gentleman who loved children and the poor." And in 1999 Sonny Cloud, a lifelong member of St. Paul's, recalled that Klair often provided Cadillac rides for Lexington children during the early years of the Great Depression. Klair himself did not drive. Cloud remembered a dark Cadillac, but Cordia Jones, the wife of Klair's chauffeur, Tom Brown, verified that the car was a dark green Lincoln.[14]

Unlike some paternalistic reformers, Klair never worked for uplift and progress for Lexington blacks. What was remarkable for Klair, however, was the identification of members of the Bluegrass elite with the rising boss. The similarity between bossism and the paternalistic oligarchy of the Old South helped clear the way for Klair and Crump and other bosses in the New South. Certainly the old gentry, holding legislative seats in Frankfort and sipping bourbon on Bluegrass verandas, saw something in the young Klair that they both understood and trusted. And Klair, the son of German immigrants, was peculiarly at home among the Bluegrass horsemen and Jockey Club crowd.

So Klair, along with the other representatives, took the oath of office, swearing to support the constitution of the Commonwealth and further swearing that he "had not fought a duel with deadly weapons within this state or out of it." Klair was to fight and win many political duels during his tenure in the Kentucky legislature.[15]

Klair served as Lexington's city representative to the state legislature until 1909, was elected to the state railroad commission in 1911, and then to another term as representative in 1917. His nomination to more than two consecutive terms was the first time in the history of Lexington that anyone was honored in this way. It was his first term in Frankfort that set the stage for a long and often dramatic career in Kentucky politics. The disputed gubernatorial contest apparently ended, ironically, when the election commission appointed under the Goebel Election Law decided for Taylor over Goebel. Goebel immediately contested the election, however, and voters from the contested eastern Kentucky counties poured into the state's capital, reportedly on free L&N rail passes, to insure that justice was done.

It was in this tense atmosphere that Goebel was shot as he made his way to the capitol on 30 January 1900. The newly appointed Committee on Contest reversed the earlier decision and declared the dying Goebel the state's next governor. A majority of both houses, meeting in the Capitol Hotel because they were blocked from entering the capitol, met and signed a statement of approval of the committee's decision. Included in the list of senators and representatives approving Goebel's election was the name of William F. Klair. His name was also included on the list of congressmen signing the "Protest, Declaration, and Judgement," a document that denounced those connected with the crime.[16]

In hindsight, Klair's devotion to Goebel, who was described by a *Louisville Courier-Journal* writer as "the first to carry the liberal banner," was remarkable considering his later conservative political loyalties and his reputation as a reactionary machine politician. On the other hand, the Klair-Goebel connection revealed the often blurred line separating bossism and reform. Calling Goebel "the greatest man that ever lived," Klair followed his lead, at least in his early, legislative career, by promoting several progressive measures aimed at benefitting the constituents in the city that he represented. Klair also learned from Goebel the slippery maneuvers characteristic of bosses and machines.[17]

While in the legislature Klair was responsible for the passage of several forward-looking measures. Appointed to the Agricultural and Mechanical College, the Municipalities, the Railroads, and the Education committees, Klair found himself in an advantageous position to reward Lexingtonians for returning him to Frankfort. The location of the State College in Lexington, and the fact that with the increasing importance of the railroads Lexington was growing into a major distribution center for the state, made the proposals of Klair's committees crucial for the city. With characteristic energy Klair went to work immediately.

During his first term in the legislature (1899–1901), he introduced a bill to appropriate $60,000 to the State College for additional dormitories, a drill hall, a gymnasium, a Young Men's Christian Association room, and a building for the normal department. The following year an additional $30,000 was proposed and passed with Klair's support. Klair also successfully sponsored a bill to change the name of the college to State University, Lexington, Kentucky, making sure that the name of the "Athens of the West" was a part of the institutional title. Years later, in 1918, during Klair's last term as representative, the General Assembly "added to the euphoria at the university with a permanent grant of an additional $200,000 each year." When news of the new bill reached the campus, the student body "paraded exuberantly along Limestone and Main streets and paid deserved tribute" to Klair, who was responsible for skillfully guiding the bill through the legislature. Carl Cone, in his history of the University of Kentucky, noted that this "epochal appropriation inaugurated a decade of growth in state support for the university." Klair's efforts to make the school into what the *Lexington Herald* in 1903 termed "the peer of western seats of learning" encouraged the institution's president, James K. Patterson, to refer to the energetic legislator as "the best friend the University has ever had."[18]

Klair considered his support for the state university to be crucial to his political success. Whatever brought prestige and wealth to the university contributed to the prestige and economic prosperity of Lexington, and whatever prospered the city ultimately brought power and influence to Billy Klair. Colleges and universities in the South traditionally have been the bastions of aristocratic privilege. By identifying himself with Kentucky's state university, the former newsboy, perhaps yearning for recognition from Lexington's old order, acquired the semblance of aristocratic prestige. Such recognition did not come quickly or easily, but Klair knew it was necessary to get things done in the Bluegrass. Toward the end of his life the city's elite admitted him to membership in the city's prestigious Lexington Club, an honor that belatedly recognized the grudging respect that Klair had won.[19]

While in the legislature—remembering his father's desertion and his own challenging and sometimes unpleasant childhood—Klair also sponsored a series of juvenile reform measures, beginning in 1906 when a bill providing for "the punishment of persons responsible for or directly promoting or contributing to the conditions that render a child dependent, neglected, or delinquent" became law. Two years later Klair sponsored bills to strengthen the existing law by defining the powers of the county courts in reference to delinquent children and by providing for their care and treatment. Klair also promoted a bill that would alleviate the abuse of child labor. Once passed, the Kentucky Child Labor Law was dubbed "one of the most advanced in the Union." In 1910, Klair's sponsorship of a co-guardianship bill that gave the mother and father of minor children co-equal rights and left decisions of their upbringing to the courts in cases of separation or divorce won the praise of supporters of women's rights around the state. Prior to the passage of the bill the father's legal claim to control his children was undisputed. In March 1910 Klair received a letter from Laura Clay, a leading suffragist and a daughter of Cassius M. Clay, expressing "the very hearty thanks of the Ky. Equal Rights Association for your successful efforts in behalf of the bill."[20]

Other bills introduced by Klair provided appropriations for the Eastern State Lunatic Asylum, for the construction of roads in Fayette County, for the repair of the Henry Clay statue in Lexington that had been struck by lightning, and for the construction of a new capitol in Frankfort. Always concerned with education despite his meager learning opportunities at St. Paul's, Klair continued to sponsor bills providing income for the state university. He also introduced an education bill that would enforce school attendance for children between the ages of seven and fourteen, and make truant officers available to investigate absences.[21]

For Klair, politics was always an extremely personal affair, doubtless one reason so many of his pet legislative projects sought to address the glaring inconsistencies and disadvantages of his childhood. Klair's advocacy of progressive measures, especially in the area of education, must have baffled some political observers in the city, but Klair followed the path of other political leaders in his rise to power. Like George B. Cox in Cincinnati, Klair rose from newsboy to boss through the shrewd development of alliances. Cox was willing to go along with Hilltop reformers in the Queen City, an alliance that proved to be "one of his most valuable assets." Cox's machine followed the advice of its reform allies and "accepted the secret ballot, voter registration, and a series of state laws which, though retaining the mayor-council form of government with ward representation, were designed to give the city a stable and more centralized government." Klair was also willing to accept structural reforms for the city charter, a pet progressive goal of reformers. The administrations endorsed by Cox also supported improvements for the University of Cincinnati, allowed housing and gambling regulation, and suppressed the operation of "disorderly brothels," this all from a leader described as "The Biggest Boss of Them All," and from a machine characterized by Lincoln Steffens as "one great graft."[22]

Klair too supported reform measures in his quest for power, for while Klair pressed for needed reforms on the floor of the statehouse in Frankfort, he was steadily building a powerful political machine in Lexington. Klair's reforms—a boon to Lexington—did not interfere with his organization of power. Indeed, the bossism of Klair—a bossism that would rule Lexington for the first four decades of the twentieth century—unlike the bossism of Dennis Mulligan was built on a base of reform.

By the end of the new century's first decade, except for a brief stint as a railroad commissioner and one additional term in the General Assembly, Klair's public career was over. His political career, however, the career that earned him the designations of King Klair, "the undisputed czar of Lexington politics," and "the most powerful man in the state of Kentucky," had just begun. His real career was staged not only in the limelight of the capitol in Frankfort, but in the shadows of a smoke-filled office on the sixth floor of the Security Trust Building in Lexington and in a resort hotel in French Lick, Indiana, as well.

Part II

William F. Klair has frequently occupied the chair as presiding officer of the House at the present and at previous sessions, filling the same with dignity and always presiding impartially and with due consideration for the rights of all the members.

Legislative History and Capitol Souvenir of Kentucky, *1910*

Lexington, Kentucky is ruled by "two mangy rats." Yes, I'm referring to Thomas Combs and Billy Klair, "The Siamese Twins of Lexington politics." . . . rats carry disease, and in my judgment, we haven't got in this community any men whose influence is as bad and who carry more moral disease about them to corrupt the people than these two men. . . . Billy Klair is properly and justly regarded as one of the most corrupt men in the politics of Kentucky.

Henry T. Duncan Jr., Lexington reformer, 1910

4

Honest Graft and the Craft of Bossism

Klair used his years in the Kentucky General Assembly in Frankfort to lay the groundwork for his organization in Lexington, making connections with the right people and seemingly making all the right political moves in his bid for power. Klair worked as hard outside the capitol as within, sometimes discussing, arguing, or lobbying with political friends and foes well into the night. A.B. "Happy" Chandler remembered that in the late hours of the evening during the legislative session, Klair could usually be found around a poker table drinking whiskey and playing cards: "He played cards ... not big cards in those times; he played poker." Once when someone asked Klair about his per diem as a legislator, Chandler recalled that Klair answered, "Well, his per diem wasn't very much, but his per nightem was quite substantial. He didn't live off his per diem; he lived off his per nightem!"[1] It was in those nightly poker sessions that Klair made the personal political connections that would serve him well in city and state politics.

A reporter for a Lexington daily intimated that "some politicians govern by the force of their personalities, and this was Klair's way." Klair's personality, polished through years of living among Lexington's poorer classes, but mingling with the city's business elite, was perfectly suited to attract a wide range of voters. His "hold on the electorate was a highly personal thing. He mixed with people, knew thousands of them by their first name."[2] When asked if he knew Billy Klair, a Lexington barber replied, "Billy Klair? Yes, I knew Billy. Always spoke to everybody, Billy did—apologized for being sober—said 'call me Billy'—knew the people, Billy did—smart man Billy was—sold newspapers when he came here—yep, sold newspapers. Billy was a smart politician all right—well-to-do when he died—yes, I knew Billy Klair. He was a great guy."[3] The public's affection for Klair, coupled with his own political instincts made more acute through an encyclopedic knowledge of the state's political history, insured political success.

Physically, there was little about Klair to distinguish him from his contemporaries. Chandler, who counted Klair as a political friend, recalled, "He wasn't anything good to look at. He wasn't prepossessing. He wasn't a big fellow, 5'6" or 7" tall. He had a florid face which was the result of drinking a whole lot." Thomas Clark remembered his round face, and that he was always "rather nattily dressed," complete with bow tie and cigar. Others recalled that "he was gregarious but not loud, open-hearted but not ostentatious. He commanded a reasonably pleasant speaking voice but used it rarely at public gathering; his mind was orderly, his syntax good, but his verb declensions were horrid."[4]

Klair used his unprepossessing appearance to advantage. When he "apologized for being sober," when he encouraged voters to "just call me Billy" and called them by name, he was following the tried and true practices of successful politicians; he identified with the people. His down-to-earth manner certainly held the key to his influence and success on the grassroots level. Lexington attorney Harry Miller Jr. recalled that during his boyhood the well-known Klair once gave him a ten-dollar gold piece, a practice that was indicative of the politician's generosity and political savvy.[5]

Using the traditional tools of patronage, favors, and a strong precinct organization, Klair systematically established a power base in Lexington, eventually developing into one of the state's most powerful leaders. Chandler explained that Klair was "a tough operator." Like other political bosses he "did politics while other people slept." Coal for poorly heated hovels, Thanksgiving turkeys, and Christmas baskets were delivered without fail to hard-pressed Lexington residents. In return, votes were delivered in election after election. Klair did not make the mistake of some aspiring politicians described by Plunkitt of Tammany Hall: "Some young men think they can learn how to be successful in politics from books, and they cram their heads with all sorts of college rot. They couldn't make a bigger mistake." Plunkitt believed that "a young man who has gone through the college course is handicapped at the outset. He may succeed in politics, but the chances are 100 to 1 against him."[6]

Klair did not have to worry about Plunkitt's admonitions about political success. As Chandler asserted, "Billy was just a two-fisted practical politician. He wasn't well-educated or well-trained but he was politically smart, and astute. . . . He was a back door fellow, a bar-room fellow, smoke-filled rooms; he was a master of all that." As an afterthought Chandler added, "He absolutely controlled Lexington."[7]

Prominent in Klair's political rise was his increasingly influential role in Democratic Party affairs. Klair secured his first party position at the age of twenty-one when he was named a member of the Fayette County Democratic Committee. In 1916, while selected as the chairman of the joint city and county committee, Klair was also named a member of the party's state central executive committee. He served continuously on the state committee until 1936.[8]

Even Klair's familial connections proved politically advantageous. On 15 November 1900, Klair married Mayme Slavin, the daughter of Patrick and Mary Slavin, who were Irish grocers in the city. Through his marriage, Klair, at the beginning of his political career, gained an entree into a very influential segment of Lexington's population, a segment on which Dennis Mulligan had depended. The marriage of a German Catholic with an Irish Catholic certainly did Klair no harm politically; historian Thomas Clark recalled that those Lexingtonians following the Catholic faith had immense power in the city at the turn of the century. Chandler, who relied regularly on Lexington voters, believed that Lexington "was a Catholic community largely . . . and they ran the city politics." James Mott, in his study of Lexington's government written in 1947, revealed that there were "probably as many persons who vehemently assert that 'the Catholics run the city' as there are those who would deny such a fact existed." The arguments reveal that Catholic influence in Lexington's city politics was at least perceived to be significant.[9]

Perhaps dismissing the fact that bossism was prevalent in the South—the former governor and senator practiced a brand of it himself—Chandler likened Klair to the better-known political bosses of the larger cities to the north. Characterizing Klair erroneously as "a typical Irish politician . . . one of the first of the so-called city bosses in the United States," Chandler asserted that Klair "pre-dates Flynn and Kelly and all of the others that I know anything about."[10] Chandler was wrong on two counts; Klair, of German parentage, was actually one of the last of the old-time bosses. His practice of traditional machine tactics was learned from experience, in the rough and tumble world of urban politics.

When asked how Klair was able to maintain political power in Lexington, Chandler replied, "Well, the Irish first. He had their solid support. Then he controlled the jobs and everybody that got a job got a job from Billy Klair. He made the organization. He had a practical organization; hard working, practical; the saloon keepers, they were all for him; the city judge was for him, the city police were for him and he controlled the patronage . . . wasn't any trouble about him running the thing. He was the boss, and they all looked up to him to be the boss. They did whatever he said. That was a good strong organization."[11] Chandler recalled that at one time "there were twenty-five or thirty saloons on one square block in Lexington down there in the neighborhood of North Broadway and Main Street and Mill Street. All those fellows were for him." During Prohibition, Klair's identification with thirsty Lexingtonians and his control of the Lexington police department went hand in hand. His "Sunday School," which was really a get-together on Sunday mornings in his office at the Security Trust Building on Short Street, included friends on the police force who "kept him in touch with what went on in town." The lower-income precincts in the city's core always served as the base of the Klair organization, and Klair was always at his best at the precinct level.[12]

In his chronicle of Kentucky personalities, *History of Kentucky*, Charles Kerr described Klair as "a man of great force of character [who] has usually been in the lead when any movement has been on foot for the betterment of the city, county, or state." Just as Klair provided benefits in his early legislative career for the city's middle and upper-middle classes in the form of educational appropriations and other progressive measures, he also took care of his own: the poorer voters huddled along the railroad tracks at the edge of the city. Klair was careful to cast a wide net in his skillful use of patronage. Benefits were given and favors granted, but Klair's favors were often genuinely beneficial to the city, unlike "Boss" Tweed's systematic rape of New York City, and unlike Dennis Mulligan's stubborn objections to city improvements in Lexington. Like the Vare machine in Philadelphia, which often appeared to favor civil service reform, Klair offered no resistance when the Lexington public school board, and later the police and fire departments, adopted the merit system. Klair found, as did other city bosses, that recommendations could still be made for positions despite civil service regulations.[13]

Klair was a master of patronage politics. In a 1947 issue of the *Atlantic Monthly*, Edward J. Flynn, the head of the Bronx County political machine in New York, revealed the importance of "taking care" of the district leaders within the organization. Klair was obviously adept at "taking care" of his lieutenants as well as lesser party hacks. On election days crews of workers were used at the polls, providing large amounts of "petty patronage." These workers were paid for the day's work and given allowances when automobiles were supplied for transporting voters to the polls. In hotly contested elections, election day expenses were often heavy, but Klair never failed to reward the party faithful.[14]

In addition to "petty patronage," Klair's positions in the county and state party organizations provided opportunities to control more lucrative patronage plums. In Kentucky, state patronage was traditionally handled by contact men in the sitting administration, while county patronage was controlled by individual county courthouse officeholders. Klair not only served as the Fayette County contact man, but year after year he, along with others who made up a small coterie of party leaders, controlled state patronage as well. In the average Kentucky county most state patronage positions came from the highway department. Fayette County might merit more than one hundred highway department jobs. In a city that included the state university and Eastern State Hospital many more positions were available for those who voted correctly on election day.[15]

Rewarding those who remain faithful to the party line has been considered "the lifeblood of a political organization." Although this assumption has been challenged by political scientists such as Frank J. Sorauf, who maintained that unskilled patronage jobs do not attract persons having abilities that make them useful to the party, Klair's reliance on Lexington's lower classes combined with his provision of services for the city's middle and upper classes proved particularly effective.[16]

The mishandling of patronage by the administration's contact man often undermined the party's effectiveness, but this was not the case with Klair. His masterful and even-handed distribution of patronage within Fayette County indicated the skill of a consummate politician. A disproportionate number of Lexington names usually cluttered the state's payrolls, showing that Klair took care of his own, and his followers delivered for him in election after election.[17]

Like George Washington Plunkitt, Klair's business was politics. Other auxiliary interests, however, fitted neatly into his political schemes and provided capital for the essential patronage that oiled the machine. While Klair had supported reform legislation in his early years in Frankfort, back home in Lexington reform-minded residents had known for some time that Klair's progressivism was suspect. While his supporters winked at Klair's active involvement in numerous enterprises, others questioned his business activities.

Turn-of-the-century Lexington provided ample opportunities for aspiring businessmen and politicians. A southern city, Lexington in 1900 "differed substantially from the great metropolitan centers of the Northeast and Midwest." The 1900 census revealed that Lexington ranked as the 153rd largest city in the United States. Despite the "boom of the 1880s" Lexington's growth in the last two decades of the nineteenth century was modest. Lexington was ranked 110th in population among American cities in 1880 and 139th in 1890. Between 1890 and 1900, Lexington experienced a 22.3 percent growth rate, reaching a population of 26,369 as the city entered the new century.[18]

As Gregory A. Waller pointed out in his study of the entertainment industry in the city, Lexington was "not the Lower East Side of Manhattan, Chicago, or Worcester, Massachusetts." Rather, turn-of-the-century Lexington was then "a small city with little heavy industry, few first-generation immigrants, a substantial African-American community, a preponderance of native Kentuckians, and a sense of itself as being southern." While small, Lexington was still large enough to have "two daily newspapers, a park and playground system, its own anti-vice campaigns and high-culture concert series, a long-standing reputation as a profitable one-night stand for touring theatrical productions, and a range of public amusement ventures: skating rinks, amusement parks, vaudeville houses, and storefront picture shows, as well as palatial movie theaters."[19]

In its population makeup, Lexington was like other southern cities in its high percentage of African American residents. In 1900, "10,132 black residents accounted for approximately 39 percent of the total population." At the same time, African Americans comprised only 19 percent of the population in Louisville and only 0.5 percent in Covington, Kentucky's two largest cities. The composition of Lexington's population was similar to southern cities like Nashville (37 percent black), Chattanooga (43 percent black), and Birmingham (43 percent black).[20]

In 1900, only 924 or 3.5 percent of the population was foreign born, although 3,160 or 12 percent were classified as being of "foreign parentage." The city's foreign-born residents came from Ireland (428), Germany (181), England (88), and Italy (50). Both the Irish and the Germans—the ethnic heritages of Mayme and Billy Klair—represented influential groups in the city, but "they accounted for only a small part of the total population, and neither constituted an insular or ghettoized subculture."[21] The 12 percent of Lexington's population described as being of "foreign parentage" compared with 38 percent in Louisville and 49 percent in Cincinnati. Compared with other turn-of-the-century cities its size, Lexington in its ethnic makeup was again more like the southern cities of Jacksonville, Montgomery, and Chattanooga, and decidedly unlike cities to the north like Bay City, Michigan, Gloucester, Massachusetts, Joliet, Illinois, and Racine, Wisconsin.[22]

Still, in Lexington the dominant presence of the Irish on the police and fire forces and in social groups like the Friendly Sons of St. Patrick, and for the Germans in the German Enjoyment Club and German Lutheran and German Evangelical churches that offered "preaching in German," attested to a visible ethnic presence in Lexington. The German Aid Society was founded in 1882, and in October 1900 the *Lexington Herald* printed a page in German.[23]

Despite the growing respect of businessmen-politicians like Billy Klair, and despite the comparatively small ethnic presence in the city, some Lexingtonians feared what they perceived to be a growing threat to traditional mores. In 1896 a writer for the *Herald* feared the impact of the limited immigration of "Arabs" to Lexington:

Lexington is an easy going old town. It isn't much in the way of manufactories, but it has the best of everything else. It has always had its poor, and its evil quarters, but they have never been the poor and evil quarters of a great city. . . . It has even always had its tenement houses, but they have been Lexington tenement houses, in some indescribable way permeated with the shiftlessness and good nature of the South. They have not been the cut-throat dens lost in the darkness of a great city. But now this more innocent phase of squalor—if I may use the term—is undergoing a sinister change. Immigration is overflowing its murky reservoirs in the great cities and settling in doubtful pools among our streets. It is hideous to think of the cancer of such old world wretchedness fastening upon the conservative poverty-principles of old Lexington.[24]

Remarkably, it was in this community and in this atmosphere that Billy Klair rose to prominence in the early years of the twentieth century. Shortly before his marriage in 1900, Klair formed a partnership with Pat Mooney and bought "The Navare," a saloon located on the corner of South Limestone and Water Streets. Five years later, the two businessmen acquired the Leland Hotel, which at the time was reputed to be "one of the best and most popular hotels in the city," from John and Joseph Skain. This enterprise ended in tragedy in 1911 when Mooney was shot and killed by an irate guest in a dispute concerning overdue rent. With his partner gone, Klair sold out on 5 November to Charles and Julius Seelbach, but he continued to remain active in other business pursuits. In 1909 he became a member of the board of the First National Bank of Lexington, serving continuously until 1913, when it consolidated with the City National Bank to form the First and City National Bank. Klair served as the director of this institution until it merged with the Fayette National Bank and then served as the director of the new First National Bank and Trust Company.[25]

Klair also served as vice president of the Lexington Union Station Company, whose terminal—built by private capital—was leased to both the Louisville & Nashville and the Chesapeake & Ohio Railroads, as vice president of the Yellow Cab & Transfer Company of Lexington, and as the director for fifteen years of the Phoenix Amusement Company. While Klair was generally successful in these various enterprises, one business venture—the Klair and Grinstead book publishing concern—won for him widespread disdain. During his years as a legislator in Frankfort, Klair witnessed the lucrative contracts given to publishers for textbook adoptions for Kentucky's school system. Elected governor in 1915, A.O. Stanley, Klair's friend and ally, signed a school textbook bill into law in 1916, his first year in office.

The bill "limited the number of changes that could be made in textbooks used by the state so that book companies could not profit from frequent and trivial changes of textbooks." Stanley explained that "an education is the only heritage the poor man can leave his children, and the cost of school books is to him often a sacrifice, but an expense that must be met." Stanley assured the parents of Kentucky's school children that new adoptions would be made only "when absolutely necessary."[26] Despite this progressive measure the governor found it necessary to seek new adoptions during his administration, but not before setting up a textbook commission to oversee the process.

The highly partisan textbook commission initially approved textbooks published by Klair's Lexington firm. Stanley admitted that "every time there is a book adoption for the public schools of the state, some sort of a row has been raised, largely fomented by the disappointed bidders."[27] The 1919 adoption was no exception. Critics pointed out "the bitter contempt" of "every honest man . . . for an administration which ruthlessly broke this solemn covenant made with the school children of Kentucky." Stanley's "hand-picked textbook commission, partisan through and through," gave to the state an adoption that, according to the critics, "caused the people of Kentucky to hesitate between a gigantic laugh and a desire to commit murder." The commission's decision to adopt Klair's "Grinstead Speller" was made although the book was yet to be published, as Klair presented the speller to the commission in galley proofs. The critics suggested that if Klair had submitted a dictionary, the work would stop "at the letter 'G.' GRAFT was far enough."[28] Eventually the court of appeals declared the adoption illegal, and Klair's speller was rejected.[29]

Klair's various business enterprises proved secondary to Klair's most successful venture. On a winter evening in 1912, Klair visited the Elks Lodge, which was next door to the Opera House on North Broadway. While there he met Tom Scott, who had just returned to Lexington from an extended stay in

Wyoming. After a game of billiards the two men had a bite to eat and began to talk. They talked about Klair's two favorite subjects—business and politics. Scott indicated that he was looking for a business connection, had considered insurance, but knew nothing about it. Klair responded, "You can learn, can't you?" and suggested that they could work together in an agency. Because neither of them "knew one iota about the insurance business," Klair believed that the new enterprise "would make for interesting times." The Klair & Scott Insurance Agency was incorporated on 29 March 1912.[30]

Klair's unpretentiousness regarding his insurance expertise was unfounded. His tenure in the legislature had revealed the opportunities available for an enterprising businessman-politician in insurance. Klair used that knowledge well, and the firm soon gained the reputation of "doing the largest gross insurance business in the state." Ensconced in a sixth-floor suite of rooms in the Security Trust Building, the Klair & Scott firm enjoyed immediate success.

Interested customers entering the offices were met by Bessie Marie Birch—at her desk to the right of the entrance—unless she was out to a sandwich and soda lunch at the Lafayette Drug Store in the Lafayette Hotel. Miss Birch ran the office, answered the phone, kept the books, and sent the bills. Insurance decisions were usually made by Scott. From his rolltop desk in a room on the opposite side of the waiting area from Miss Birch, Scott kept morning hours before retiring for lunch and afternoon leisure at the Lexington Club. Klair worked at a large table in the same room with Scott. Scott's daughter-in-law remembered that Klair did not linger at his office table. He would arrive in the morning, stay long enough to go through his mail, and then leave to conduct his main business of politics—in the saloons and on the streets of the city, or in Frankfort whether he was a member of the General Assembly or not.[31]

Although Nancy Graves asserted in her study of the Lexington boss that Klair's interest in helping others prevented him from accepting "anything in return," the *Lexington Herald* revealed that while he was in the legislature he often defended various business interests, including those with which he was "vitally connected." Those interests included insurance.[32]

The insurance connection was not unusual for aspiring political bosses. Chicago's first ward political boss and city alderman, Michael "Hinky Dink" Kenna, as well as Edward Hull Crump, the Memphis boss, were in the insurance business. In the Klair & Scott agency it was understood that Scott would look after the insurance work while Klair handled the political end of the business. The business-political connection was understood. Like Plunkitt of Tammany Hall, Klair was a master of honest graft. Like Plunkitt he "seen his opportunities and he took 'em." When Thomas Clark—in Lexington during the Klair years—was asked if the Klair & Scott firm had been involved in insurance graft, he replied, "I don't think it was graft, per se. I think there were very generous contributions, and a very generous amount of work for the election of the governor. And they got the business; and the business was at a top price. They got the patronage without having to bid for it."[33]

Certainly the distinction that Plunkitt made between honest and dishonest graft was applicable to Klair's insurance dealings. Clark surmised that Klair & Scott carried a "tremendous amount" of the state's insurance. "Happy" Chandler believed that "they had it all, I think, had virtually all of it." In 1934 the *Courier-Journal* reported that since 1 January 1932 Klair had "written insurance on State property for which his firm, Klair & Scott, has been paid in excess of $19,000 in premiums. In addition the firm has been paid $2,610 as premiums on bonds of elected State officers." The Klair & Scott firm also wrote insurance for Keeneland, the race course and grandstand built in 1936, six miles west of Lexington.[34] Klair's connection with Kentucky's racing interests were legendary. In 1937, the year of Klair's death, the *Cincinnati Enquirer* reported that Klair & Scott had $444,550 out of a total of $2,618,441 of the state's insurance before the creation of the board of charities and correction, which apportioned the state's fire insurance among all the agents of the state.[35]

From his office on the fifth floor of the Security Trust Building, Charlie Wiley, elected to Kentucky's General Assembly in 1936 and later as Lexington's mayor, called Klair "a shrewd politician" and recalled that Klair "had fire and theft insurance on all the concrete bridges in the state."[36] Actually the firm's largest single contract was with the University of Kentucky. As "the best friend the University ever had," Klair was also befriending himself.

When in 1925 Henry K. Milward wrote Frank L. McVey, the university's president, asking to "be favored with a share of the insurance on the new addition to the Chemistry building," McVey responded that the "matter of insurance on the new Chemistry Building is placed through one agency. This is done in order to concentrate the matter of insurance and make it unnecessary for the University to deal with more than one concern. The Klair & Scott Agency have the insurance." In 1932 McVey assured Johnston Miller of Taylorsville that "for fifteen years the University has placed its insurance through one agency, relying upon the agency to make such distribution as seemed wise." The year before, Scott informed the executive committee of the board of trustees that a five-year note would cost the university, for all buildings, approximately $49,450.[37]

In 1936, under Governor Chandler, a system of self-insurance by the state eliminated the lucrative state contracts held by the Klair & Scott agency. Chandler recalled that Scott, whom Klair often referred to as an "office boy," "fell out with me worse than anybody because I passed a law requiring the state to carry its own insurance. That made him furious because he had that state insurance policy that made him about $100,000 a year and all he had to do was write insurance on fire-proof buildings. It was a racket, sort of." Klair's part in the "racket" netted him enough money for the *Courier-Journal* to report that at the time of his death he was one of Lexington's wealthiest men: "The democratic leader reputedly gave away thousands to charities. He is also said to have placed thousands into political campaigns to insure election of the candidate he was backing." The newspaper added that although the Klairs occupied an unpretentious home in the western part of the city, they were "wealthy enough to have built several mansions."[38]

Klair was not the only member of the Lexington machine to share in the results of the boss's inside influence. By the end of the century's first decade the Klair machine was firmly entrenched in the city. Although Klair had established himself as something of a progressive during his early years in the legislature, he soon alienated himself from Lexington's reform element. Klair supported Henry T. Duncan, the "Mulligan ally turned crusading reformer," in Duncan's bid for the mayor's office in 1899. When members of Duncan's reform regime, in Klair's words, "would not play ball," however, Klair eventually attached himself to the reactionary courthouse ring. When questioned about this bit of political maneuvering, Klair stated simply, "Well, Frank Bullock always hangs up something." By joining forces with Bullock, the Fayette County judge, Klair found that his operation ran more smoothly. Bullock welcomed Klair to the fold. In a matter of time Klair was the leader of what Mayor Duncan's son, Henry Jr., referred to as Lexington's "Big Six." In addition to Representative Klair and Judge Bullock, the "Big Six" included Louis des Cognets, a contractor and lieutenant of Gov. J.C.W. Beckham, Ernest Ellis, also a contractor, Thomas Combs, the mayor of Lexington from 1904 to 1907 and later a state senator, and John Skain, the college-educated mayor of the city from 1908 until 1912 and—along with his brother, Joseph—the former owner of the Leland Hotel. While the composition of Lexington's "Big Six" changed over the years, the one member that remained constant was Billy Klair.[39]

With several members of Lexington's political power structure involved in the contracting business, local newspapers repeatedly expressed concern over bids for street construction and coal contracts within the city. In 1911, when reformers had wrested control from the entrenched Fayette County court-house machine, the new county judge immediately approved a new coal contract that would apparently save the city hundreds of dollars. The *Lexington Leader* reported that the new contract called for the payment of $2.90 per ton, while Bullock—the former judge and also the head of the Home Construction Company, a concern that Klair served as a member of the board of directors—had paid $4.00 per ton to Louis des Cognets and Company without competitive bidding. Both Bullock and des Cognets, loyal members of the Klair machine, had benefitted from lucrative town and county contracts. With Bullock out as county judge, even the *Herald,* reluctant to agree with the rival *Leader,* expressed concern over the huge difference in road building in the county and that of street repair and construction within Lexington: "Wherein is the difference between the construction of the roads of Fayette County and the streets of the city of Lexington, that the taxpayers of Lexington should pay between two and three hundred per cent more for the construction of the streets than the construction of the roads cost?" The question of course was rhetorical. The difference was in the fact that the county's roads were controlled by the group of reformers who called themselves Fusionists, while the city's road department answered to the commands of Billy Klair.[40]

In 1909 Henry T. Duncan Jr., following in the reform footsteps of his crusading father as the Fusionists' leader, charged that several years earlier Louis des Cognets, as president of the Lexington Street Railway Company, had provided $1,500 for Thomas Combs's campaign fund with the understanding that, when elected mayor, Combs would grant des Cognets's company the right to lay tracks and run interurban cars into the city on Georgetown Street. Duncan further maintained that during Combs's tenure in the mayor's office expenditures for the repairs, reconstruction, and building of county roads alone amounted to $976,742.68, with most of that amount paid to favored contractors, such as Bullock and his Home Construction Company, without competitive bidding. Pointing to the county administration's extravagance, Duncan charged that the average cost of maintaining the courthouse was $15,000, while Louisville, Paducah, Newport, and Covington each ran their courthouses on less than $4,000.[41]

Companies favored by the machine raised the ire of the *Herald,* a newspaper often appreciative of the benefits Klair had brought to the city: "We will not respond now, by publishing a list of those who are directly or indirectly interested in the Central Construction Company and the Home Construction Company, which together have received contracts from the city and county aggregating tens of thousands of dollars. [These companies] are engaged in doing public work. They have been awarded contracts at prices which seem excessive."[42]

Road and street building had long been a lucrative source of "honest graft" for urban machines. Lexington's experience was no different. An ambitious streetcar system, begun with the construction of the first mule-car lines during the days of the Mulligan ring and during the formative years of the period of what was hailed as the "new Lexington" in the 1880s, provided thousands of dollars for machine coffers. The streetcar system had been viewed as the symbol of Lexington's transformation from town to city. A 1906 chamber of commerce publication proclaimed that "in the march of progress, no more important factor exists in our modern cities than the street railway service, and nothing does so much to extend the growth, and invite population and permanent investment, as a well-equipped, well-managed electric railway system. The people of Lexington have reason to feel a large measure of pride in their street railway."[43] The promotion of a mass transit system for Lexington, hailed by political hacks and reformers alike, revealed that bossism and reform were not mutually exclusive. What was good for Billy Klair and his machine was sometimes good for the city as well.

From 1880, when the earliest efforts at mass transit were being made, to 1930, when motorized vehicles were replacing the streetcar, Lexington's population doubled. In that period the largest increase occurred in the first decade of the twentieth century—during the heyday of the electric railway system and during the formative years of the Klair organization—when the population rose from 26,369 in 1900 to 35,099 in 1910. By 1930 Lexington had become the state's third largest city, after Louisville and Covington, with a population of 45,736.[44]

As the city spread out along streetcar lines emanating from the city's core, Billy Klair's machine branched out as well. The genius of Klair was that, unlike Mulligan, he was able to recognize and take advantage of the opportunities available in an expanding community. His advantageous linkage of bossism and reform was soon overshadowed by his more useful coupling of business and politics. The boss's generous distribution of Klair & Scott Agency calendars—handed out on election day or tucked into Christmas baskets—symbolized the more profitable connection. In short, as the city grew, Klair grew also, in wealth, influence, and power.

5

The Age of Progressivism and Beyond

B ecause of its growth and prosperity, and because of the enlightened educational opportunities provided in the "Athens of the West," Lexington, Kentucky, dubbed the "Queen City of the Bluegrass" by businessmen-reformers in the 1880s, had a unique opportunity to play a leading role during the period that has been called the Age of Progressivism. The city's roots of traditionalism, buried deep within the soil of the conservative South, along with the legacy of bossism established by Dennis Mulligan and perfected by Billy Klair, prevented any radical departure from the patterns of the past, however.

In Lexington the "Fusion Movement" was initiated in 1909 on what reformer Henry T. Duncan Jr. termed "the part of the upright, courageous and unpurchasable people of this community, irrespective of party lines against the most corrupt, daring and criminal political machine that ever had its grip upon the throat of the public." As the son was predicting "dire things" if the people allowed the continuance of the machine by electing the "Official Family Ticket," the apt name for Klair's slate of candidates, Henry T. Duncan Sr., Lexington's former mayor, opposed Klair in the race for city representative to the state legislature. Believing that Fayette County, under machine control, was regarded as the most lawless and corrupt county in the Commonwealth, the Fusionists, made up of dispirited Republicans and disgruntled Democrats, waged a bitter campaign against the machine.[1]

Concentrating their attack on Klair and former mayor Thomas Combs, the Fusionists lambasted past machine administrations, citing numerous instances of graft and voting fraud. Reminiscent of Dennis Mulligan's "sunburnt rock" escapade, Combs was accused of permitting thousands of feet of heavy lumber to remain in sewer trenches instead of requiring them to be taken to other trenches. Instead, still more lumber was purchased, presumably from the Combs Lumber Company, for each additional trench that was laid. Combs was also accused of destroying ballots and stencils used in an election which included a decision on the issue of $200,000 of bonds for building a city hall. In favor of the bond issue, Combs was seen by two men "sitting in the Mayor's office . . . stuffing into the open grate and burning the ballots, books, stencils and everything else used at that election." According to the Fusionists, Combs responded unabashedly that he burned the ballots because there were only 19 votes for the bond issue and 262 against. Later, when the returns were reported from that precinct, the bond issue passed by a vote of 194 to 99.[2]

Despite the reformers' accusations, Klair's candidates, except for the office of police judge, prevailed in 1909. Amid cries of voting irregularities Klair defeated Duncan in the race for city representative by the narrow margin of 3,061 to 2,929. Accusations of voting fraud continued to hound the Klair machine for years after the initial blasts by the Fusionists in 1909.[3]

The reformers' attacks continued in the 1910 elections with the publication of the so-called "deadly parallel registration lists." Although the Fusionists had been unsuccessful in procuring election victories in 1909, their claims of the promotion of increased honesty in registration and voting methods were substantiated by a comparison of the 1905, 1907, and 1910 registration lists. Focusing on the McNamara saloon building, a cold storage warehouse, and black tenements on the lot at the corner of West Main and South Spring Streets, the reformers accused the Klair machine of padding registration rolls with the names of floaters, repeaters, and "phantoms who had no existence." The Leader declared that neither "the Tammany Democracy of New York nor the Republican Machine of Philadelphia . . . ever did anything so flagrant or daring as to register 94 'voters' from a small group of buildings on a single city lot, which now [1910] in an open and clean registration shows up with only eight voters."[4]

In 1911 the machine was again accused of election irregularities. Samuel Wilson, the embarrassed Democratic Party chairman, reported that the Lexington Democrats were "cleaning up their act." Continued accusations of tactics such as the "old certificate buying trick"—purchasing fraudulent voting registration certificates distributed to friendly voters on election day—were leveled at the machine, however. J. Franklin Wallace, the antimachine candidate for mayor, accused police chief J.J. Reagan "and his band of pirates of swooping down on my lithograph cards" and destroying more than $200.00

worth of antimachine advertising. Reformers also criticized the machine's campaign style. A few days before the election, prospective voters were escorted by Klair and Thomas Combs—in 1911 a member of the state senate and chairman of the Senate Committee on Religion and Morals—to a nearby park for a preelection bash. A *Leader* article headlined "Whisky and Beer Were Plentiful at Fort Spring" reported that electric interurban cars, loaded down with a tempting supply of refreshments, gathered up crowds on Spiegel Hill and other suburban centers, continuing on in a gala procession to the park for added attractions.[5]

The reformers' most virulent attacks in 1911 were reserved for Klair in his bid for a position on the state railroad commission, although that position was considered less important than his stranglehold on the Lexington electorate. Described as "something that nobody understands," the railroad post was generally manned by fellows who "didn't do very much." With such headlines as "Chosen Few Approved by King Klair," the state's newspapers concentrated on the machine's domination of the Democratic Party. The *Louisville Post* reported that Klair was "now the undisputed Democratic boss of Lexington" and printed an editorial cartoon depicting a discerning "Miss County Unit" searching for a satisfactory lodging place. As she approaches the "Democratic Harmony Flats" she finds conditions in such an uproar that she decides to move on to the "O'Rear House" (O'Rear was the Republican candidate for governor). Back at "Billy Klair's Café" a campaign poster proudly boosts Klair's candidacy for railroad commissioner.[6]

In Lexington, the Duncans again led the assault against Klair. In late November Henry Duncan Jr. announced the deplorable state of a city ruled by two "mangy rats," attacking the rule of the city by a machine which fought, as one editorialist observed, "without gloves." With his strained voice barely audible because of countless tirades against the hated machine, Duncan admitted that he was referring to Klair and Thomas Combs, "the Siamese Twins of Lexington politics": Duncan whispered passionately that "Rats carry disease, and in my judgment, we haven't got in this community any men whose influence is as bad and who carry more moral disease about them to corrupt the people than these two men." Present during the "mangy rat" speech, Klair leaned against a tree only a few feet from the podium, puffing contentedly on his ever-present cigar. After Duncan, referred to by the *Herald* as "Sir Galahad," had delivered a particularly vindictive assault on "King" Klair, a Klair supporter in the standing audience, undoubtedly a recipient of the boss's largesse, remonstrated, "Shame on you!"[7]

Referring to Klair as "properly and justly regarded as one of the most corrupt men in the politics of Kentucky," antimachine forces turned their attention to Klair's voting record during his tenure in the legislature and questioned whether Klair as railroad commissioner would represent the railroad laborers or the railroad companies. Indicative of the degree to which he had abandoned Goebel's stand against railroad domination, Klair was now recognized by reformers as the candidate of the railroad interests, his legislative career marked "by a tender solicitude for the interests of the corporations." The *Leader* stated that Klair had "been largely instrumental in the defeat of various bills in which the brotherhoods of railway men were intensely interested."[8]

Despite his legislative record, or perhaps because of it, Klair was easily elected to a four-year term as railroad commissioner of the Second District, consisting of thirty-two counties, at a yearly salary of $3,000. During his tenure Klair's decisions disappointed but did not surprise those who had linked him with the railroad interests. Klair backed Goebel's old foe, the L&N, in the passage of a bill that forced Western Union to remove or lease any lines located immediately on the railroad. Klair refused to accept gifts of cash and clothes from elated L&N officials but was less obstinate concerning a gift of one of the first Victrolas ever made. Making the most of a lucrative position, Klair frequently used free rail passes issued by the companies until the passage of the antipass law, and when several coal mines canceled insurance contracts with the Klair & Scott firm, it was alleged that coal cars mysteriously failed to make scheduled stops in eastern Kentucky. Klair's abuse of the commission post was so obvious that he was unable to gain reelection in 1914. Following one of the few setbacks in his political career, Klair observed wryly, "My constituents have handed me my resignation."[9]

Klair's performance during his stint as railroad commissioner was indicative of a growing indifference to, and indeed an abandonment of, the cause of reform, a fact that the Duncans and other Fusionists had known for some time. A reform reputation had certainly served him well during the years of his rise to political fame and fortune, but it was increasingly apparent that reform was not the catalyst of his political agenda. Nor was Klair motivated ultimately by the prospect of financial gain or by the prestige afforded a person of his position. His successful attempts to stay out of the public eye and his lack of material ostentation precluded these temptations. Klair made money to give it away. Instead, Klair followed the well-worn path of other political bosses in a quest for power. This quest for power, a hallmark of political bossism, prompted Klair's political actions.

Klair's stand on the significant issues of the day—race, woman's suffrage, governmental restructuring, and prohibition—were all inspired certainly not by any allegiance to reform but by his struggle for power. Klair's mark on the city was undeniable. But the city's continued acquiescence to his designs was not simply the result of his successful quest for power. Postwar Lexington, with its growing southern identity, proved particularly receptive to Klair's political savvy and control. The patterns of paternalism, however altered in the structure of the boss system, refused to die in postwar Kentucky. In New South Lexington, however, in contrast to the Lexington of the Old South, white Lexingtonians alone were included in the boss's paternalistic system.

The race question and the issue of voting rights were intertwined in the Lexington of the New South. Following the Civil War, blacks drifted into the city from surrounding Bluegrass farms, and concerned white Lexingtonians, regarding the influx as a serious problem, mobilized support for measures to safeguard the city from the specter of "Negro domination." A change in the city charter included poll taxes for city elections. Other changes moved the 1870 city elections to February, well before the Fifteenth Amendment went into effect on 30 March, and extended the term of office for city officials from two to three years.[10]

With the coming of black male suffrage, as much as it was impaired by the city's new poll taxes, Lexington politicians made intense efforts to woo the city's growing population of black voters. At the same time blacks made mild assertions of their rights and privileges. In 1885 the *Arkansas Evangel,* a Baptist publication, deemed a Lexington meeting so important that it printed an article entitled "Colored Men Securing Their Rights." Black leaders throughout Kentucky met in Lexington and made plans to join "The Mutual United Brotherhood of Liberty of the United States," an organization targeting Jim Crow laws that restricted black access to hotels, restaurants, and railroads. Despite such efforts the city continued to treat its black population as a second-class citizenry into the twentieth century. While black individuals faced few opportunities for advancement, black voters grew in importance in the eyes of Lexington party officials.[11] Unlike some other white political bosses in other southern cities, Billy Klair was unsuccessful in his efforts to secure widespread black support. Because Lexington's black voters traditionally supported Republican candidates, Klair was often forced to find ways to discourage the city's black voters from reaching the polls. In 1909 Klair's cohort, Thomas Combs, was accused of initiating a "rough house" in a precinct where a large number of blacks were waiting in line to register. When this tactic failed to divert blacks from going to the polls, Klair began the practice of using black repeaters to increase the Democratic count. In 1906 the Klair machine was accused of purchasing from 1,500 to 1,700 illegal voting certificates for a few hundred hireling repeating voters.[12]

While this practice undoubtedly made a difference in election day results, Klair was never able to procure a majority of the legitimate black votes. In 1917 the *Lexington Leader*, stating that Klair and his managers were "making strenuous efforts to induce the Negroes of Lexington to vote for him," believed that "it is hardly likely that they will succeed to any appreciable degree." Klair had gained disfavor with the Lexington black community in an earlier legislative term by supporting House Bill No. 347, which would prevent the building of a school for blacks in Shelby County. A plan had been formulated to build Lincoln Institute there at a cost of $37,000 as an industrial school to educate blacks in "industrial arts and callings." Klair's bill, which was directed against the plan, was eventually passed over the veto of the Republican governor, Augustus E. Willson. The recalling of the incident in the *Leader's* "Colored Notes" section in 1917 illustrated Klair's continuing inability to woo black voters.[13]

Klair eventually admitted defeat in this area, claiming "nigger domination" by the Republicans. The *Lexington Herald*, usually sympathetic to the Klair machine, quoted a local black editor's remark that "when organized and capably led, the negroes shall become members of the Police and Fire Departments and of the various city boards." The fear of black dominance, striking a sensitive chord in the minds of Lexington's white citizens, was never realized. In response to the accusations the Republicans and later the Fusionists, led by Henry Duncan Jr., declared that the "only kind of negro domination I fear is that which may occur as the result of the work of demagogue politicians in this city who style themselves Democrats." The *Herald* retorted that "the only possibility of the Republican city ticket being elected is due to that negro vote."[14]

Race remained a significant issue in Lexington politics as in other cities. Klair's inability to gain black support was a conspicuous failure when compared to the success of bosses in other cities. Of course, Republican bosses like George B. Cox in Cincinnati were aided by their affiliation with the party of Lincoln, but Democratic bosses like Nashville's Hilary Howse and Edward Hull Crump of Memphis appealed to black voters as well. While Cox worked to smooth racial antagonisms in Cincinnati, the Howse machine "rose to power by mobilizing at least some of Nashville's black citizens, paying poll taxes, and granting favors to win their votes."[15] In Memphis, Crump perfected the art.

Crump turned to a member of his inner circle, Frank "Roxie" Rice, to oversee the registration and voting of blacks, a work that "entailed not only rounding them up in wagons on election day, but paying their poll taxes and treating them to barbecue and beer." Although he distanced himself from such activities, Crump "arduously courted the black vote," a practice—lamented critics—that "stemmed primarily from 'buying' their votes." Crump's tactics were so successful that blacks in Memphis "became a tightly controlled part of his machine."[16]

Unlike Cox, Howse, or Crump, Klair's failure in Lexington was more akin to Louisville's experience under the Whallen Democratic machine in the early years of the twentieth century. John Whallen found it unnecessary to "court the black vote" at all. At election time blacks "were closely questioned and their right to register challenged" by Democratic election officials. Fearful of police retaliation, many Louisville blacks simply stayed at home on election day. In *Life Behind a Veil: Blacks in Louisville, Kentucky, 1865–1930*, George C. Wright suggests that to fight the solid black Republican vote, Whallen and the Democrats encouraged black "shadies" to form Negro Democratic clubs. These clubs became bases to intimidate blacks to vote the right ticket. Wright asserts that "Negro thugs, as much as anything else, kept many blacks from viewing the Democrats as a respectable party." When Whallen's tactics failed, he like Klair resorted to playing on white fears that Republican victories would lead to "nigger domination."[17] Both Whallen and Klair relied increasingly on the fraudulent use of black "repeaters" to garner black votes illegally.

In Lexington, despite his inability to sway black voters, Klair remained victorious in election after election. In 1909, for example, Klair won a slim victory over Duncan by a majority of only 132 votes, with Duncan receiving practically the solid black vote. The slim margin was indicative of the erosion of Klair's power, which was based in part on his reliance on black repeaters and floaters. Accusations of voting irregularities against the Klair machine became so widespread and Fusion officials kept such a vigilant watch on election day activities that Klair despaired, "There was nothing doing, as you couldn't get next to a Negro with a $100 bill."[18]

Only later did Klair successfully forge alliances with members of the black community. Klair supported, for example, Green P. Russell, a two-time president of what is today Kentucky State University. A former principal of Lexington's black schools, Russell's political connection with Klair was no doubt strengthened through Kentucky State's insurance contracts with the

Klair & Scott insurance firm. The Russell-Klair alliance was an exception.[19] Klair was never able to add Lexington blacks to his base of support.

Black reluctance to support the Klair machine was also instrumental in influencing Klair's response to the woman suffrage movement. Kentuckians, and especially Lexingtonians, led the suffrage movement in the South. After the Civil War, national leaders Carrie Chapman Catt and Susan B. Anthony toured the state. In 1881 the Kentucky Woman Suffrage Association was founded, "the first such group in the South." This group later "transformed itself" in 1888 "into the broader-based Kentucky Equal Rights Association (KERA)." As president of KERA for twenty-four years, Lexington's Laura Clay was recognized by the 1890s "as the leading southerner in the National American Woman Suffrage Association (NAWSA)." Clay's father, Cassius Clay, despite his reputation as an antislavery reformer, had been decidedly opposed to women's rights. As witness to the "inequalities involved" in their parents' divorce, Laura and her three sisters eventually became strong supporters for rights for women.[20]

For Laura Clay and other Kentucky women's rights supporters, progress came slowly. And in one specific case a woman suffrage victory, gained early on, was overturned, largely because of the maneuvering of Billy Klair. Women had been able to vote in school board elections in Kentucky's second-class cities—those cities having populations between 20,000 and 100,000 (Lexington, Covington, and Newport)—since 1894. In Lexington, women's support for the Democratic Party had been negligble since the turn of the century. Perhaps women reformers, those active in reform politics in Lexington, admired the reform Republicanism of Theodore Roosevelt. Others railed against the corrupt inefficiency of the Democratic machine. In the city's school board elections of 1901, only 662 women registered as Democrats, while 1,997 were listed on the Republican rolls. Counting male and female registrants, Republicans outnumbered Democrats 4,393 to 4,073. Despite these statistics, the Democrats carried the election by 572 votes. The victory was "far from an honest triumph," however, as even the *Lexington Herald* admitted. The polls where women were to vote remained closed until noon, eliminating any opportunity for voting by black domestics. In addition, all election officials were Democrats. The *Herald* concluded that the "ordinary Negro found it was almost impossible for him to vote at all."[21]

The importance of the school board elections in providing patronage for the Lexington machine was evident. Fearing other Republican registration majorities in the future, Klair along with Sen. J. Embry Allen introduced bills in January 1902 to disenfranchise women residing in second-class Kentucky cities. To concerned progressives within the Democratic ranks, Klair explained that "1,900 colored women and only 700 white women registered and voted" in the last city election. His insistence that "colored women practically controlled ... school elections" in Lexington did not explain how the Republicans had managed to lose in 1901.[22]

Clay and other Lexington women sought to derail the legislation by organizing the Committee on Retention of School Suffrage for Women. With representatives from the Fayette County Equal Rights Association, the Woman's Club of Central Kentucky and the Woman's Christian Temperance Union, the committee was nonetheless unable to overcome the political clout of Billy Klair. Klair's fear of the negative political potential of black women voters and his argument that white women would not bother to vote resulted in the Democratic legislature's repeal of school suffrage for women in the state's second-class cities in 1902. Under pressure from Lexington women led by Laura Clay, Klair revealed his true fears by offering a substitute bill which would exclude only "the ignorant and illiterate class from the polls." This revision, aimed at disenfranchising Republican-voting black women, was rejected, and the original bill became law by a vote of 67 to 20 in the House and 23 to 12 in the Senate. In his study *Laura Clay and the Woman's Rights Movement,* Paul Fuller stated that this "was the only instance in the history of the movement where the franchise, once won, was taken away by action of the legislature." The repeal indicated how insignificant reform had become in Klair's struggle for control of the Lexington electorate. Resulting from a longstanding fear of black rule in Lexington, the repeal also illustrated the importance of race in the politics of Lexington and "the central role that race played in the history of the southern woman's rights movement."[23]

According to Fuller, the Klair-Allen legislation had a far-reaching effect on the national suffrage movement. Forced to alter their goals because of the social attitudes made plain in the battle over the repeal of Kentucky's law, suffragists, especially in the South, tended to be "confirmed in a racist mold." Realizing that their loss of the franchise occurred because too many illiterate black women voted, Kentucky's woman suffrage leaders began to back school suffrage for women who could read and write. When suffrage for all women was lost, "they reacted by trying to gain it for their own elite group."[24]

For Laura Clay the defeat was an especially bitter disappointment. Ironically, at the same time that the Klair-Allen legislation progressed through the

House and Senate to the governor's desk, Clay was appointed to the chairmanship of the Increase of Membership Committee of the NAWSA, her rise to national prominence coming in the wake of "the painful and embarrassing defeat in her own state."[25] In Kentucky, Madeline McDowell "Madge" Breckinridge, great-granddaughter of Henry Clay and the wife of Desha Breckinridge, editor of the *Lexington Herald* and the son of the ex-Confederate William Campbell Preston Breckinridge, became president of KERA in 1912. That same year Breckinridge led the fight to regain school suffrage, reversing the defeat of her predecessor Laura Clay. After Kentucky ratified the Nineteenth Amendment—one of only four southern states to do so—in 1920, Breckinridge cast her first and only vote for president in November 1920. She died a few weeks later. Breckinridge and Clay, two Lexingtonians, had made a remarkable contribution to the fight from their base in Billy Klair's Lexington.

As for Billy Klair, both his fear of the attraction of the Republican Party for black women voters and his belief that white women would continue to neglect their duty to the Democrats shaped his attitude toward the woman suffrage movement until the ratification of the Nineteenth Amendment. At the same time, the rise in the movement of Madge Breckinridge, the wife of newspaperman Desha, a Klair admirer, complicated matters for him. Desha Breckinridge endorsed Klair in his bid for railroad commissioner. "Though we have disagreed with him on numerous occasions and disapproved of his course in numerous matters," Breckinridge wrote, "we are fond of him and believe that he was one of the most efficient representatives ever sent from Lexington to Frankfort." While disagreeing with Klair's tactics, Breckinridge concluded that "no one could have accomplished more for the material benefit of Lexington than has Mr. Klair during his services in Frankfort."[26]

In September 1911 the Breckinridges hosted a dinner meeting at "Aylesford," their home on Linden Walk. The guest list, dominated by leading "machine" members, was reported in the 3 September edition of the *Leader:* Frank A. Bullock, county judge of Fayette County; William Preston Kimball, chair of the Democratic city and county committee; John Skain, the machine-backed mayor; George S. Shanklin, member of the county election commission and the fire and police commission; Louis des Cognets, an influential businessman; and Billy Klair, "conceded to be the most influential man in his party in this city and county."[27]

Around the time of the dinner party at the home of Madge Breckinridge, Klair's regard for issues important to women was in the process of revision. As with other issues, Klair's stance on woman's rights was less than consistent. In 1910 his support for a co-guardianship bill, giving mothers and fathers of minor children equal rights and leaving questions of the upbringing of children in cases of separation or divorce up to the courts, won praise from leaders of the woman's movement, notably Laura Clay.[28] His support of the co-guardianship bill and the regranting of suffrage in school elections in 1912, a reversal of his earlier victory, was not an indication of the waning of Klair's power. Instead, his changing reactions to Kentucky's woman suffrage movement was vintage Klair, yet another indication of his use of practical, personal politics in his quest for power. His support of certain women's reform measures important to Madge Breckinridge was a small price to pay for the favorable press her husband could provide.

Another indication of Klair's shrewdness as a politician came with Lexington's decision in 1911 to adopt a commission form of city government. The plan would organize Lexington's government around departments headed by a group of "commissioners" elected at-large. This progressive measure was first tried in Galveston, Texas, after the city administration was found wanting in the aftermath of a catastrophic tidal wave and flood in 1901. In Lexington, the commission movement began in December 1909 with the naming of a committee to study the plan. The chairman of the committee, Judge Charles Kerr, lectured in support of the new plan to law students at the State University. His address was entitled "Cities Should be Managed and Controlled as Any Business Corporation, rather than Treated as Political Organization— Old Forms No Longer Adequate."[29]

Lexingtonians debated the issue throughout the following year. J. Ernest Cassidy led the anticommission forces, while Kerr enjoyed the surprising support of the city's machine-elected mayor, John Skain. The commission issue complicated the November 1910 elections for reformers and machine politicians alike. With headlines such as "The Old Machine Makes Last Stand" the *Lexington Leader* continued to lambaste the Klair organization, despite the fact that Klair appeared to back the progressive commission plan. Stating that the crafty Klair had attempted to "make people believe that the Machine leopard has changed its spots," the Fusion Party, beaten soundly by the machine the year before, stepped up its campaign.[30]

In reality the Fusionists were placed in a difficult position. To the surprise of many, Klair and Thomas Combs, as members of the General Assembly, had allowed the bill, granting cities of the second class the right to change their form of government, to become law. As a result the reformers were faced with the prospect of the hated Klair giving his blessing to their pet progressive project. The *Leader* pointed out the irony of the situation by printing the remarkable argument against the commission plan that was heard daily on the streets of Lexington: "I know things are bad and that any change ought to be an improvement, but I am afraid of any bill that 'Billy' Klair and 'Tom' Combs put through the legislature. There is a 'nigger in the woodpile,' somewhere, and I am not going to take any chances on the new charter."[31] The newspaper suggested that if Klair and Combs had prevented the passage of the charter amendment in the General Assembly, it would have been more appealing to Lexington's forward-looking citizens.

Klair actually surprised the reformers with his support of the new charter. After all, his influence in naming Lexington's mayors since 1904 made any change in the old mayor-council system, which he had mastered and dominated, a nuisance for the Klair machine. The "widespread impression" was that Klair would not permit a change, but unlike Dennis Mulligan in his stubborn resistance to the charter changes of the 1880s, Klair illustrated his political acumen by supporting an amended version of the original measure in the General Assembly. A stipulation was added permitting a return to the old form of government after a four-year period if the residents of a city were dissatisfied with the commission plan.[32]

The reformers attempted to disavow Klair's support by pointing out that Klair was simply yielding to public pressure. In arguments that echoed the criticisms of the Mulligan ring in the 1870s, Lexington's twentieth-century reformers questioned how "any stranger visiting Lexington, and taking note of its physical condition, its utter lack of civic pride and municipal advancement, [could] hesitate for an instant to try anything different from what we now have." Despite such arguments the Lexington electorate failed to pass the commission plan in 1910. Although Fusion candidates swept most of the city offices, the commission plan failed by 747 votes.[33]

Reformers and machine politicians immediately began a strange yearlong campaign in favor of the commission plan. Reformers argued that despite a clause in the city charter of 1886—admonishing members of the police and fire departments to limit their election day activities—the police and fire departments had been for years little more than a "political annex of the ruling party organization," a condition that would be remedied by the departmental structure of the commission plan. In response, George S. Shanklin, a longtime member of the machine, presented a petition with 1,999 names of Lexington residents favoring the commission form of government. Not to be outdone, the reformers countered by distributing a pamphlet entitled "Commission Government in Brief," which asserted that Klair and Combs were not responsible for the proposed amendment to the city charter. The pamphlet assured Lexington voters that "the proposed amendment to the city charter as presented now to the voters is the identical charter prepared by the committee of business men and differs in no wise as it is finally presented to the voter . . . from the original copies handed by the committee to Senator Thomas A. Combs and Representative W.F. Klair in the last session of the Legislature. Not even an 'i' dotted or a 't' crossed, nor was there a punctuation changed from the original bill." This comedy of accusations and rebuttals continued until the commission plan was finally adopted on 7 November 1911 by a majority of almost two to one, and the plan officially went into effect on 1 January 1912.[34]

While the reformers rejoiced, Lexingtonians patted themselves on the back. The acceptance of the progressive measure was seen as another important step in Lexington's rise from a backward town to an enlightened city. Far from being a triumph for the reformers, however, the decision by the Lexington electorate to change the structure of the city's government played into the hands of a grinning Billy Klair. Klair looked with favor on a plan that would replace a mayor, eight aldermen elected at-large, and two councilmen from each of six wards with a commission representing the city-at-large. Under the new plan there would be less danger of reformers being elected from Lexington's eastern wards. The concentration of reformers in these wards had posed a definite threat to Klair's control for several years before the new charter was accepted. Klair realized that he still could elect and control the commissioners in an at-large system. The increased centralization of Lexington's city government actually worked to Klair's advantage. Recent studies by political scientists and sociologists conclude that bosses built their machines in the wake of centralized charter reform.[35] By consolidating his own power, while at the same time dispersing the reformers' power and influence, Klair remained the dominant voice in Lexington politics for another quarter century.[36]

The headline of the *Lexington Leader* proclaimed "The People Speak with Voices of Thunder and the Lexington Machine Is Broken." In 1912, a year in which the crusading Theodore Roosevelt was leading the Bull Moose Party in an ill-advised bid for the presidency, the city of Lexington experienced its first year under the "progressive" commission form of government. Although Lexington was enjoying progress in the form of a growing population and an expanding economy, that progress was not evident in the workings of the city's new commission government. The machine was not broken. It continued on in its new commission form.[37]

After five years under the commission plan, Klair was still in control. Following his failure to win a second term for railroad commissioner in 1914, Klair attempted a return to the legislature in 1917. The *Lexington Leader* lashed out at its old enemy in characteristic fashion. In fact, editorials from the *Leader* would lead a newcomer to Lexington to believe that under the dictatorial rule of Klair the city was without benefit of five commissioners. Even the editors of the *Herald*, while noting their fondness for Klair and remembering his industriousness as a lad "selling newspapers on the street a quarter of a century ago," proclaimed that politically "he has been our enemy ever since he entered politics." Although the *Herald* admitted that the law establishing the commission plan could not have been enacted without his support, the editors also refused to forget that the Lexington boss had once attempted to "destroy" the *Herald* as punishment for the newspaper's opposition to the liquor interests. Nonetheless, the 9 October 1917 edition of the *Herald* included a remarkable, if somewhat murky, endorsement of the boss: "We, therefore have no political reason to advocate his election. But we believe he should be elected than that his opponent should be elected."[38]

Just as the vote on the commission plan dominated election day conversations six years earlier, the liquor question was the overriding issue in 1917. Despite the Commonwealth's historical association with bourbon, Kentucky was one of the first states in the South to support temperance. A strong temperance movement, initiated before the Civil War, reemerged "in the postwar decades with renewed confidence."[39] The legislature enacted Kentucky's first local option law in 1874, and by 1915, 106 of the state's 120 counties had adopted prohibition, and "only twenty-three towns in the state still granted licenses to saloons."[40]

Lexington remained decidedly among the "wet" communities. Ironically, leaders of the Woman's Christian Temperance Union and the Independent Order of Good Templars hailed from dripping "wet" Lexington, and the Anti-Saloon League had strong supporters in the city. Lexingtonian George Washington Bain presided over the twenty-four-thousand–member Order of Good Templars, and Frances Estill Beauchamp, another resident of the city, led the WCTU. Prohibition advocates agreed that liquor "destroyed families, corrupted elections, and provided power to a 'Beer Trust' or a 'Whiskey Party.'"[41]

If Billy Klair's support of commission government was vague in 1911, his stand on the issue of Prohibition was understood clearly by all. A former saloon operator himself, Klair had profited handsomely from the lucrative liquor trade of his Leland Hotel, and his taste for whiskey was well-known. Klair was identified as a supporter—indeed, as a leader—of "the liquor interest" in the state. As a member of the legislature, the budding boss made deals around a poker table, playing cards and drinking whiskey. Klair's reputation alone, for drink and for shady political deals, made him a ready target for supporters of Prohibition.

Despite its long-standing opposition to the liquor interests, the *Herald*'s endorsement of Klair for the legislature resulted from the newspaper's confidence that Prohibition was inevitable, with or without the support of Lexington's city boss: "The Legislature will by an overwhelming majority, if not by a unanimous vote, submit to the voters of the state a constitutional amendment drawn in accordance with the views of the Forward League. It is ascribing far too much power to Mr. Klair to think that he . . . could prevent the passage of such an amendment, which is decreed by the fates. Whiskey will not be sold in Kentucky again. . . . It will not be sold in Kentucky when the present supply is exhausted."[42] The *Herald* proposed that neither "Mr. Klair nor any other individual can prevent the coming of prohibition or the granting of suffrage to women."[43]

The *Herald*'s argument proved sound, but the coming of woman's suffrage and prohibition, movements that Klair earnestly opposed, did not deter the boss from his quest for power. On 2 November 1917, only four days before the election, Governor Augustus O. Stanley arrived in Lexington to offer Klair his support in his bid for a legislative seat. William Townsend, the Democratic campaign manager, met the "slightly inebriated" governor at Union Station and escorted him to the Phoenix Hotel, where he was able to recuperate in time to deliver a stirring speech that evening at the Opera House in Klair's behalf. During the speech, the "dripping wet" Stanley echoed the *Herald*'s belief that "the next legislature certainly would submit a bone-dry prohibition amendment to the State constitution." The colorful governor went on to defend Klair's stand as the representative of his Bluegrass constituents; Lexington and Fayette County had repudiated prohibition in an earlier referendum by a majority of thirty-four hundred votes.[44]

While the prohibition amendment was a certainty, the *Lexington Leader* realized that the issue would not make or break Klair. The *Leader* concentrated instead on Klair's lack of loyalty to the Democratic Party, giving as an example his support in 1908 for the Republican W.O. Bradley over the Democrat J.C.W. Beckham in a race for a U.S. Senate seat. In response to the *Leader*'s question "Was Klair a true Democrat?" Governor Stanley asked if "the editor of the *Leader* is a fool or does he think you are fools?" Putting Klair and his Democractic fidelity on trial, Stanley called on prominent Democrats as witnesses to the boss's integrity and party loyalty. Klair was obviously found not guilty, at least by the Lexington electorate, as he defeated his opponent, A.B. Thomason, by the staggering margin of 3,162 to 1,225. Except for the North End precinct, Klair carried all 39 of the city's precincts.[45]

Klair's victory was the result of his popularity and the smooth running of a well-oiled machine. On election day the veteran organizer was on the "firing line" early, keeping up his activity all day, traveling from precinct to precinct in an automobile, distributing rewards, and keeping in close contact with his loyal lieutenants.[46] As these activities ensured election victories for the machine, reformers had railed against such tactics, especially when they led to the defeat of a reform candidate.

The reformers' censures proved useless. In 1917, following Klair's overwhelming victory, Lexington's reformers finally conceded defeat, even admitting a certain fondness for the personable boss. At the same time, the reformers revealed the source of their opposition and distrust of Klair. In their words, the city's progressives believed that Klair's record "as a politician of the machine type is out of harmony with the spirit of progressive democracy that is sweeping over the world today." As an example of Klair's objectionable methods, Dr. A.J.A. Alexander, a reform-minded Democrat and chairman of the Democratic Forward League, recalled that when a particular vote was taken in the legislature Klair had placed gunmen on the floor of the House to intimidate members of the majority, an action that caused "such a riot of force and fraud as to make the session one of the most scandalous in the history of the state."[47] Although Klair was not adverse to the rare threat of force on the floor of the General Assembly, or calling out thugs to disrupt the vote on election day, his use of tactics of intimidation was usually much more subtle.

The *Leader* suggested that Klair, now returning to Frankfort, could use his influence to secure an "honest vote" on the prohibition amendment and to enact a "real civil service law for cities of the second class." During a previous term in the legislature Klair had continued to keep the reformers off-balance by introducing and securing the passage of a bill placing Lexington's firemen and policemen under civil service rules. Klair's shrewd use of machine tactics, combined with well-timed and well-chosen reform causes, continued to serve the masterful boss during his last stint in the General Assembly.[48]

Despite frequent stabs at progressive reform—commission government, civil service laws, woman suffrage, prohibition—Lexington continued in the conservative mold of a southern city as the nation entered the First World War. Cries for clean government continued to fill the editorial pages of the Lexington dailies, but the city was slow to change. As the city prepared for war along with the rest of the nation, demands to clean up other aspects of city life were voiced as well.

For some time since the European war began in 1914, Lexington movie-goers had viewed motion pictures of the battlefields at the Ben Ali Theater. After the sinking of the *Lusitania* in 1915, and with Germany's resumption of unrestricted submarine warfare in February 1917, some Lexingtonians began to contribute to the British-American War Relief Fund. The city's influential German population, which included Billy Klair, found it more difficult to rally to the Allied cause. *Herald* editor Desha Breckinridge urged President Woodrow Wilson to take immediate action. Patriotic rallies held at Woodland Auditorium indicated growing support for America's involvement in the war, and when a declaration of war was passed by Congress on 6 April 1917, Lexingtonians responded enthusiastically.[49]

On 14 April, more than fifteen thousand patriotic Lexingtonians gathered at Cheapside for a rally that featured martial music and a moving address by Governor Stanley. The rally prompted the city to action. Many college students left their campuses to enlist. At the University of Kentucky all able-bodied male students were enrolled in four military organizations. The students continued to attend classes, but they moved to company barracks and drilled for an hour or so each day. The Student Army Training Corps was housed in two-story wooden barracks on the corner of Rose and Winslow Streets. This site became Camp Buell, named after the Union general Don Carlos Buell.[50]

The city's university students were not the only members of Lexington's population to take an active part in the war effort. Dr. David Barrow, a local surgeon, organized the Good Samaritan Base Hospital Unit No. 40. Mobilized on 24 February 1918, the hospital unit totaled 223 enlisted personnel, 100 nurses, and 48 medical officers. Consisting largely of local men and women, the unit left for England on 5 July 1918.[51]

Lexington was designated as a mobilization site for Kentucky troops soon after the war was declared. The establishment of an army camp near Lexington, considered a coup for the Lexington business district, was not an easy acquisition. Although Lexington was presented in glowing terms as a safe place where one could raise a family by chamber of commerce publications, by World War I parts of the city had acquired a decidedly unwholesome reputation.[52] Serious complaints against prostitution in the city had begun in the first decade of the century, although various "disorderly houses" had operated in Lexington since the 1790s. After the Civil War certain sections of town were identified as "red light" districts. The earliest, "Babylon Block," was later replaced with "Rat's Row" and "The Hill." A grand jury report in 1911 referred to "The Hill" as "a disgrace to the city." Reporting again in 1913 to Judge Charles Kerr, a grand jury indicted the owners and operators of various "resorts" along "Rat's Row." Included in the report was an indictment against Belle Breezing for running a bawdy house at 153 Megowan Street, and for selling liquor without a license.[53]

Breezing's establishment, which *Time* magazine referred to as "the most orderly of disorderly houses," had by the 1890s become "one of the largest and most lavish establishments south of the Mason-Dixon line." Catering to Lexington's elite—"successful, influential and socially prominent men of the community"—and also to wealthy out-of-town patrons, the popular madam allowed no gentlemen downstairs who were not dressed in proper evening attire. Belle's house, a stately brick mansion, was located near the center of the so-called vice district, in close proximity to the other, less pretentious establishments of Blanch Patterson, "Snooky" Simpson, Lizze Hill, Barb Burnell, and "Mother" Board.[54]

By 1915 the Lexington vice district included Megowan Street (now Northeastern Street) and extended from 345 Wilson Street to East Short Street. An argument for the "segregation" or separation of prostitution in a restricted area had been made for some time. Prostitutes were checked for venereal disease once a week, and the police made regular rounds through the district, not so much to arrest offenders as simply to maintain order. Some arrests were made, but as John D. Wright concluded in *Lexington: Heart of the Bluegrass*, "there does not seem to have been a consistent or persistent attempt to stamp them out entirely."[55] Dependent on votes from operators, practitioners, and frequenters of the houses, Billy Klair refused to tamper with a proven base of support. In 1915, however, in the face of growing concern, Lexington's machine-backed mayor J. Ernest Cassidy appointed, with Billy Klair's blessing, a committee on social hygiene. This committee, which later became the city's vice commission, brought in experts from the American Social Hygiene Association, an organization presided over by Harvard's Charles Eliot and whose membership included Cardinal Gibbons and Jane Addams. The results of their investigation, published in the vice commission's report to the city commission, shocked Lexingtonians to action.[56]

The extent of the problem was laid out clearly. The commission defined a parlor house in the segregated district as an entire building devoted to the business of prostitution. Parlor houses also existed outside the vice district, along with single rooms or "assignation houses that were used for immoral purposes." Each parlor house was presided over by a "madam who transacts all business, collects the money, secures inmates, makes all the arrangements with the inmates, pays all the bills, and secures customers."[57]

During the investigation the commission visited twenty-eight parlor houses within the district, twenty-seven additional houses outside the district, and twenty-two assignation houses. In addition the investigators were solicited by thirteen prostitutes to go to five different hotels. These numbers, when contrasted with the findings of a similar investigation in Richmond, Virginia, a southern city four times the size of Lexington, illustrated the extent of the city's vice problem:

Parlor houses in Richmond	*Parlor houses in Lexington*
Within the district 24	Within the district 28
Outside the district 29	Outside the district 27
Number of inmates, counted 178	Number of inmates, counted 156
Number of inmates, estimated 211	Number of inmates, estimated 188
Population 150,000	Population . . . . .40,000[58]

Almost all of Lexington's prostitutes were from outside the town, coming from Louisville, Cincinnati, and Cleveland, and increasingly from Knoxville, Huntington, Dayton, and Hamilton, cities which had recently closed their segregated districts. The customers of these houses were found to be "as a general rule, boys, students, laborers, clerks on small salaries and strangers in the city." On Saturday and Sunday evenings, groups of noisy, often intoxicated young men crowded along the streets of the district. Cabs and taxis brought patrons to the doorsteps of the more expensive establishments. Many of the customers were under twenty years of age, much younger "than the investigators have found among the customers of other cities." Upon arrival at the disorderly houses the young patrons were treated to liquor and dancing. The dancing was described by the vice commission investigators as "vile, vulgar, and degrading to the extreme." The commission concluded that the "liquor and dancing are the dangerous stimuli that make it almost certain that every caller will become a customer, even if his sole purpose at first is merely curiosity."[59]

Although the commission wanted it understood that it did not "assume an attitude of hostility or censure towards the City Commissioners or the police for not having satisfactorily dealt with this perplexing problem in the past," they reported that police stationed in the district were there merely to prevent disorder. They revealed that officers were seen in "certain houses" and that one officer recommended a house to a prospective customer. The commission found the sanitary conditions of the houses appalling, describing a typical house "filled with dirty furniture, the halls are dirty, and the whole atmosphere is foul with unhealthy odors."[60] The commission's conclusion of the overall impact of Lexington's houses of prostitution in the city contrasted sharply with the chamber of commerce's portrayal of an elegant southern city of culture and enlightenment: "The slot-piano, with its cheap and trashy music, the indecent dances of the brothel, the sale of liquor, the steady presence of pimps and madams—all these things play their part to stimulate the sex-instinct and so increase the demand, and therefore the supply. In addition to all these things, madams and owners of the houses have boasted to our investigators that this is a wide open town and that nobody bothers them."[61]

According to the commission, the most serious result of the city's negligence in the area of vice was the detrimental influence on the children of the city. The School Census of 1915 listed 10,598 school-age children. Noting the "generous provision" made for them in the area of education, the commission also emphasized that the child's environment made important contributions to character and ideals. The commission, asserting that each child had the right of protection from vice, played its trump card in its war against evil by stating, "The presence of a section in our town, where vice in its most degrading form is tolerated, is a menace to every boy and girl in Lexington."[62]

The commission made the telling revelation that more children lived in the Fourth Ward, "where this open sore of Lexington is located," than in any other ward in the city. The census numbered 1,756 white and 1,633 black children, for a total of 3,389 school-age children in the notorious ward. This total equaled one-third of all the children in Lexington. The Constitution Street Public School was located in full view of the rows of disorderly houses. The principal of the school related to the committee that on leaving school at the age of fourteen, many of the school's former students went to work in one of the nearby houses. It was common for both black and white children to be seen playing in the street as scantily clad "inmates" watched, smoking cigarettes, from parlor house windows.[63]

This last volley, aimed squarely at the city's disregard of a well-known problem, found its mark. The resulting public outcry and the hope of presenting Lexington as a logical site for the military mobilization and training site that eventually became Camp Stanley encouraged Mayor Cassidy and the city's board of commissioners to pass the city's first antivice ordinance in December 1915. As Lexington churches observed "Purity Sunday," reformers cheered the commissioners' action.[64]

After the passage of the ordinance, Cassidy, intent—in 1917—on publicizing yet another progressive accomplishment for the city, assured Raymond B. Fosdick, chairman of the Committee on Training Camp Activities, that "if there is a single disorderly house in Lexington we are not aware of it." The unbelieving Fosdick was astonished at the mayor's revelation "in view of the well known conditions in Lexington, which even a superficial investigation would uncover." Fosdick eventually called on yet another commission to investigate. The commission sent back their findings with the terse statement: "To sum up: prostitution and liquor are running riot."[65]

Devoted to the securing of the military site, Lexington officials sent a portfolio of materials to the Central Department of the U.S. Army. The packet included assurances from the board of commerce, the Rotary Club, and the editors of the *Lexington Leader* and the *Lexington Herald* that the city would give a "square deal" to all military personnel. Adequate rifle and artillery ranges were guaranteed and "pure food assured." Military officials were reminded that the original list of 140 saloons had been cut to 105, a number that would eventually be lowered to 75. Strict law enforcement was promised, and the blight of prostitution, while not completely eradicated, would continue to be combated. Despite Commander Fosdick's dismay at the ineffectiveness of the antivice ordinance, the city's persuasiveness paid off, and Camp Stanley was established on Garrett W. Wilson's Lansing Farm, a 245–acre tract located on the north side of Versailles Pike west of Hamilton Park. Three-hundred "box barracks" were erected to house the new arrivals, and the city's store owners rejoiced at the added business.[66]

Despite the rash of promises made by city officials to secure the camp, and although Belle Breezing's establishment as well as several other less-publicized houses were shut down, Lexington's police officers continued to ignore the problem of prostitution in the city. The fact that the new Camp Stanley commander declared the city's "red light" district off-limits for his soldiers was evidence enough that prostitution had not been wiped out.

With the nation's declaration of war, most Lexingtonians turned their attention to the war itself. While all Lexingtonians experienced the effects of rationing—"meatless" Tuesdays and "wheatless" Wednesdays—the war made life especially uncomfortable for some of Lexington's residents, including Billy Klair. Those Lexingtonians of German heritage faced intense anti-German sentiment: "Selections of literature by German authors were scissored out of school textbooks, no German or Austrian music was played or sung, and even the harmless name of kindergarten was to be banned as a 'Hun name' and replaced by 'primary circle." And Governor Stanley, Klair's ally and friend, vetoed a measure that would have forbidden the teaching of German in Kentucky's public schools. Certainly Klair's German heritage, albeit assimilated through the years into the culture of the Kentucky Bluegrass, made the war years a particularly uncomfortable period for the boss.[67]

All Lexingtonians, regardless of ancestry, rejoiced when news of the armistice was announced in November 1918. The news brought welcome relief from the sacrifices of the war that at home had been coupled with the city's struggle with the nationwide epidemic of Spanish influenza. In Lexington, more than 1,000 cases were reported, and "at least 51 people had died." The epidemic at the end of the war "swept through the troops at Camp Buell on the University of Kentucky campus," and Lexingtonians succumbed to the outbreak regardless of class or economic status.[68]

The recognition of some of Lexington's less seemly traits by the Lexington elite before the war—briefly put aside during the war years—continued after the war. For Lexington, as in other urban areas, an obvious and noticeable problem was the deplorable state of the city's housing. According to the 1920 census, Lexington was essentially a city of single family homes, with 10,720 families living in 9,500 dwellings. Although approximately 200 "double houses" and small apartments were scattered throughout the city in 1920, practically no large apartment houses served as dwelling places. Lexington had long been famous for the architecture of its private dwellings. The wide range of styles, which included Federal, Greek Revival, Neo-Gothic, Italianate, Renaissance Eclectic, and Richardsonian Romanesque designs, lent an air of urbanity and elegance to the city.[69]

The Comprehensive Plan of Lexington and Its Environs, printed in 1930, revealed that "in most of Lexington's residential districts the homes are up to the best American housing standards." Even the new "double houses" and apartment houses of the "efficiency type," located for the most part along High, Maxwell, Rose, and Broadway Streets, with some immediately north of the central business district, were well-built, well-situated domiciles. Small apartments, which could house from four to six families, had only recently been built in some of the best outlying residential sections of the fast-growing city. The 1924 *Housing Survey of Lexington,* printed for the city's board of health, asserted that it "is possible to walk through street after street in the southern and southeastern parts of the city and scarcely see a house which is below standard."[70]

On the surface visitors admired the charm of Lexington. The city's architecture told the story of a place full of culture and "historic associations." The city's elite, ensconced in the historic homes around Gratz Park and Transylvania College's Old Morrison, basked in the glow of architectural refinement. Despite the descriptions of beautiful, well-landscaped, and architecturally appealing home places, neglect of particular housing areas and dramatic shifts in the city's population caused increased concern for observant Lexingtonians.

The flight of Lexington's white middle class to the suburbs followed the pattern of other growing cities. At first following the streetcar lines along routes emanating from the city's core, the automobile freed the middle class to move into the interstices and into developing subdivisions at the fringes of the city limits. Between 1910 and 1930, 65 percent of the increase in Lexington's white population found housing in outlying subdivisions. Among the eleven thousand residents moving to the new areas in that twenty-year period were many that came from the Fayette County countryside to enjoy the advantages of life in a thriving city. Others, however, involved in the "white flight" syndrome, moved away from the city's older residential districts because of the intrusion of commercial establishments, and because of the shifting of the city's black population. In contrast to the white population, most of the increase in the number of Lexington's African American residents occurred in the older sections of the city. Only about 20 percent of the city's black population moved to outlying Georgetown Street, a new black subdivision.[71]

This shift in population caused concerned residents to notice the decline of some of Lexington's older neighborhoods. Eventually the established but traditionally poor neighborhoods, such as Chicago Bottom, Brucetown, Davis Bottom, Goodloetown, Yellmantown, Pralltown, and Irishtown, received most of the new attention directed toward the city's blighted residential districts. These areas, described by Lexington reformers as mostly "poor colored neighborhoods," were founded originally as philanthropic ventures by wealthy residents such as John A. Prall, a Lexington lawyer, who "laid out Pralltown far down on South Broadway" after the Civil War. Prall built row houses for the city's blacks, "in whom he was so deeply interested," according to the standards of the day, with generous open spaces for air and light. By the 1920s, however, these houses had degenerated into dilapidated shacks, far from sanitary and "so badly out of repair that they should be vacated, unless practically rebuilt."[72]

Pralltown was not an isolated example of poor housing in the city. The conductors of the city's housing survey found dozens of Lexington streets in similar decline, neighborhoods of "three room frame houses and flimsy shacks . . . crowded together, many of them dilapidated, damp, unsanitary, which do not qualify even as shelters against inclement weather." Many of these "blighted neighborhoods" in the center of the city's historic areas could be traced to the servant quarters of an earlier day, placed conveniently out of sight in the rear of Lexington's fine old mansions.[73]

The mansions themselves were undergoing change. Many had been rebuilt and made into apartment or rooming houses. Few were still maintained as private residences. The rebuilt houses, occupied by several families, soon lost their original charm, becoming overcrowded, depressing dwellings with inadequate facilities. Housing conditions were blamed for an increased reliance throughout the 1920s on charitable organizations. In 1923 the Family Welfare Society reported under the heading "Why They Came" that poor housing and sickness were the two greatest reasons for welfare requests. Out of the 343 families asking for help in 1923, 222 individuals came because of bad housing conditions, while 217 reported needs because of sickness.[74]

The extent of the effects of poor housing for the entire city was emphasized in the board of health's *Housing Survey of Lexington*. In 1923 nurses from the Public Health Nursing Association made 10,995 calls to 4,606 patients. The caseload included 162 new cases of tuberculosis in addition to the 981 cases on hand at the beginning of the year. A total of 4,161 treatments were given to 663 new patients suffering from venereal diseases. The board summed up the fears of many health officials with the statement that "a cook, a laundress, a chauffeur, a nursemaid, a barber, a clerk, coming from a home where there is infectious disease, brings the germs to daily work."[75]

Housing was a problem for Lexington's poorer residents, regardless of race, although statistics showed a predominance of poor black housing. When the influx of Irish immigrants came to the city in the mid-nineteenth century to work on the railroad building projects, the railroad companies built cheap housing for the workers along the tracks in Irishtown and Davis Bottom. These projects were in close proximity to the black neighborhoods. By the 1920s dwellings in the Irish sections were in a deplorable state, and housing for Lexington's blacks was even worse. Cards filled out by public health nurses after their visits to many of the city's ramshackle residences indicated that out of the families visited, eighty-six were black and forty-eight were white. A prominent black physician summed up the growing concern of black and white Lexingtonians over the city's poor housing conditions: "We have to take the alley standard out of the lives of our people, as well as taking the families out of the alley."[76]

The individual who did more than any other Lexingtonian to take the "alley standard" out of the lives of the people was Madeline McDowell Breckinridge. After overcoming a near-fatal bout with tuberculosis, Madge Breckinridge served at the forefront of other urban reform endeavors in addition to her work as president of the Kentucky Equal Rights Association. In 1908, influenced by the settlement house programs of Jane Addams in Chicago, Breckinridge began to solicit funds for her plan to start a similar project in Lexington. With a $10,000 donation from the Lexington Board of Education and a sizable $30,000 grant from Robert Todd Lincoln, the eldest son of the martyred president, Breckinridge completed the building of the Lincoln School in 1912. Located on the corner of West High Street and De Roode Street, the school "provided classrooms, a laundry, cannery, swimming pool, and both afternoon and evening programs for the parents of the day students." Elizabeth Cloud, trained at Addams' Hull House, served as the school's first principal.[77]

The irony of the Lincoln School, named after the son of the Great Emancipator and built by the daughter-in-law of one of John Hunt Morgan's raiders, was typical of Lexington's diverse but productive past. Despite such efforts, the problems of poverty and poor housing continued to plague the city. According to the housing survey, the filthy, disease-ridden houses "which are shelters, but not homes, [produced] lack of thrift, bad working habits, criminal standards, low earning ability, and improper living standards." The Lexington underclass continued to concern city officials into the 1920s and 1930s, as the additional crisis of the Great Depression approached.[78]

As it turned out, the fetid neighborhoods, representing the underside of the community, and hidden behind the embarrassed whispers of Lexington's elite, were fertile grounds not only for venereal disease and crime but also for the aggressive manipulations of a political machine. For it was in the notoriously poor districts that Billy Klair built his machine, providing minimal services for a desperate people.

Political and social change were evident in Lexington during the first three decades of the twentieth century. As the city grew in population and expanded economically, battles over commission government, prohibition, civil rights, and women's rights were fought, and concerns over the city's vice and housing problems were raised. Hulking in the background, casting a long shadow over the affairs of the city, was Billy Klair's political machine. Often presenting the semblance of progressive reform, but usually relying on heavy-handed machine tactics, Klair skillfully guided Lexington's Democratic organization in his quest for power.

For Klair, reform was not the end, but the means to an end. The party was not sacred for him. His frequent desertions of the Democrats as a member of the statewide organization known as the bipartisan combine would attest to that. It was his quest for power and the maintenance of power that became all-consuming. In the end, when all of the calendars, Thanksgiving turkeys, and Christmas baskets were delivered, and after all of the votes were counted, it was not the leader's deeds that really mattered. It was his ultimate designs. In the first two decades of the twentieth century, those designs made Klair the leading political power of Lexington. In the 1920s and early 1930s, Klair's power and influence would extend beyond his local domain, and would cause individuals like John Y. Brown Sr., a political opponent, to refer to the Lexington boss as "probably the most powerful man in the state of Kentucky."[79]

Lexington set aside the week of 31 May through 6 June 1925 to celebrate the sesquicentennial anniversary of the city's founding. The Sesquicentennial Jubilee Celebration of Lexington, Kentucky, culminated in a festive historical pageant, various episodes of which honored heroes of Lexington's past and celebrated turning points in the city's history. The last episode honored the city's role in the Great Crusade, a war in which "Lexington played a full part, giving her best without stint."[80]

The pageant was appropriate. For all of its failures, Lexington could stand with a confidence that belied its nagging problems. The ambition and vision of the city's progressive leadership was made tangible in the sesquicentennial celebration. The pageant presented Lexington as a vibrant city, as in many ways it was. But the pageant also carried a symbolism that was lost on most Lexingtonians at the time. Like Lexington's history, the pageant was a charade, masking the failures and glossing over the hard realities of the city's past. For Lexington, the realization of the vision presented by the pageant would not be derived from mere speeches and pageantry but would only follow in the wake of a national disaster.

King Klair and the Bipartisan Combine

B y the time Billy Klair and other Lexingtonians celebrated 150 years of history in 1925, the city's political boss had extended his power and tight control over his local domain to the larger sphere of state politics. The charade of Lexington's sesquicentennial parade was played out on the larger stage of state politics. And it is impossible to interpret the drama of state politics in the 1920s properly without referring repeatedly to Billy Klair, or King Klair as supporters and opponents alike called him during the decade.

King Klair established a foundation for statewide political influence during his public career as a legislator in Frankfort. His admirer and sometime critic Desha Breckinridge had admitted in 1911 that "it is true that the whisky men are for him," but the editor also praised Klair for the statewide reputation already garnered by the young politician:

During the years, totaling nearly twenty, in which he has been in Frankfort, either as a page or as a member of the Legislature, he has done innumerable services for innumerable men, scattered over Kentucky. When a page there, he won the friendship of men of every section, representing every view; active, courteous and accommodating, with marked ability and he always seized the opportunity to do a favor for anyone who gained his friendship or commanded his admiration. As a member of the Legislature he pursued the same course, so there is scarcely a county in the State in which he has not acquaintances, and few, if any, in which he has not friends attracted by his personality or under obligations to him for some act of courtesy.[1]

It was a logical extension of power and influence for the boss. Klair used his experience in the state capital to build a statewide following, but his reputation as the boss of one of the Commonwealth's leading cities served him well, too. After all, Lexington, along with Louisville and Covington, represented the urban domain of the Roaring Twenties in a largely rural state.

In Lexington, both Prohibition and woman suffrage led to temporary political setbacks for Billy Klair's machine at the beginning of the decade. Lexingtonians, however, continued to adhere to the boss's paternalistic agenda in the Roaring Twenties. At first glance, the rise of Billy Klair in a southern city was remarkable considering the degree of respect given to a son of German immigrants by many Lexington blueblood, bourbon power brokers. Klair played the role of paternalistic political master for poor and dispossessed white residents of Lexington, relying on their votes in election after election, but he eventually gained the support of the Bluegrass elite as well.

It was during the 1920s decade that Klair rose to the height of his power, exhibiting a political acumen learned and mastered through years of political maneuvering. A photograph of a mass political rally on Cheapside in the 1920s to elect representatives from the Third District to the state central executive committee of the Democratic Party gave ample notice of Klair's continuing popularity. Members of the crowd, several thousand strong, held banners and signs hailing Klair as the party's choice.[2] Klair was chosen to represent the district successively from 1916 to 1936. Because "the chief business of [the committee was] to supply the party with leadership necessary to the organization and conduct of campaigns," and between elections to be involved in "the influencing of matters of patronage," Klair's involvement in Democratic Party work facilitated his rise to statewide influence.[3]

Despite woman suffrage and Prohibition, Jazz-Age Lexington provided the perfect backdrop for Klair's political machinations at home. Kentucky ratified the Nineteenth Amendment on 6 January 1920, and Gov. Ed Morrow signed the suffrage bill implementing the amendment into law. Men and women made up the crowd at a mass rally for the Democratic Party on Cheapside on 3 May. A few women became politically active themselves in the 1920s—following the lead of Laura Clay and Madge Breckinridge—but it was not until the 1930s that a woman was elected to a major municipal post. Florence Shelby Cantrill, the great-great-granddaughter of Isaac Shelby, Kentucky's first governor, and the surgeon Dr. Ephraim McDowell, secured the support of Klair and won a seat in the state legislature in 1933. Cantrill eventually became Lexington's first woman city commissioner as a member of Klair's "Home Town Ticket" in 1936.[4] Billy Klair had come a long way since his fight in 1902 to repeal suffrage for women in school board elections, but the impact of women voters in post–Nineteenth Amendment Lexington did little to alter machine control in the city. As Lexington chronicler John D. Wright concluded, the "fears of many men that the American political scene would undergo radical transformation because women could vote were hardly justified."[5] In Lexington, Billy Klair still held sway.

Neither was Klair deterred by Prohibition. Despite strong temperance support, support that led to Kentucky's first local option law in 1874, Prohibition did not come to Lexington until statewide and national Prohibition in 1920, but even then it was not enforced in the city. Kentucky humorist Irvin S. Cobb noted that Prohibition was so strictly enforced in the state that at times "a thirsty stranger may have to walk all of a half a block to find a place where he can get a drink." In Billy Klair's Lexington, the boss's control of the police department insured lax enforcement of the Eighteenth Amendment. Historian J. Winston Coleman Jr. made home brew in his Lexington basement and recalled later that "each family [in the city] had a favorite bootlegger from whom they got their liquor."[6]

As with charter reform in the previous decade, Klair's masterful maneuvering in the 1920s kept Prohibition from mounting any formidable threat to the power structure within the city. Another issue, however, provided another opportunity for Klair when he attempted to broaden his sphere of influence throughout the state. Along with bourbon whiskey, tobacco, and coal, horse racing—both thoroughbred and harness—has long been associated with the Commonwealth. By the 1920s, only Kentucky and two other states continued to have legal betting at racetracks. When reformers attempted to outlaw parimutuel wagering—a system of racetrack betting in which those backing the winners divide, in proportion to their wagers, the total amount bet after a percentage has been taken by racetrack operators—in the 1920s, Klair's alliance with Bluegrass horsemen proved critical to the future of the horse industry in the state. The stakes were indeed high, particularly for Klair's Bluegrass, upper-crust constituency. And although Klair had been forced to devise nuanced responses to local threats posed by commission government and woman suffrage, his response in the 1920s—as with his earlier response to Prohibition—to an antipari-mutuel wagering movement was not uncertain. It was both this issue and Klair's alliance with the Jockey Club that brought Klair statewide notoriety in the 1920s.

Klair actually relied on a tried and true method that had proven effective in earlier battles. He forged effective alliances with sympathetic, and sometimes divergent, groups to meet his ends. His cultivation of diverse constituencies in Lexington ranging from the city's underclass to the Bluegrass elite proved effective in establishing a base of local power. In the 1920s Klair's close association with the Jockey Club, and his more ambiguous connection with a group known as the bipartisan combine, brought varying degrees of approbation and castigation.

Political alliances were, of course, not new to Klair and other politicos in the state. Indeed, Klair's first brush with state politics in Frankfort, in 1898, provided intense training in the art of factional politics. J.C.W. Beckham, elected as house speaker in that session, and William Goebel, chosen as president pro tem of the senate, represented two political factions. The Goebel assassination two years later illustrated an extreme result of state political factionalism. As state historians Hambleton Tapp and James C. Klotter noted, when that regular session of the General Assembly convened on 4 January 1898, "two later-to-be 'bosses' and political masterminds of the Democracy, Percy Haly of Frankfort and William F. ("Billy") Klair of Lexington, made their debut"—Haly as sergeant-at-arms of the house and Klair as assistant sergeant-at-arms of the senate.[7]

If he was introduced to factional politics in that 1898 legislative session, Klair became an active participant during his legislative tenure and then as the boss of Lexington in the first two decades of the twentieth century. Then in the 1920s Klair found ample opportunity to perfect the art.

In his study of Kentucky politics, Robert Sexton argued that, in essence, Kentucky factionalism was "molded by personalities, or power groups, and ideological labels were at best tenuous." And local factionalism, according to Sexton, often influenced politics throughout the state. Sexton described local factionalism as "an underlying theme" of Kentucky politics.[8] Once included in a group of power brokers in Lexington dubbed the "Big Six," Billy Klair eventually overshadowed other members of that group, and by 1930 the "undisputed czar of Lexington politics" was included in a statewide "Big Six," a group of local political bosses who also "controlled power in Kentucky." This statewide junta included Klair, Ben Johnson of Nelson County, Michael J. "Mickey" Brennan of Louisville, Albert W. "Allie" Young of Morehead, and Frankfort's Percy Haly, Democrats all. Maurice Galvin, a Republican from Covington, was also recognized as a member of the group.[9]

Each of these individuals had built substantial power bases. Together, these six men named governors, allotted patronage, and generally "controlled power" in the Commonwealth. Four members of the group—Klair, Johnson, Brennan, and Haly—were Catholic. Realizing that "statewide election stood out of their reach" because of their religion, they "thus turned to being the men who controlled the office they could not win."[10]

Of the "Big Six," only Haly stood politically apart from the others. He allied with J.C.W. Beckham, and it was "through Haly's political genius that Beckham won the governorship in 1900, reelection in 1903, and a seat in the U. S. Senate in 1914." Vilified by opponents as a political boss and described by one scholar as "the preeminent political organizer of his day," the "General" died in 1937, having developed pneumonia while directing flood relief efforts in Louisville.[11]

While Haly directed Beckham's reform-minded campaigns and "counseled others on how to win and retain office," other members of the "Big Six" represented another major faction of the state's Democratic Party.[12] Ben Johnson had long opposed the Beckham-Haly faction. Bardstown's "Boss Ben" perfected the art of patronage politics, first as a state legislator, as a collector of internal revenue for the Fifth District, and then as a member of the state highway commission. Johnson had sought the Democratic nomination for governor in 1911, "but stepped down before the primary because of opposition to his Catholicism."[13]

Mickey Brennan became "the unchallenged leader of the Democratic party in Louisville." Coached by the Whallen brothers, "the controlling influences of the Democratic party in Kentucky at the turn of the century," Brennan, the son of Irish immigrants, displayed "a sharp wit, a keen memory, a knack for organization, and ambition" as he followed his mentors to statewide political prominence.[14] Not a Catholic, Allie Young practiced law in Morehead and was elected to the state senate in 1923, a position he held until his death in 1935. In northern Kentucky, Maurice Galvin, a Catholic and a Republican, was elected as commonwealth's attorney in Kenton County, "a heavily Democratic area." Like Johnson, Galvin served as a collector of internal revenue. He was later successful in several business pursuits, all the while keeping a hand in statewide politics.

Although a Republican, Galvin developed a close friendship with Billy Klair. Together with Johnson, Brennan, and Young, Galvin and Klair formed a "formidable coalition of political leaders [that] made and unmade Kentucky governors for two decades." The group, representing the Bluegrass, eastern coal counties, and urban centers in central and northern Kentucky, became a formidable, if sometimes ambiguous, force in the state. Dubbed the "bipartisan combine," the coalition generally protected railroad, coal mining, liquor, and racetrack interests in the state by supporting like-minded candidates regardless of party affiliation.

Although he sometimes benefitted from the support of Klair, Happy Chandler remembered bipartisan combine members as "reckless and ruthless." Chandler asserted that if "the Democrats insisted on nominating a candidate they didn't cotton to, they would unite behind the Republican" and then concentrate on trying to control his program in the legislature.[15]

Through his earlier opposition to Beckham, Klair had already learned the effectiveness of working with disgruntled Democrats and with Republicans across the state. Members of the Haly-Beckham faction accused him of party disloyalty. When Klair ran for railroad commissioner in 1911, W.P. Walton, a well-known newspaperman in the state, editorialized that the "Nomination of W.F. Klair to be railroad commissioner proves three things,—that the whisky men are in the saddle, that a man can bolt the Democratic nominee with impunity and be rewarded therefore, and that the power of the man he bolted [former Governor Beckham] is waning, all of which we deplore."[16]

Still, Klair's work for the party and his continual membership on local and state Democratic committees insured that he would remain a valued force in the Democratic Party. In nominating Klair for chair of the Democratic city and county committee in 1916, George R. Hunt said that "no Democrat of his age in Lexington or Fayette County had given as much of his time and effort and money to the cause of Democracy." When elected, Klair responded that he intended to "put every man to work" and that under his leadership the committee "would do its best to maintain Democratic traditions and Democratic ascendancy in Lexington and Fayette County."[17] Klair was also elected to the Democratic state central committee in 1916, a tribute to his growing statewide reputation. Through the state committee, Klair actively promoted "the Democracy" in venues outside Lexington. When Louisville appeared to be "hopelessly Republican," the state committee named Klair, Allie Young, and Dan Talbott of Bardstown to a subcommittee "to see what could be done." After meeting with Mickey Brennan, the subcommittee decided to name Elam Huddleston as county chairman. Huddleston apparently decided, like Klair, to "put every man to work," and Louisville was soon returned safely to the Democratic fold.[18]

By 1920 Klair was recognized as a power in the party. At the same time it was clear to friends and foes alike that he represented the "Stanley faction" of the party, associated with liquor, coal, and horse racing. Ironically, it was during the administration of A.O. Stanley that a "Corrupt Practices Act" and a state antitrust law were passed. The General Assembly established a state tax commission, set up a budget, and modernized the revenue system. More funds were set aside for education, and it was the "wet" Stanley that agreed to let Kentucky voters decide on a state constitutional amendment for Prohibition. Stanley's reform accomplishments were so extensive that "with his term of office, the Progressive Era reached its apex in Kentucky."[19] Yet after Stanley resigned as governor in 1919 to take a seat in the U.S. Senate, reformers aligned with Beckham and Haly castigated the "Stanley faction" as the embodiment of reaction.

Klair's involvement in the embarrassing textbook fiasco of the Stanley administration, his identification with the railroad interests, his defeat for a second term on the railroad commission, and his early work to defeat woman suffrage and Prohibition made him a conspicuous target for reformers' jibes. Roughly analogous to the bipartisan combine, the "Stanley faction" also included James Buckner Brown, Johnson Newlon Camden, and James Campbell Cantrill in 1920. Brown got his start in banking in Louisville through connections with the Whallen brothers. By 1911 he served as president of Louisville's First National Bank and the Bank of Commerce. Then in 1919 Brown directed the merger of three different banks into the National Bank of Kentucky. This institution, under Brown's presidency "was to dominate Kentucky banking during the 1920s."[20] Brown, "colorful, careless, and reckless," made millions and liked to display his wealth with expensive outings to casinos in French Lick, Indiana.[21] The French Lick Springs Hotel had been established at the turn of the century by Thomas Taggart, the three-term mayor of Indianapolis and political boss in Indiana. The resort and nearby casinos soon became a popular gathering place for politicos on both sides of the Ohio River.[22] There, Brown entertained friends lavishly and often paid off their gambling debts. With Billy Klair as a frequent guest, French Lick served as a location for political strategy sessions as well. In the 1920s, Brown bought the *Louisville Herald* and the *Louisville Post,* merged them into the *Herald-Post,* and used his editorials to counter the antigambling views of the *Courier-Journal*'s Robert W. Bingham.

Like Brown and Klair, Camden was also aligned with various business interests in the state. Though admitted to the bar, the highly educated Camden chose not to practice law, involving himself in business pursuits, including thoroughbred horse breeding and coal, rail, and oil development in eastern Kentucky. Camden served as chair of the Kentucky Racing Commission and as president of the Kentucky Jockey Club in the 1920s.[23] J. Campbell Cantrill served in the state legislature with Klair and was elected in 1908 to the U.S. House of Representatives, serving there until his death in 1923. Cantrill had opposed woman suffrage, "believing it would do irreparable harm to the Democratic party," and consistently voted against legislation to regulate business.[24]

While the Beckham faction had strong support in the state's rural areas, the faction of the party to which Klair subscribed was "largely an urban faction." The split was not so much demographic in nature, although politicians like Klair and Brown worked from city bases. Robert Sexton argued that Kentucky's factional politics divided around "urban cultures and rural cultures irrespective of geographic lines."[25] The stands that Klair espoused in the Roaring Twenties were more closely identified with urban values that disturbed rural Kentuckians who looked to Beckham and antimachine, antigambling, and antiliquor candidates to support.

As a member of the "Big Six," as a leader of the group within the Democratic Party known as the "Stanley faction" early in the decade, or as a participant in the bipartisan combine, Klair made the most in the 1920s of his already established reputation as a political wheelhorse. And in the shifting sands of state politics one political constant was Billy Klair, who played a significant role in election after election in the 1920s and early 1930s. Although politicians like John Y. Brown Sr. recognized his power, Klair never attained the status of his contemporary Anton J. Cermak, the boss of Chicago described as "one of the most powerful leaders in Democratic politics and the most successful 'boss' in the history of Jeffersonian ranks." By 1933, on the eve of his death after being shot at the side of President-elect Roosevelt, Chicago's Cermak was "absolute boss of that city and the state of Illinois."[26] In Kentucky, Klair worked closely with politicians inside and outside his party to achieve his ends. His power was significant, if not absolute. A few examples will illustrate Klair's role in statewide races.[27]

The May 1920 Democratic state convention met in Louisville and, "marred only by the efforts of a Beckham lieutenant, Elwood Hamilton, to unseat the Lexington Boss Billy Klair," unanimously endorsed James M. Cox for president.[28] The election in November indicated the power of the state's Democratic Party: In the first presidential election in which women could vote, Kentucky led the nation in voter turnout (71.2 percent), and while other border states were won by the Republican Warren G. Harding, Cox carried Kentucky by four thousand votes.[29] The results, however, were different in the race for a U.S. Senate seat. Hamilton's unsuccessful strike at Klair at the beginning of the May convention indicated that all was not well within the party. While

Kentucky went for Cox in the race for president, a Republican candidate, Richard P. Ernst, beat out the incumbent Beckham in the race for the U.S. Senate.

Ernst, from Covington, worked as a corporation lawyer across the river in Cincinnati, where the brother of Covington's political boss, Maurice Galvin, had served as mayor. Critics argued that because of his connections in the Queen City, Ernst "sought to be Ohio's third senator." When the votes were counted, the Democratic incumbent had tallied seven thousand fewer votes than had Cox in the race for president. In a reversal of the presidential race, Ernst defeated Beckham 454,226 to 449,244. Beckham had failed to vote on the suffrage question, and the perception of his opposition to woman suffrage was certainly glaring in this first election in which women could vote. More damaging, however, was the close alliance between the Ernst supporter Maurice Galvin and his "close personal friend" Billy Klair. His crafty silence in central Kentucky and "the factional alliance between Covington Democrats and Klair"—Sexton noted that conceivably "Klair simply asked the Covington Democrats to ignore" Beckham—spelled doom for Beckham.[30]

In the 1923 race for governor, Klair's ally, J. Campbell Cantrill, appeared to be the front-runner for the Democratic nomination against Paducah's Alben Barkley, the forty-five-year-old congressman who would eventually, of course, become the "dominant state politician of the twentieth century." Barkley took strong stances on key issues—unusual for a Kentucky politician—and "took on" the labor, railroad, and coal lobbies, and promised to end pari-mutuel betting at Kentucky's racetracks.[31] In short, Barkley challenged many of the causes that Klair and the bipartisan combine cherished. It was no coincidence that Elwood Hamilton, an attorney in the firm of Beckham, Hamilton, and Beckham and the individual who had tried unsuccessfully to unseat Klair as a delegate to the state convention in 1920, served as Barkley's campaign manager.[32]

In his speeches, Barkley lashed out at the "crooks and corruptionists" and identified himself with the progressive tradition of Woodrow Wilson and Gifford Pinchot of Pennsylvania. Barkley claimed that the racing and coal interests, just like the old "racing lobby and liquor lobby," had a stranglehold on Kentucky politics. Barkley intended, he stated, to "take its filthy hands from the throat of Kentucky."[33] In Barkley's campaign, Billy Klair and Maurice Galvin "drew special criticism," Klair being labeled as a chief "corruptionist." When Klair was charged with working to obtain the state's insurance contracts, Barkley supporters noted that the insurance for the University of Kentucky had recently been raised from $25,000 to $500,000 and the contract given to the Klair & Scott firm by Republican governor Edwin P. Morrow.[34]

Barkley saved his most eloquent diatribes to lambaste Klair's connection with the Kentucky Jockey Club. Formed in 1918 "to bring business efficiency" to Kentucky's race tracks, but also "as a further aid to a thoroughbred industry under siege," the syndicate was encouraged especially by Matt Winn, the Churchill Downs promoter who had more than anyone else built the Kentucky Derby into the world's premier horse racing event, and by two staunch friends of Billy Klair: Thomas A. Combs, a state senator and former Lexington mayor, and Johnson Newlon Camden, the Bluegrass millionaire. Although the Jockey Club was initially respected as a progressive attempt to bring efficiency to an important Kentucky business, it eventually became a target for another progressive concern. Essentially a monopoly, the Club purchased the state's four premier thoroughbred tracks, Churchill Downs in Louisville, Latonia near Covington, the Kentucky Association track in Lexington, and Dade Park in Henderson, and became a target of antitrust charges. Camden also served as the chair of the state's racing commission, the commission charged with regulating the industry. Because the Club's profits depended on the monopoly granted by the state, officials and supporters found it necessary to maintain the support of the General Assembly. With a Billy Klair-dominated General Assembly and Maurice Galvin serving as a paid lobbyist for the Jockey Club, Barkley and other opponents of Klair's faction saw another example of the bipartisan combine at work in the state.[35]

In the campaign, Barkley gained the support of Beckham and Haly and, by this time, Robert Worth Bingham, a onetime supporter of the Jockey Club. Initially, Bingham had viewed the organization "as a way of promoting the agricultural interests of the state." Bingham's son, Barry, remembered that his father had served on the board of the Club. When he "saw that the resources and prestige of the organization were being diverted to the support of the politicians who made up the bi-partisan combine in control at Frankfort," Bingham "vowed to fight the influence of that group." Ironically, in his fight Bingham allied not only with Beckham and Haly, but also with Republican A.T. Hert, forming bipartisan connections of his own.[36]

Bingham had purchased the *Louisville Courier-Journal* in 1918 and, reversing the course of Henry Watterson, used the paper's pages to espouse reform initiatives such as Prohibition and woman suffrage. When Bingham placed Percy Haly on the paper's payroll, he left little doubt about his stance on Democratic Party factionalism. As James C. Klotter wrote in *Kentucky:*

Portrait in Paradox, 1900–1950, "three men now forged a new triumvirate— Bingham, the publicist; Haly, the planner; and Beckham, the politician."[37]

In 1923 Barkley joined the triumvirate, at least temporarily, but lost the primary to Cantrill by some nine thousand votes, the only defeat of his illustrious career. When Cantrill died of a ruptured appendix shortly after the primary election, it was up to the Democratic state committee, now dominated by Klair and James Brown, to choose a new nominee. The committee chose William Jason Fields from Olive Hill, who went on to defeat Republican attorney general Charles I. Dawson in the general election.

Although Fields was nicknamed "Honest Bill from Olive Hill," Klair's enemies looked warily at any indication of collusion between the new governor and, in Hamilton's term, "the old gang." Hamilton wrote to Barkley in January 1924, "It seems right now that the old gang is pretty much in the saddle at Frankfort, thereby causing much dissatisfaction." The writer worried that "of course nobody can anticipate what Fields will do, though it looks like he is rapidly getting where it will not be possible to throw the old gang in the discard." Hamilton expressed "utter disgust with things at Frankfort" and left little doubt that Klair as a member of "the gang" was in control for the time being: "Billy Klair organized the Legislature and started it off, but a very vigorous fight is being made on the old element there, with more headway being made than ever before."[38]

When Fields announced a plan for a $75 million bond issue—to be paid off with a gasoline tax, an automobile license tax, and an increase in property taxes—for highway and prison construction, for education, and to eliminate the state debt, critics saw in the proposal the hand of Billy Klair. Klair had a long history of connections with the road construction business in Lexington and Fayette County; Bingham and others feared another example of the boss's use of "honest graft." At an "anti-bond demonstration" during a joint session of the legislature, Beckham delivered a "ripping good" talk and "made many good friends," according to Donald McWain in a letter to Barkley. McWain believed that the "$75,000,000 bond issue is dead," but that "they seem to keep William Jason as closely guarded as a man could be. How long he will stand for these tactics I do not know, but it looks like he would break from that gang some time."[39]

As the 1924 Democratic state convention approached, James Brown orchestrated a planning session at Louisville's Seelbach Hotel. Given to lavish gatherings, Brown invited seventy leading Democrats to propose "several steps designed to bring about unity" at the convention. Although supporters of

Barkley attended, the session was dominated by Klair and Brown, and other members of the "hard-core Cantrill faction" of the party.[40] As the bosses planned, Fields chafed at accusations that his program was determined by the sinister schemings of Klair. In an open letter to the *Courier-Journal,* Fields responded to an editorial that referred to "Billy Klair and his pals who are running the administration." Fields replied that "charges that Billy Klair and his pals are running my administration is a wilful and malicious lie." Fields struck out at Bingham as the source of the accusations: "No group or individual save myself is running my administration which fact is well known to The Courier-Journal and which is the cause of its animosity toward me." Instead, the governor pointed to another faction, and wrote, "If I were controlled by an individual and [that] individual was your lord and master Mr. P. Haly, or his Courier-Journal group, I would have the constant indorsement and praise in your editorial columns."[41]

Upon convening in Lexington, Democrats were prepared to endorse William Gibbs McAdoo for president, but the *Courier-Journal* suggested that significant planning had already been conducted before the delegates arrived: "Lexington is a hospitable city and the delegates will enjoy a jaunt to it, but as far as the business they are supposed to transact is concerned they might save railroad fare and time and remain at home." The editorialist lamented that "Billy Klair and his pals have already transacted that business" and that "Billy and his pals will take a new wrap on the party reins for another four years." In a final sally, the writer concluded that "Mr. McAdoo of course can have the State delegation. That is a small matter in comparison with four years' assured control of the Government of Kentucky."[42]

The *Courier-Journal* assured its readers that Billy Klair was in control. When the convention met in Lexington's Woodland Auditorium, Bingham's paper covered the event with an article entitled "Fields/Klair Captains Oil Machine Cogs" and with the 15 May front-page headline "Barkley Leads Attack on Bi-Partisan Ring; Attempt to Oust 'Billy' Klair Voted Down." Still reeling from his primary defeat the year before, Barkley assailed machine control of the party in a speech delivered to convention delegates: "We have heard much in Kentucky of this sinister bi-partisan control at Frankfort. I serve notice . . . to these political hucksters of the very liberties and honor of our people, that their days are ended. . . . These corruptionists should be driven to the penitentiaries."[43]

Klair was not sent to the penitentiary, but a motion was made by a member of the opposing faction to replace him on the Democratic state central committee. The move to oust Klair, promoted by a barrage of *Courier-Journal* editorials before and during the convention, prompted Lexingtonian W.P. Kimball to come to the boss's defense. Speaking in Klair's favor before the vote, Kimball told the delegates that he remembered Klair "as a barefooted newsboy who helped support a widowed mother and educated brothers." "Not a day passed," Kimball asserted, "without his doing a favor and good act for someone." The speaker decried accusations about the bipartisan combine, "this interlocking system they talk about" is "a joke intended to fool old women." Klair had "never been a lobbyist and never had a dishonest dollar." Instead, Kimball praised Klair as "a kindly little fellow doing good for humanity" and begged for unity: "These miserable, contemptible fights, we know where they come from, are intended to do harm, not good."[44]

Before Kimball could continue with further praise, representative Henry A. Pulliam, a Barkley ally from McCracken County, called out, "Will the gentleman yield to a question?" Kimball asked who had made the request. "Pulliam!" came cries from the crowd. Kimball responded, "That wall-eyed fool from Paducah?" With that interchange, the vote was taken, with 1,799 delegates voting for Klair and only 367 against the boss. Called to the podium after his victory, Klair "declared his pleasure in the confidence of the convention" and assured the delegates, "I never at any time in my life received or accepted any money from any corporation or person, not even a dime." Klair added that "the only time I have ever lobbied in Frankfort has been for some friend. That is what I like to do, help my friends."[45]

From his base in Lexington, Klair's circle of friends, as well as enemies, widened considerably during the 1920s. While Klair had mastered the art of bringing together disparate constituencies in his hometown, the rancorous divisions evident at the 1924 state Democratic convention led to Republican victories in November. Calvin Coolidge won the presidency, A.O. Stanley lost to Frederick M. Sackett Jr., the Republican candidate, for reelection to a U.S. Senate seat, and in a referendum on the $75 million road bond issue, Kentucky voters defeated the measure 374,328 to 275,863.[46]

Klair's short-lived victory and notoriety from the 1924 convention came at a high cost for the party. He helped plan strategy for the convention, and he organized the 1924 General Assembly as well. In the end, however, he accomplished very little of the governor's agenda in the face of continued factionalism within the party. As for Fields, the governor was "not experienced enough and strong enough to mobilize forces to overcome the factionalism that destroyed his hopes and caused him to resort to petty public bickering with opponents."[47]

Klair no longer served in the legislature, but with his control of Lexington intact he continued to be an ever-present participant in legislative sessions in Frankfort. Late in 1925 Klair worked to secure his choice for House speaker. Henry Pulliam, Klair's erstwhile antagonist from Paducah, had intended not to seek the speakership, but reconsidered when Klair met with G. Lucien Drury about the position. In a letter to Barkley, Pulliam feared that Klair might get his choice by default. Candidates supported by Pulliam were either ill or inept: "Whitsell Hall . . . is sick and refuses to make an active campaign," Pulliam wrote in a letter to Barkley. Furthermore, "J. H. Baughman says he gets mixed up on parliamentary procedure and could not handle the job. J.O. Evans of Winchester is all right except being somewhat deaf. Belknap would be good except that he is luke warm on the issues." Pulliam lamented that "one by one they have been eliminated until it looks as if the Klair element will get the organization by default on our part in not putting a candidate in the field unless I get it myself." Pulliam asked Barkley to write letters to representatives in his behalf and included a list because "there are some who would be useless to approach."[48]

Pulliam's candidacy proved fruitless, however, as Drury became speaker, another indication of Klair's influence. Unlike some of the representatives themselves, Klair continued to use his mastery of parliamentary procedure effectively. In his study of Kentucky's General Assembly in 1926, Henry B. Simpson concluded that "if a lobbyist succeeds in securing the support of a group leader who is a good parliamentarian his prospects will be greatly strengthened." While Klair failed to achieve passage of the governor's bond issue, through his parliamentary expertise he fought off a strike at an "interest" with which he had enjoyed a long association from his base in the Bluegrass. Pulliam charged Klair, along with Galvin, with attempting to have the House adjourned before a bill to place "a five-cent tax on bets through the parimutuel" could reach the floor. When Henry J. Meyers, a Klair-Galvin ally from Covington, made a point of order that the action setting the adjournment time could not be rescinded, Pulliam charged that Klair and Galvin "have been in cloak-room conference with other race track-coal lobbyists in contact with Mr. Meyers in the House rest-room." Pulliam claimed that because of the adjournment consideration of the tax on racetrack gambling and other measures could fail to reach the floor as the session drew to a close: "I am against such tactics that are shutting off consideration of some twenty bills in order to kill one bill which they oppose."[49] Klair's "smoke-filled room" and parliamentary manipulations, whether conducted in his Security Trust Building office in Lexington or in a capitol restroom in Frankfort, continued to frustrate political opponents in the 1920s.

With the woman suffrage and prohibition issues settled at the beginning of the decade, pari-mutuel wagering provided the political issue that dominated the 1920s. Campaigns against racetrack gambling and evolution mobilized moral crusaders intent on championing legislation to eliminate the evils. During a three-week evangelistic crusade in Louisville in March 1923, Billy Sunday pronounced that the "issue is not political, it is moral." Some Kentuckians reasoned, however, that politicians like Alben Barkley, rather than evangelistic crusaders, had the power to drive "the money changers from the temple."[50]

When Barkley decided to challenge incumbent Richard Ernst for a U.S. Senate seat in 1926, however, he was more intent on winning an election than crusading for a righteous cause. If anything, his failed 1923 campaign for governor had taught Barkley the necessity of compromise. Reformers and Barkley supporters looked to him to fight the "old gang" and to attack "the monopoly of the Jockey Club and their collusion with mine owners, text book dealers, and the railroads," the litany of concerns with which Billy Klair was involved. Reformers lumped various interests together under the major evil of bipartisan control of the state: "As long as the coal and Jockey Club interests controlled Kentucky, progress for the common man, the farmer, the laborer, or the school child was impossible." Reformers and members of the opposition faction made clear that efforts to tax coal and do away with racetrack gambling were tied together; "both were attempts to depose entrenched monopoly."[51]

In *The Anti-Race Track Gambler,* publisher M.P. Hunt linked gambling with other moral issues, arguing that bosses like Klair used Kentucky racetracks as they had used liquor and saloons on the local level. In light of Klair's political career, his argument is compelling. Hunt wrote, "Just as the brothel and saloon had to keep a hand on local politics, this gigantic exponent of commercialized vice is forced to keep a hand on state politics."[52] It indeed was through the Jockey Club and the "horse racing crowd" that Klair built statewide support, much as he had used his business connections with various saloons to establish a base of support in Lexington.

Barkley's supporters hoped that he would be able to overcome Billy Klair's bipartisan organization. In April 1926 Dr. J.L. Vallandingham, a representative from Lexington and a Klair foe, assured Barkley that "we stand together on some great things that will mean much for Kentucky." Vallandingham reminded Barkley that he "was one of the many Central Kentucky votes that stood for you a few years ago against this infernal 'Billy Klair' Catholic dominated machine and have not back slidden one inch." The writer asked Barkley to "remember me to your Rep. Henry A. Pulliam."[53]

Despite the encouragement of Vallandingham, Pulliam, Hamilton, and others, Barkley, remembering his 1923 defeat at the hands of the machine, decided to placate "the old wets, the Klairs and Browns, and convince them he was a reasonable man." When Barkley supporters implored the candidate to use his influence to keep Klair from organizing the General Assembly, Barkley refused, claiming that "state legislative politics were none of his business." Barkley's overtures to Klair's faction were successful. Although it was rumored that Governor Fields would seek the Senate nomination, Fields wrote Barkley in April that "you have a clear field, so far as I'm concerned."[54]

Klair's faction made way for Barkley for several reasons. Barkley had obvious strengths—energy, a devoted following of "energetic reformers," and "dynamic speaking ability"—and he had indicated that from Washington he would pose no threat to the interests back home in Kentucky. Certainly, for Klair, Barkley in Washington was more attractive than Barkley in Frankfort. As with Boss Platt's decision in New York to place Teddy Roosevelt on McKinley's ticket in 1900, "the legend of a conspiracy to 'kick Barkley upstairs'" developed in 1926 in Kentucky. It was more than a legend. When the votes were tallied, Barkley's strength in Klair's central Kentucky—a reversal of the 1923 primary—helped him defeat the incumbent by a twenty thousand–vote plurality.[55] On the surface the senatorial election of 1926 appeared to reunite Kentucky's Democratic Party, a party fragmented through years of factional turmoil. The following year's gubernatorial election, however, would indicate clearly that Kentucky's political factionalism had not ended and that the bipartisan combine remained active into the late 1920s.

In 1927, Beckham sought the Democratic nomination for governor as expected, running against Klair's choice, former House speaker Robert T. Crowe of Oldham County. Based largely on a significant edge in rural western Kentucky, Beckham won the primary and faced Republican Flem D. Sampson in the general election. Beckham again based his campaign on his opposition to racetrack gambling, calling for an end to pari-mutuel wagering, a measure that had replaced the old method of bookmaking. Ironically, the original pari-mutuel wagering bill had become law under Beckham's watch as governor in

1906.[56] Beckham's decision to make betting the cornerstone of his campaign placed Klair in a difficult position. Although he had waged unremitting war against Democratic opponents in primary elections and had sometimes offered only a lukewarm, nominal endorsement of Democratic candidates in general elections, Klair had never officially backed a Republican in a gubernatorial contest. Until 1927, his position on the Democratic state executive committee had precluded that. In 1927, however, the battle lines were drawn clearly. It would be either Beckham or betting.[57]

In his study of Kentucky politics, Robert Sexton regarded the 1927 election "as a Kentucky classic for both buffoonery and treachery." The *New York Times* suggested that "students of Democracy will find little to encourage them in the whole spectacle." And John H. Fenton concluded in *Politics in the Border States* that the election "marked the close of a chapter in the state's political history." Fenton wrote in 1957 that during the thirty years since 1927 "no candidate has presented himself who has seriously challenged the position of the ruling oligarchy of the state."[58]

In the campaign, Sampson ignored the gambling issue completely. Believing him to be a "safe" candidate, Klair and his faction bolted Beckham to support the Republican, and the bipartisan combine "saw its finest hour." Klair's decision was indeed dramatic. As a young man, Sampson had worked in Knox County as a law partner with Caleb Powers, the man indicted in 1900 for conspiracy to assassinate William Goebel, Klair's early political idol. But Klair had abandoned his previous connections and his early reform bent. The week of the election, Klair took out full-page ads in the *Lexington Herald* and *Lexington Leader* endorsing Sampson. In the ads, Klair made clear the reasons for the endorsement: "Beckham's election means the end of racing in Kentucky." "It is an election that will determine the fate of the sport that is linked with Kentucky in the minds of the world—horse racing." It was even rumored that should Beckham win the election, the Jockey Club was prepared to move the Kentucky Derby to Chicago.[59]

Klair's ads and repeated rumors paid off for the bipartisan combine's candidate. When the returns were counted, Sampson had defeated Beckham, 399,698 to 367,567. It was clear that Democrats had voted split tickets, since the remainder of the Democratic slate from lieutenant governor to auditor was elected. It was also clear that Billy Klair's backing—even for a Republican—was crucial. In central Kentucky's Seventh District the Democratic majority of 18,000 in the 1923 election was reduced to only 2,500 in 1927. Lexington gave Beckham only 37.5 percent of its vote, as the gubernatorial candidate ran 4,000 votes behind the Democratic candidate for lieutenant governor. Fayette Countians went for Sampson over Beckham, 12,974 to 7,640.[60]

Klair's decision to support the Republican insured Beckham's defeat, but the decision also had repercussions for Klair. On the day of the election the *Interior Journal* claimed that "no more bitter or senseless campaign has ever been waged in Kentucky politics than the war on the present democratic ticket waged by a man trusted as a party leader." The writer referred to James Brown, but even more surprising than Brown's defection was that of Klair: "For the first time in Democratic political history in Kentucky, James B. Brown has been able to take with him into the republican party in this election William F. Klair, of Lexington. No matter how hot the primary fight, no matter who won in it, Klair has always been regular." Referring to the endorsement of Sampson in the Lexington papers, the editorialist was "of the opinion that before allowing his name to be attached to that advertisement Mr. Klair, in all political decency, should have resigned from the Democratic state executive committee." While admitting that Klair had a legal right "to bolt his party ticket," morally Klair "has no right to be a Judas Iscariot or a Benedict Arnold to the party which has honored him and in which he occupies, by virtue of his membership in the executive committee, a position of leadership."[61]

Like others in the party, the writer expressed disappointment in the Democratic leader. "We have not always agreed with him, but we have always been compelled to respect his party regularity." Perhaps "Klair is preparing, like Jim Brown," concluded the writer, "to take his place in the republican ranks." Charles Hardin, the state chairman of the party, and other leaders were bitter at Klair for his defection. They laid plans to expel the boss and other bolters from leadership positions. In the April 1928 meeting of the executive committee, Hardin led committee members to pass a resolution barring all Democrats who had failed to vote for Beckham from participating in county, district, and state conventions, conventions that would determine the party's presidential nominee as well as party leaders for the next four years.[62]

Unwilling to accept dismissal from party leadership, Klair fought back. He asked for another committee meeting to reconsider the "bolter resolution" and through Brown's *Louisville Herald-Post* warned that a purge would spell defeat for the party in fall elections. Klair specifically claimed that the resolution, if carried out, would cost the party fifty thousand votes.[63]

At that point, realizing the imminent danger to the party, Alben Barkley advised Hardin to withdraw the resolution and "placate the Klair faction."

From his seat in the U.S. Senate, Barkley understood that the state party fight had larger implications. The serious nature of the split was evident; even Klair's foe, Elwood Hamilton, was willing to compromise. Hardin called the state executive committee for a second meeting on 18 May to reconsider the original resolution that "all persons shall be qualified to vote in the county and legislative district conventions . . . who at the November elections . . . voted for all the Democratic nominees whose names appeared on the ballot." At the insistence of Barkley, Hardin agreed to a second meeting although he assured party members, "I resent the suggestion of Billie Klair and others that the Democrats will lose to the party thousands who bolted, if not permitted to take part in the convention." Hardin claimed that "the position taken by Billie Klair is that if they are not permitted to vote in the conventions, they will not support the nominees and the principles involved in the coming State and national elections."[64]

While it was understood that Alfred E. Smith would be the party's choice for president in 1928, Hardin maintained that the primary issue at the state convention was again not the party's presidential nominee, but rather "shall bolting Democrats or loyal Democrats organize the party?" Hardin waxed poetic when describing Klair and his recent defection: "I am the rider of the wind, the stirrer of the storm. And the place I left behind me is still with lightning warm."[65]

For his part, Klair, the "stirrer of the storm," had no choice but to compromise. At the second executive committee meeting it was agreed that Barkley would be named temporary chairman of the convention. In return, Klair and other bolters would be seated and Barkley would limit his remarks in the opening speech to national matters. Klair survived in his party leadership role, though barely. A resolution to expel Klair from the executive committee was narrowly defeated in his Lexington district, and his opponents gained control of the party machinery in six of the remaining eight districts.[66]

The state convention opened inauspiciously in June when a fist fight erupted in a meeting of the credentials committee between the official Klair delegation and a rump delegation from Lexington. The Klair delegation was eventually seated to hear Barkley's plea for harmony in his opening address. Harmony prevailed, but only on the surface. Hardin was reelected as chair of the state executive committee, assuring the party in the words of a writer for the *Interior Journal* "of a chairman for the next four years absolutely free from the taint of the Klair-Fields . . . Jockey Club combination." In contrast, Hardin was described as a presiding officer "in whom there is no guile, a political knight sans peur, sans reproche, an honest, every-day, old-fashioned demo-crat, loyal and faithful to the core."[67]

The main work of the convention was to choose the party's nominee for president. In New Yorker Al Smith, the Catholic, "wet" son of Irish immi-grants, and product of Tammany Hall, Kentucky Democrats chose a candi-date remarkably similar to Billy Klair. The *Western Recorder,* the state organ of the General Association of Baptists in Kentucky, asserted that the same op-ponents of Prohibition were now the great supporters of Smith's candidacy: "These interests are a reincarnation of the old liquor crowd that long con-trolled Kentucky." According to the *Western Recorder* the state bosses and the "sporting elements" in league with the "urban aliens" sought to control the state through their support of Smith.[68] In background and in ideology, Klair and Smith mirrored one another.

If there was any Kentucky leader who could lead the fight for Smith—a "wet, urban, Catholic"—in the dry, rural, largely Protestant state, it was Billy Klair. But Klair was a local leader with local concerns, and his ideological bent ended at the state line. That is not to say that Klair's actions had an impact only on the local and state levels. It was the disunity of the Democratic Party, a legacy of Klair's decision to bolt in 1927, that spelled doom for Smith in Kentucky in November 1928. When Klair, now politically weakened from his recent battles, failed to secure his choice for Smith's campaign chairman in Kentucky—Barkley gained the position—Klair offered only lukewarm sup-port for Smith throughout the campaign.

The *Louisville Herald-Post,* the newspaper of Klair's friend James Brown, actually endorsed Herbert Hoover. While Klair, stung from the backlash of his recent defection, did not openly support the Republican in 1928, neither did he enthusiastically support Smith. In a letter to Klair's ally, Thomas Rust Underwood, successor to Desha Breckinridge as the editor of the *Lexington Herald,* Lt. Gov. James Breathitt expressed his dismay: "It is disheartening to me that conditions that are purely local should be allowed to become involved in a National campaign." Breathitt wrote that "with the prospects of electing a Democratic President, we [should] bury our animosities for the time, call an armistice for a few months and unite in the single purpose of carrying the state. After the election if the boys want to renew hostilities among them-selves, let them go to it, but let us have no division in our ranks when the enemy is upon us."[69]

Breathitt's concern was justified. Klair's weak, nominal support, coupled with lingering divisions and hostilities within the party, led to a 177,000–vote plurality for Hoover, the largest majority for a Republican to that time. Hoover's victory in 1928 left the Democratic Party "in tatters" in Kentucky.[70] With a Republican governor elected in 1927 and the state going for a Republican president in 1928, both the result of Democratic Party fights instigated by Billy Klair, the Lexington boss found that maneuvering on the state level was a greater challenge than in the friendly confines of Lexington. If Klair's party was "in tatters" in 1928, the following year a more serious challenge— economic in nature—awaited the Lexington boss, the rest of Kentucky, and the nation.

Part III

The modern American city was the product of the forces of industrialism and big business. So too was the city boss. Though its first appearance had been earlier, the big city machine took its more familiar form in the 1870s or eighties, mimicking the large businesses that had helped to create it. Like business, the machine existed to make a profit. Businesses made their profits by exchanging goods for money, and investing it; machines did so by exchanging jobs and services for power, and investing it.

James W. Mooney

All you have to remember is one name: Roosevelt. . . . Sure. F.D.R. Nobody else but. Because he's the man, sport, who really put the skids under your uncle, and he did it years ago. It's just that it took until now to catch up with him. . . . Well, of course, the old boss was strong simply because he held all the cards. If anybody wanted anything—jobs, favors, cash—he could only go to the boss, the local leader. What Roosevelt did was to take the handouts out of the local hands. A few little things like Social Security. Unemployment Insurance, and the like—that's what shifted the gears, sport.

Edwin O'Connor

7

Bossism and Reform in the Great Depression

As stock prices fell drastically on Wall Street in late October of 1929, Lexington residents seemed to be more concerned with local politics and the University of Kentucky's undefeated football team. The gridiron exploits of John "Shipwreck" Kelly and especially the political shenanigans of Billy Klair, by then the undisputed czar of Lexington politics, made for more entertaining reading than did accounts of economic ruin.[1]

Edward Dabney, chairman of the board of the First Security National Bank and Trust Company, believed "the depression that followed [the crash] affected Lexington and Central Kentucky less than the rest of the state and other parts of the country." "Happy" Chandler, Kentucky's lieutenant governor and later governor during the depression years, maintained that "Kentucky climbed to no great heights and sank to no great depths. The mood of the state was down, but people of this state responded well when they had to." An editorial in a local newspaper proclaimed in November 1930 that "Lexington may be glad that Lexington is Lexington. Disturbing factors elsewhere do not so greatly affect this city which has so many interests and so many different factors in prospective development." The same editorial cited the largest enrollment in the history of Lexington's universities and colleges as an indication of the city's comparative prosperity.[2]

Thomas D. Clark, in 1931 a newly appointed instructor in the University of Kentucky's Department of History, expressed a deeper concern than did the local dailies. Clark recalled that he was worried about three things during the depression, "getting fired, having enough money to buy the essentials and what would be the future of our country." The struggling young professor's concern was based on the fact that within a year his monthly salary was cut from $180 to $100. Although few Lexington residents were involved in stock speculation compared to larger urban areas, Clark stated that "there were a great many U.K. professors dabbling in the stock market. In fact, they were bragging how much money they were making. They didn't have much to say about the crash."[3]

Despite the losses of university professors and a few others, no accounts of starvation and extreme hardship appeared on the pages of Lexington's newspapers in the early years of the depression. Lexington was seemingly immune from many of the problems faced by the larger urban centers. After all, Lexington was not dependent on heavy industry as were the great metropolitan areas to the north. Instead, in 1929, Lexington remained a university town, and an agricultural and trading center, inhabited by many wealthy farmers and merchants.[4]

According to the 1930 census, Lexington was Kentucky's third largest city with a population of 45,736, following only Louisville with 307,745 inhabitants and Covington with 65,252. Of its population, 32,360 Lexingtonians were native white, while a substantial number, 12,759, were black. Only 612 residents were listed as foreign-born. Of the city's gainfully employed, the largest number, 4,694, were occupied in domestic and personal services, 4,511 were involved in the manufacturing and mechanical industries, 3,735 were listed under trading, 2,610 under professional services, and 1,945 under transportation and communication occupations. Only 785 were listed under agriculture, but this small figure does not indicate the large number of farmers residing immediately outside the city limits. Nor is it indicative of agriculture's immense influence on Lexington during the depression years.[5]

According to the Federal Writers' Project contributors to *Lexington and the Bluegrass Country*, by far the most important industry to the city was tobacco: "Over the immense loose-leaf tobacco floors . . . and out from the warehouses where the farm product is cured and stored annually, passes a crop that in cash value to the city and its environs far outranks any other product. This rural production sets the pace for the trade activity within the city, and a good tobacco year is a good year for the city as a whole."[6] The publication revealed that "the traditionally superior" Bluegrass livestock industry was next in economic importance to the city, and asserted that "the environs of Lexington stand in an unusual and pleasant relationship to the urban area itself. It might be said that the industries of Lexington lie outside the city, and that the social interests of the industrial area lie within the city."[7]

Nestled in the heart of the Bluegrass region, with its thriving tobacco and horse farming industries, Lexington could point to its balanced and growing domestic, professional, trading, manufacturing, and mechanical industries. Home of "the largest loose leaf burley market in the world," the city also boasted of a continuing public and private building program. The business and commercial elements in the city were indeed optimistic. In 1930, a section on the front page of the *Lexington Herald* was reserved daily for the "Looking Up With Lexington" column, in which quotes from local businessmen were printed, emphasizing the city's prosperity, a prosperity that would undoubtedly continue in the coming years.[8]

The *Herald* column mirrored the attitude of the nation's leadership in Washington. When a delegation approached Herbert Hoover in June 1930 requesting "immediate expansion of federally sponsored public works," the president responded, "Gentlemen, you have come sixty days too late. The depression is over."[9] The president's optimism was not shared by all segments of Lexington's society. In January 1930 it was reported that between fifty and sixty men sought shelter each night at the Lexington police station. While shelter was provided, not until 18 January did donations from local bakeries allow the transients to be given food as well. Unable to find work in Lexington, the men would spend the night and continue their search the next day. To provide for the increasing number of needy transients, as well as an occasional resident unable to get a meal elsewhere, a more permanent "soup kitchen" was set up in the city hall garage. The *Lexington Herald* reported that on 28 November 1930, "88 unfortunates" crowded into the garage and ate a meal of stew, coffee, milk, and bread donated by concerned residents.[10]

Of Lexington's permanent residents, 962 were classified in the 1930 census as "persons out of a job, able to work, and looking for a job." By 1937, 2,719 individuals (1,703 male and 1,016 female) were totally unemployed and wanting work. An additional 1,506 (1,189 male and 317 female) were listed as "partly employed and wanting more work."[11]

Unemployment had not been a problem in Lexington during the 1920s. Men could always find work in one of the city's tobacco warehouses or on the farms in the surrounding countryside. Many Lexington city dwellers of the poorer sort provided for themselves from the produce of small garden plots. The few that were temporarily without means to buy a good meal would usually be cared for by concerned individuals or by one of Lexington's churches. If all else failed, one of the local magistrates was available to dispense emergency money from a fund at his disposal, and Billy Klair used proceeds from his thriving insurance business to provide Thanksgiving turkeys and Christmas baskets in exchange for votes on election day.[12]

Beginning in the winter of 1929–1930, however, even Klair's beneficence proved insufficient. Lexington's older residents had not remembered the depressions of the 1890s as being so severe. Jobs increasingly became hard to find. Lexington's tobacco auctions annually provided employment for more than two thousand persons during the sales season, but they were no longer sufficient in meeting unemployment needs. Likewise, traditional means of relief provided by Lexington's churches or the local boss were inadequate. Despite the fact that the end of winter improved Lexington's situation somewhat by absorbing some of the unemployed into the spring farm operations, Mayor James J. O'Brien, a Klair subaltern, found it necessary to appoint an unemployment relief committee to study the relief problem and to propose solutions. That no large-scale relief program was in the works was evident when the committee proposed the innovative plan of employing men to paint house numbers on street curbs.[13]

The stumbling efforts of Klair's machine-backed city administration were supplemented with the increased activity of local charity organizations. Agencies such as the Salvation Army and the Travelers Aid Society for transients, and the Family Welfare Society for unemployables such as children and the elderly, had attempted historically to provide for the needy. Even the Lexington chapter of the Boy Scouts of America, through door to door solicitation, found temporary work for twenty-one men during the city's "Spring Clean-up Week."[14]

As winter approached in 1931, the mayor's unemployment relief committee initiated a drive for the donation of canned goods to supplement the police department's "soup kitchen." On 1 October, a bureau for the registration of the unemployed was opened in the courthouse. The amount of $162.50 remaining in the funds of the mayor's committee was added to the $150.00 appropriation of the fiscal court and placed under the supervision of Ed Wilder, the executive-secretary of the Lexington Board of Commerce.[15]

A few weeks later a "six-weeks plan" was launched. Housekeepers, businesses, and farmers with available work were urged to fill out and mail blank pledges printed in the local newspapers to the employment bureau. Within two weeks, 581 residents had registered for work through the bureau. The almost total inadequacy of the plan was made clear when employment was found for only one carpenter, one practical nurse, one plumber, and "one man for yard work" in a typical day of the bureau's work.[16]

In the early years of the depression, the administration in Lexington was slow to grasp the problems that the city faced. Some Lexingtonians despaired and concluded that drastic measures were necessary. Looking back on the depression years, a Lexington socialist, once active in the Kentucky Workers' Alliance, stated, "They didn't think it was a permanent thing. . . . The immensity of the problem hadn't been grappled with." Throughout the United States, Americans were faced with an unprecedented situation. In Lexington, important changes, while not revolutionary, were made in the city even before a new president inaugurated a "new deal for the American people."[17]

The Great Depression unleashed a new wave of reform energy—of the structural reform variety—in Lexington that had been building during the latter years of the 1920s. Although the commission plan of city government favored by Lexington's reform-minded business leaders had replaced the old mayor-council system in 1912, the subtle maneuverings of Billy Klair had made the city's commission little more than an arm of the democratic machine. While Klair had promoted the commission plan and sponsored the bill in the state legislature that allowed it, he had no difficulty in fashioning it to conform to the machine mold.

In 1928, concerned citizens launched a campaign to change the city charter to a city manager format, a plan first tried in Staunton, Virginia, in 1908. By 1914, the National Association of City Managers had been organized and structural reformers heralded city manager government as a model of progressive efficiency.[18] In 1929, a bill was introduced in the state legislature by John Y. Brown that would allow cities of the second class to have a city manager form of government. In a board of directors meeting of the new Charter League, organized by W.T. Congleton, one of Lexington's more prominent businessmen, it was suggested "that a meeting be arranged with William F. Klair to learn if he would oppose any features of the bill." Porter Land, a member of the House Rules Committee and "under obligations to Billy Klair," supported the bill. However, to appease the powerful, well-connected Klair an amendment was attached to permit the manager system to go into effect only at the end of machine-backed Mayor James J. O'Brien's administration. The bill quickly became law, much to the delight of the city's progressive businessmen, and with this obstacle out of the way the Charter League went to work to secure the city manager form of government in Lexington.[19]

The goals of the Charter League had widespread support in Lexington. The League of Women Voters, the board of commerce, the *Lexington Leader*, the Rotary Club, the Optimist Club, and the Kiwanis Club all favored the city manager plan. The "movement became so universal in Lexington that in the spring of 1928 fourteen organizations sent representatives to a meeting endorsing the plan."[20] Billy Klair was less than enthusiastic. Although in cities like Cleveland, Ohio, city managers were chosen by party bosses, Klair knew that the reform tide in Lexington, encouraged by the hard times of the depression, presented the first real threat to his control of the city since the early years of the twentieth century.[21] The boss's fears were justified by the results of the 1931 elections.

In the municipal elections on 4 November 1931, more than 16,600 Lexingtonians, the largest number in the city's history, went to the polls. The Charter League's plan of government was chosen, and its entire ticket elected by an overwhelming majority. The new mayor, W.T. Congleton, and a commission of four immediately began interviewing for the important city manager position, and on 22 November 1931, Paul Morton, a native Kentuckian coming from a similar post in Alexandria, Virginia, was chosen from a list of forty-one applicants as Lexington's first city manager.[22]

Under the new system, the job of running the government was taken out of the hands of a local politician and given to a professional—the city manager. Although a few boards and commissions, such as the public library board and the board of health, were still controlled by the mayor and the commission, the most important areas of government were organized into departments under the direct control of the manager. For example, departments of public welfare and public works were organized, paving the way for the implementation of the federal programs to come. While the centralization and increased efficiency derived from the department setup produced greater potential for dealing with the city's depression problems, the choice of an outsider for the powerful manager's post presented a serious challenge to the Klair machine.[23]

In a statement printed in the *Lexington Herald*, Mayor Congleton outlined the immediate plans of the new administration. Although no effort would be made to "clean house," a direct challenge was issued to machine patronage when Congleton asserted that each government position would be subjected to close scrutiny and positions would be combined whenever possible. The city budget would be drafted and the entire system of city government would be reorganized. These plans for a revamping of the city government became a reality when Morton began his duties in January 1932.[24]

At thirty-seven years of age, Paul Morton was energetic, well-qualified, and as machine supporters soon learned, "tough as nails." One of his first acts was to notify twenty city employees that their services would no longer be needed after 4 January, making it clear that inefficient workers and machine hacks would not be tolerated. Morton stated that "efficiency, economy, and centralized control are requisites of city manager government." The new manager presented a direct challenge to the Klair machine: "We are here to build up public service, efficiency, and economy, rendering a dollar's worth of service for a dollar's pay, at the smallest cost possible to the taxpayer."[25]

By the end of 1933 the city manager and commissioners pointed with pride to the accomplishments of the administration's first two years. Tax deductions had saved Lexington taxpayers a total of $96,803.26, or a reduction of 28 percent according to the *Louisville Courier-Journal.* Operation costs of the city government were reduced by $216,313.54, and a cash surplus was achieved for the first time since 1915. Ever critical of the Klair organization, the *Courier-Journal* reminded its readers that the city manager regime under Morton "finished the last year's business with a cash surplus of $11,000 . . . despite having paid off a debt of $48,000 inherited from the Klair-O'Brien Administration." Greater efficiency in the various departments was evident, although the continuing depression and rising unemployment had made charity demands unusually heavy. The reorganized Department of Public Welfare had increased the budget of the contributions and charities division by $15,322.84. Long strides had been made since Mayor O'Brien's unemployment relief committee reported $162.50 in the relief fund.[26]

When voters went to the polls in 1933, the *Courier-Journal,* indicating a real interest in the affairs of Louisville's sister city, announced that "Lexington has the opportunity of deciding whether to continue the present excellent regime, which has saved the taxpayers so much money, eliminated graft, and given the city such good government, or whether to turn the city hall back to the Klairs." The impressive accomplishments of the first two years of the first administration under the city manager plan insured a 63 percent plurality for the Charter League ticket in the city elections of 1933. Although the *Courier-Journal* claimed that the elections pitted the Charter League against the Klair machine, the *Lexington Herald* denied that Klair took an active part in the campaign. The *Courier-Journal* asserted that the "Klair machine in Lexing-

ton, which two years ago fought desperately to prevent non-partisan government and the employment of a city manager in that city, but was defeated, is
making a desperate effort to recapture the city government there with a ticket
of four commissioners who oppose those elected on the ticket with Mayor
W.T. Congleton." Thomas Rust Underwood, Klair's friend and the general
manager and managing editor of the *Herald,* claiming that "there was not a
word of truth" in the *Courier-Journal*'s accusations, responded that Klair "has
taken no active part in the city election this year" and that any "observer of city
political affairs would know this."[27]

Regardless of Klair's involvement, the results of the 1933 elections insured that Morton and the Charter League ticket would continue to bear the
responsibility for implementing the New Deal programs of the president elected
the year before. Local implementation of federal relief and recovery programs
introduced a new dynamic in local efforts to deal with the deepening depression and provided another challenge for Billy Klair.

By 1935 Paul Morton's city manager administration, disregarding the role
of the federal government's New Deal work programs, took credit for a new
storm sewer, a sanitary sewage plant, two community centers, and a public
health center. A modern airport was almost finished, and the construction of
a new city jail was under way. In typical Morton fashion, the city manager
published a campaign booklet, *Two Short Years: The Story of a Change,* listing
additional advances. The tax rate continued to decline, operating expenses for
the city government were cut, a modern accounting system and a central purchasing plan were installed, garbage collection was taken over by the city, a
police radio system was installed, and $50,000 was added to appropriations
for charities.[28]

The youthful Morton also brought national recognition to the city. The
Charleston Gazette carried an article on Lexington's many improvements, officials from Corpus Christi, Texas, expressed interest in Morton's streets and
sanitation record system, and Lexington became the subject of numerous articles in journals, such as the *National Municipal Review, Manufacturer's Record,*
and *Southern City.*[29]

Morton's record was impressive considering the fact that so many accomplishments were made without the backing of Klair and his dormant machine. In some cases, such as Morton's attempt to revamp the police and fire
departments, the fearless manager confronted the machine directly. Appalled
to learn upon taking over his duties that in 1931 Lexington had more homi-

cides per capita than any other city in the United States, Morton was determined to change police protection in the city. Morton confronted Ernest Thompson, the police chief and "Klair subaltern," forced him "to wear a uniform," and "gathered evidence for a case against the chief." Although "Paul Morton was told [that] Thompson was put in by the gang and should stay," the manager "fought him just the same."[30]

Thompson suggested that his confrontation with Morton resulted from differing ideas about the application of the law: "Morton believed the law applied the same to all people. I never thought you should treat a bank president the same as you would a low-down gambler or crook." Although Morton was unable to fire the chief, Thompson eventually resigned only to be elected sheriff of Fayette County. With Thompson out of the way, Morton shifted his attention to the morale of the city's police and fire corps. Firemen recalled Morton's instructions to the city's policemen and firemen: "'If you ever need anything, money, etc., come to me,' and he would really see that we were helped. He personally helped us at the fires and saw that we got coffee and sandwiches if we needed them."[31]

Morton's usurpation of patronage activities usually performed by Klair surely offended the Lexington boss. Indeed, the city manager's intention to use Klair's previously proven methods to accomplish his own ends further blurred distinctions between bossism and reform in this southern city. Although the lack of machine support hindered many of Morton's projects, his determination to bypass the approving nod of Billy Klair earned him the respect of more than a few Lexingtonians. A Lexington druggist remarked, "Morton was tops. He had to please the Commission and fight the old gang." A janitor recalled, "He was a great manager. He straightened out the police and fire departments. If they didn't like it, they could quit." A Lexington barber stated simply, "The politicians could not control Morton."[32]

Despite his success, Morton's continual battles with the machine, along with the enticement of a pay increase, prompted him to resign from his position in Lexington in May 1935 to take another city manager post in Trenton, New Jersey. His resignation, along with the resignation of Mayor Congleton, spelled doom for the Charter League administration, and after the resignations the Charter League declined, becoming a "generally disunited and apathetic organization." In November 1935 the Home Town Ticket, pledged to select a home town city manager and stocked with "old gang politicians," swept the city elections with a 63 percent majority. Although Klair had denied the accusation before the election that James J. O'Brien would be given the manager's job, the erstwhile machine supporter took his oath of office the day the commission began their duties.[33]

Despite a brief interlude during the tenure of Paul Morton as city manager, Klair again controlled Lexington's administration in 1935. Klair had not been idle during his brief exile from political dominance. While Paul Morton and his city manager regime curtailed some of the boss's activities at home, Klair worked to strengthen his statewide influence. It was perhaps his increased emphasis on the state level in the late 1920s and early 1930s, coupled with his disregard—at least compared with his previous attention to detail— for local politics, that exposed his local organization to the successful attacks of the reformers.

Outside the city, Klair's presence continued to be felt as he worked to strengthen his statewide influence. As the Great Depression had an impact in altering local government structures in Lexington, the economic decline also altered the makeup of the bipartisan combine on the state level. After the Wall Street crash, stories of business and bank closings were carried in newspapers across the nation. None of the reports shocked Kentuckians more, however, than news of the fall of James B. Brown's National Bank of Kentucky in the autumn of 1930. With the bank's downfall, "the reverberations shook the very foundations of the Democratic Party." While Robert Sexton's contention that the National Bank of Kentucky was "the most important national bank to close in the entire country" is arguable, the coinciding fall of Brown, a pillar of the bipartisan combine, had a dramatic effect on state politics.[34]

The fall of the bank and the personal bankruptcy of its founder forced Brown "to retire from active participation" in the Democratic Party, an event not altogether bad for Billy Klair. It was Brown who had led Klair to abandon the party to support the Republican Sampson in 1927. As Sexton suggested, Brown's departure "somewhat cleansed the liberal faction of a disreputable element."[35] Although Brown was no longer a viable participant in the political affairs of the state, Billy Klair remained. Significantly, it was Billy Klair who would continue the French Lick, Indiana, strategy sessions, a tradition established by the flamboyant Brown.

From his position of power as the leading member of the bipartisan combine, Klair employed his organizational skills to make himself indispensable to Democrats aspiring to state offices. And Klair's influence was such that the legislative sessions were organized under his guiding hand. Thomas Rust Underwood, editor of the *Lexington Herald* and later a U.S. congressman, recalled the extent of Klair's influence on the state level: With his "indefatigable energy and his passion for details, he could plan the course of each and every important bill. Moreover, persons seeking the position of Speaker of the House of Representatives sought his advice prior to the caucus meeting."[36] Much like Huey Long in Louisiana, Klair continued to roam the halls of the capitol and the chambers of the House and Senate into the 1930s, even though he was not an elected member of those bodies.

Outside the General Assembly, Kentucky's highway department became increasingly important as a source of patronage in the depression years of the 1930s. Since the passage of the Federal Highway Act of 1921, which increased federal aid for road projects, Kentucky's expenditures for highway building had increased as well even before the depression hit. In 1927 more than two-fifths of Kentucky's $28,400,000 budget went for roads, and by 1931 almost half the state's expenditures were funneled through the highway commission. At the same time legislators cut funding for public schools drastically. By the depression decade the highway commission had become "a source of patronage, campaign funds, and power over legislation and local bodies," and Ben Johnson, chairman of the commission and an ally and friend of Billy Klair, had acquired immense power.[37] From Johnson's position as chair of the commission, he fashioned a statewide machine of his own:

He could offer not just a job but livelihood for destitute relatives of influential men, grateful men, who in turn would be expected to repay the favor. The promise of a road meant jobs for local contractors, increased business for merchants (now closer to their customers), and the hope of success for farmers who had seen their perishables ruined by slow transportation. A decision by Johnson on state contracts and state sinecures could mean prosperity or failure to large numbers of Kentuckians who had few alternatives in the bleak days of the Great Depression. In times of plenty men casually looked to Johnson for aid; in hard times they sought it desperately.[38]

In 1930 the Republican governor Flem Sampson realized that the "highway commission represented the most politically important force in government" in the state. Despite the support of Klair and Johnson in the 1927 election, Sampson dismissed Johnson as chairman of the commission and attempted to create his own Republican machine through his appointive powers. A campaign to take the power to appoint the commission out of the hands of the governor was initiated by Johnson's son-in-law, J. Dan Talbott, a druggist in Nelson County. Klair and another political ally, Senator Allie Young of Morehead, lined up with Talbott in the effort, and with Klair's backing, Young introduced a bill in the Senate calling for a reorganization of the highway department.[39]

The bill provided for seven highway districts. The commissioner from each district would be appointed by the president pro tem of the Senate, who was a Democrat, instead of the governor. The bill was later amended so that the governor, the lieutenant governor, and the attorney general would appoint the commission. Because the latter two men were Democrats, the Republican Sampson would still lose control. The amended bill, making no pretense of being anything but a highly partisan piece of legislation, went on to state that "after a new governor (presumably Democratic) was elected in 1931, . . . the power of appointment would rest solely with him." While the reorganization bill, commonly referred to as the "ripper bill," was being debated, Klair launched—through his General Assembly allies—an official investigation of the highway department's conduct under the Sampson administration.[40]

When the bill passed over Sampson's veto, the *Courier-Journal*'s sarcastic response, "Rip, Rip, Hurrah," proclaimed the Democratic victory over Sampson. Ben Johnson was soon appointed as one of the new commissioners, along with Charles Fennell, Klair's personal friend from Lexington. The new commissioners lost no time in placing Johnson back in the commission chair. Klair's influence in the naming of the commission insured that Lexington and Fayette County would not be neglected when road projects were determined. Lexington construction companies received a healthy share of highway bids, and Lexingtonians were especially blessed with patronage positions and employment.[41] Klair ironically never received full credit for the increased road building activity in Lexington because his coup in state politics in 1931 was coupled in the same year with the defeat of his machine by the Charter League's ticket. It was Paul Morton, the new city manager, who claimed credit not only for procuring New Deal work programs from Washington but also for additional aid from Frankfort. Billy Klair had unwittingly aided his rival's efforts back home.

Still, the highway coup only increased Klair's reputation for power politics, a reputation that was admired by friends and grudgingly admitted by political foes. A writer for the *Mt. Sterling Gazette and Kentucky Courier* referred to the reorganized highway commission as "a steam roller." "It was soon found that some horsemen were needed to help the Roller work properly and the four horsemen of Kentucky, Mr. Johnson, Mr. Billy Klair, Mr. Brennan and Mr. Glenn [a Barkley ally known as "Ferryboat" Glenn because he went from side to side] were chosen."[42] The writer set up a mock conversation in which a father explained to his son the finer points of Kentucky politics:

William Frederick "Billy" Klair. A confident "King Klair" was at the height of his power in the early 1930s. (Courtesy Lexington Public Library)

(Left) Dennis Mulligan, an Irish businessman and politician, introduced Lexington to boss politics in the late nineteenth century. (E.I. Thompson in Kerr and Wright) (Below) Lexington's muddy Main and Limestone Streets on the eve of the Civil War. (UK Special Collections)

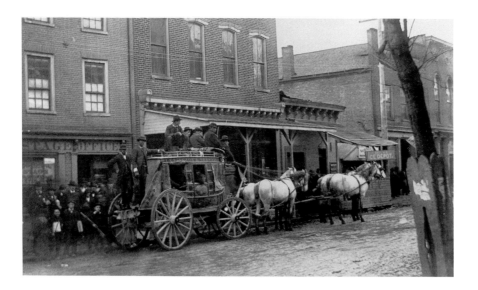

Young Billy Klair (holding a rifle) stands behind this stagecoach at its stop on the south side of Short Street, just west of Mill in 1881. (Kentucky Historical Society, Special Collections and Archives)

The construction of the stone Richardsonian Romanesque courthouse from 1898 to 1900 coincided with Billy Klair's rise to power. (UK Special Collections)

Billy Klair, pictured second from left in the third row from the top, was a member of the 1908-1909 House, the last legislature to convene in the old statehouse in downtown Frankfort. (Kentucky Historical Society, Special Collections and Archives)

The House chamber in the old statehouse during the 1908 session. (Kentucky Historical Society, Special Collections and Archives)

Early twentieth-
century residences
like these gave
Lexington an air
of gentility and
refinement.
(Wynelle Deese)

(Right) As a young legislator, the diminutive Klair acquired something of a reform reputation. (Cone, *The University of Kentucky: A Pictorial History*) (Below) In 1869, James K. Patterson assumed the presidency of the A&M college that would become the University of Kentucky. Before he retired in 1910 he praised Billy Klair for his work in the state legislature on behalf of the institution, calling Klair "the best friend the University has ever had." (UK Special Collections)

Through his close association with the Kentucky Jockey Club, Klair supported racing at the Kentucky Association Track located at Fifth and Race Streets. This photograph was taken during a meet around 1910. (Wynelle Deese)

As a member of Kentucky's General Assembly, Billy Klair supported appropriations for the Eastern State Lunatic Asylum, located in his hometown. This postcard of the institution was published around 1905. (Wynelle Deese)

Two Typical Kentuckians

This postcard of a "Kentucky Colonel" lifting a bourbon-laced mint julep represented the Old South stereotype familiar to New South Lexingtonians. (Wynelle Deese)

(Above, left) Madeline McDowell "Madge" Breckinridge, a philanthropist, leader in the women's suffrage movement, and admirer of Billy Klair. (UK Special Collections) (Above, right) Desha Breckinridge, son of W.C.P. Breckinridge, husband of Madge, and publisher and editor of the *Lexington Herald*, was "fond of" Klair, although he confessed that "we have disagreed with him on numerous occasions and disapproved of his course in numerous matters." *Lexington Herald-Leader*) (Right) Laura Clay, the National American Woman Suffrage Association's leading southerner, once praised Klair for his sponsorship of a co-guardianship bill. Klair's support for the woman's movement later proved less than consistent. (UK Special Collections)

In 1915, pedestrians, electric streetcars, and motorized vehicles vied for room on Lexington's Main Street. (UK Special Collections)

(Left) Thomas Skillman Scott, Klair's insurance partner in the Klair & Scott firm. (Marjorie R. Scott) (Below) The Klair and Scott insurance firm was located in a suite of offices on the sixth floor of the Security Trust Building on the northeast corner of Short and Mill Streets. (Wynelle Deese)

Klair (*second from right*) and A.B. "Happy" Chandler (*far right*) with other politicos at Thomas Taggart's French Lick Springs Resort in the early 1930s. (UK Special Collections)

Mayor James J. O'Brien was a trusted Klair subaltern. He posed here at City Hall with a lion cub to promote the film *Trader Horn* in April 1931. (House and Carter, UK Special Collections)

Looking west from Mill Street down Short Street in 1932, Klair's beloved St. Paul's Church towers in the distance. (UK Special Collections)

St. Paul's Catholic Church on West Short Street boasted the city's first turret clock. Billy Klair's home stood only a short distance from the church. (J. Winston Coleman Photographic Collection, Transylvania University Library, in Kerr and Wright)

This group of leaders in the city manager administration broke ground for a storm sewer project, Lexington's first Public Works Administration (PWA) project, on 14 May 1934. From left to right, Walter G. Rehm (president of the board of commerce), Mayor W.T. Congleton (with shovel), F.W. Phelps (city engineer), Leo Butler (president of Northern States Contracting Company), and City Manager Paul Morton (with pick). (House and Carter, UK Special Collections)

Gov. Ruby Laffoon's administration proved inadequate in leading the state through the early years of the Great Depression. Here, the governor posed with Miss Kentucky (Evelyn Dean from Lexington) at Joyland Park just north of the city on 18 August 1932. (House and Carter, UK Special Collections)

When John Y. Brown Sr. challenged Klair for the Fayette County post on the state's Democratic central executive committee, a mass convention on Cheapside adjacent to the Fayette County courthouse settled the matter on 9 April 1932. Supporters for Brown congregated on the north side of the square (*right*), while the Klair faithful gathered on the south side. The *Herald* reported that the event drew the largest crowd since the free silver election of 1896. (UK Special Collections)

Klair backers at the mass convention on 9 April 1932. As the Klair supporters swelled steadily to the south of Cheapside, it became evident that the boss's power remained strong. (UK Special Collections)

Billy Klair's Lexington, circa 1925. (Kentucky Historical Society, Special Collections and Archives)

But what did they do with the Steam Roller, daddy?

They put it in the Highway Garage at Frankfort to be used against the Republicans in November.

Are you going to help ride the Steam Roller, daddy?

No, sonny, I am one of those independent voting and thinking men, who are going to demolish that instrument of war at the coming election. And there are thousands of others. Now, sonny, do you know what a Steam Roller is?

Yes, daddy, and I am going to build me one to kill all the little boys around here who won't do what I want them to.

That is what the Johnson-Klair Steam Roller did to the real Democrats at Lexington.[43]

Although the father assured the son that "thousands" of "thinking" voters would "demolish that instrument of war at the coming election," Klair's skillful planning insured that his choice would gain the governorship in 1931. Klair again displayed his parliamentary expertise as he maneuvered to secure the state democratic convention for Lexington. When a motion to locate the convention in Lexington was overruled by the Louisville delegation, Klair had another representative discreetly move that the convention be held on 12 May. After the motion carried, the delegates discovered that the date was during the week of the Kentucky Derby. After much debate, it was decided to hold the convention in Lexington after all rather than compete with the Derby in Louisville.[44]

The 1931 convention, held in Lexington's Ben Ali Theater, was again dominated by Klair. The *Louisville Times* reported that Klair "pulled important strings" and helped give the nomination to Ruby Laffoon, a circuit judge from Madisonville. Frederick Vinson, a member of the U.S. House of Representatives and later secretary of the treasury and chief justice of the Supreme Court, nominated Laffoon. Laffoon went on to defeat his Republican opponent, Louisville's mayor, William B. Harrison, in the general election. Although Klair eventually broke with the Laffoon administration, he wielded considerable influence during the Laffoon years.[45]

In November 1931, immediately after the election, the governor-elect met with party powers at French Lick to "outline a program for the forthcoming legislature." The highway commission was central in the group's discussions, and Laffoon was adamant that he alone should have the power to appoint the commission. Although Klair was influential in amending the "ripper" legislation that provided for appointive powers for the governor alone after 1931, it was clear that Klair was unwilling to allow Laffoon to have the final say in commission appointments. At the same time, it was already evident that Laffoon had a mind of his own. He intimated to Vinson in a 29 May letter that there "were some disappointments to me that took place in the Lexington Convention—some things were done that I did not endorse and it is regarding some of these matters that I want to discuss with you."[46]

Klair seemed more at ease with Laffoon's cousin than with the newly elected governor. J. Dan Talbott concluded that Klair "was working hand-in-hand with Polk Laffoon to run the government of Kentucky with Governor Laffoon as their front man."[47] Talbott's conclusion proved less than accurate when the "balding, limping, but amazingly resilient" Laffoon, never comfortable with the manipulations of Klair, challenged the Lexington boss directly by dismissing Charles Fennell from the highway commission. Although Fennell was considered "a neutral during the time Johnson was chairman of the commission," sometimes voting with Johnson and sometimes with the "administration faction" led by Commissioner Thomas Rhea from Russellville, the *Herald* reported that Laffoon removed Fennell, "wielding the sharp ax which in the last few months has 'decapitated' politically, three members of the Highway Commission." Klair's break with the Laffoon administration was complete when Klair refused to support Rhea, Laffoon's choice for governor in 1935. Instead, Klair eventually backed Lieutenant Governor "Happy" Chandler for the state's top position.[48]

As lieutenant governor, Chandler had maneuvered to better his chances in the 1935 gubernatorial race. While Governor Laffoon was traveling with heir-apparent Rhea to Washington in order to meet with President Roosevelt, Chandler, acting as governor for the out-of-state Laffoon, called a special session of the legislature to pass a bill requiring party nominations by primary instead of by convention. Upon returning to the state, an indignant Laffoon was "obliged to sign a bill authorizing a 'double' primary, one requiring a second run-off between the highest finishers if no one received a majority in the first contest."[49]

Chandler had never respected the aging Laffoon. In his autobiography, *Heroes, Plain Folks, and Skunks: The Life and Times of Happy Chandler,* he asserted that "a stranger watching Ruby Laffoon lean on his cane and limp down the statehouse corridors might feel twinges of sympathy. The old man wasn't much to look at, either. In his early sixties, he was hulking, unprepossessing, balding, with unflattering big nose and ears. I didn't feel sorry for him. Gover-

nor Laffoon was an accident looking for a place to happen." A brilliant campaigner, Chandler knew that he would have an advantage in a primary but
that in a convention the Laffoon-Rhea forces would have the advantage.[50]
Perhaps Chandler misjudged the extent of Klair's control of conventions in
the 1920s and 1930s, as well as Klair's alienation from Laffoon. Nonetheless,
Chandler's bold move worked to his advantage in 1935.

Originally pledging his support for Frederick A. Wallis, his neighbor from
Paris, Klair was freed to change his choice to Chandler in 1935 after Wallis's
elimination in the first primary. His support for Chandler resulted in a 63
percent Fayette County majority for the young lieutenant governor over Rhea.
The boss's continued strength in and around Lexington was evident, as Chandler had polled only 36 percent of Fayette County's vote in the August primary before Klair had announced his support in the run-off election in the
fall. In the November general election Chandler had little trouble in defeating
the Republican nominee, Circuit Judge King Swope.[51]

Klair's support did not mean that the erratic young governor would fall into
line behind the boss's leadership. Following Chandler's election in November, a
Christmas parade float in December bore "a wrecked car" with a placard pro-
claiming, "Old Bi-partisan Machine," "Didn't We Knock Hell Out of It?"[52]
Klair's relationship with Chandler soured because the new governor was unwilling to return Charles Fennell to the highway commission. Chandler continued to consider Klair his "good friend," however, and late in life recalled, "I
didn't have any trouble with him. I got along well with him. I know one afternoon late in the hotel somebody asked Billy 'Are you for Happy?' and he put
his arm around me and he said, 'I'm for Happy; the people are for him.' He said,
'I'm for whoever the people are for.'"[53] As with Billy Klair, Happy Chandler's
identification with the people served him well in his political career.

In November 1935, Klair was only two years away from his death in 1937.
His final years in the early 1930s had been filled with political struggles on
the local and state levels. In Lexington, the victory of the Charter League in
the municipal elections of 1931 was certainly a setback for his local machine.
In Frankfort, opposition from John Young Brown proved worrisome to the
aging boss. Brown first met Klair through Tom Scott, Klair's partner in the
insurance business. As a young law student at the University of Kentucky in
the 1920s, Brown asked Scott for a part-time job, and Scott put Brown to
work distributing placards among central Kentucky business houses. When
Brown asked Scott to introduce him to the Lexington boss, Scott, impressed

by the young man's initiative, obliged. Klair was likewise impressed and eventually supported Brown's successful candidacy for a post in the Kentucky House of Representatives in 1929.[54]

At a French Lick meeting with Laffoon in 1931, Klair suggested that Brown should be Speaker of the House. After some discussion, Klair was confident that the young representative had been decided upon as Speaker. Laffoon later changed his mind and instead of Brown promoted Tom Dunn. J. Dan Talbott and Allie Young continued to back Klair's choice of Brown, but Laffoon, already indicating his recalcitrance toward Klair's influence, refused to back down. In "customary pre-session Democratic caucus, the Governor found that he could muster only 17 votes for Dunn while Talbott held 54 votes securely in his hands for Brown."[55]

Apparently, at some point before Brown was elected as Speaker, Klair approached Brown with his desire to name the House committees. When Brown refused to strike the deal, the *Lexington Herald* reported that "from that day Mr. Klair exerted all his influence to prevent this affiant securing the speakership." In contrast to this report, Talbott and Young asserted that Klair, while withdrawing his support, made no effort to oppose Brown's election.[56]

Chandler recalled that soon after Brown's election as Speaker a tearful Klair visited him at his Versailles home to tell him of his disappointment that Brown would not allow him to name the House committees. Chandler remembered that Klair "had always named the House committees, especially the ones of business, and he was most influential with them." Chandler recalled that Klair "cried because he had helped John Brown and John Brown had broken his word to him or he had not properly understood him because he had told Billy Klair that he was going to name the committees."[57]

The hurt caused by the misunderstanding between Brown and Klair was slow to heal. In 1932, Brown showed the brashness of a political upstart by challenging Klair directly for the Fayette County post on the state Democratic central executive committee. The *Lexington Herald* announced the battle in the 3 April 1932 headline "Personal Attack Is Made on W.F. Klair by John Y. Brown; Will Run for Committee" and in a 5 April editorial, "A Regrettable Fight in the Democratic Party of Fayette County."[58] Brown's challenge resulted in a remarkable gathering in Lexington on 9 April 1932. On that day what was described as "one of the most interesting political contests ever staged in Central Kentucky" developed when the county mass convention was held on Cheapside next to the Fayette County courthouse.[59]

In *Kentucky Politics,* Malcolm Jewell and Everett Cunningham stated that the "county meeting generally is an efficient device by which the dominant faction in a county can formalize its selection of delegates to the state convention. . . . Attendance at the county mass meetings is usually small and is generally confined to active political workers, local office holders, state workers, and perhaps a few interested citizens." Newspaper reports revealed that the 1932 meeting was no usual contest. The *Herald* claimed under the title "A Notable Event on Historic Cheapside" that the crowd was the largest number of citizens of Fayette County assembled there since the free silver election of 1896. Estimates of the crowd ranged from twenty-five hundred to six thousand.[60]

In mass convention fashion, the representative was decided "by division, with the friends of Mr. Klair taking the south side of the square next to Main while Mr. Brown's supporters will take the north, or Short street side of the square." On the day of the contest, marching bands took up their stand on the opposing sides. The *Herald* reported that Klair's supporters, coming from the far reaches of the county and city and arriving in bus and truck loads, formed companies on Main Street and marched in military fashion into the square.[61] As the Klair supporters swelled steadily to the south of Cheapside, it became evident that the boss's power remained strong. The contest was settled when Brown, acknowledging the large majority for Klair, made a motion that the election of Klair "be made unanimous without a count either by the chairman of the meeting or the tellers."[62]

Although Happy Chandler remembered that after "1930 . . . Brown opposed [Klair] and didn't allow him to have as much influence as he had before," the contest on Cheapside in 1932 revealed that Klair's influence remained strong into the 1930s. The *Herald* asserted that "for some twenty years after his retirement as a member of the Kentucky legislature he was the campaign manager of the victorious candidates for Speaker of the House. With his advice, they mapped their plans. He was also the leading figure of the Democratic state central committee, the leading party organization, during that time."[63]

But that time was changing. The Great Depression made sure of that. Klair continued to the end of his life as a power in state politics, and after Paul Morton's tenure as city manager, only a brief interlude in the early 1930s, Klair's organization continued on in Lexington as well.[64] But it was a different Lexington, changed from the friendly, small city in which Billy Klair had thrived for so long. As with most everything else in the United States—north and south—the depression changed bossism and reform in the southern city of Lexington.

8

Lexington's New Deal

In 1932 and 1933 American attitudes toward charity and responsibility for unemployment were changing. Traditionally, charity was considered under the aegis of churches, private organizations, and the local political boss. When these sources failed to meet the growing relief demands of the crisis of the 1930s, many were convinced that government—local, state, and federal—must take more responsibility. In Lexington, with Billy Klair spending more time and energy in Frankfort and in French Lick strategy sessions, a more efficient, departmentalized city manager format replaced the slipshod efforts of the former machine administration.

The sharing of responsibility for depression problems among local, state, and federal governments was of course a key issue in the presidential election of 1932. Although Lexington voters had supported Hoover instead of the Catholic Al Smith in the 1928 election, the inadequacy of the Republican's policies prompted many Lexingtonians to change allegiances in 1932. Lexington's changing attitudes were reflected at the polls. The 65.1 percent in Fayette County that voted Republican in 1928, became a 56.6 percent plurality for the Democrats in 1932. Whether or not these figures represented a rejection of Hooverism or a vote of confidence for Roosevelt, Lexingtonians anxiously awaited the results of their decision. Billy Klair's sardonic response echoed the sentiments of many Lexingtonians: "Kentucky voted for Mr. Roosevelt, and I hope Mr. Roosevelt remembers that when he begins distributing the Federal pie. We have been eating corn bread for years. We need a little pie."[1]

"A little pie" came soon enough, but ironically, because of his defeat by the Charter League in 1931 and again in 1933, Billy Klair had little to do with distributing federal largesse in the early stages of the New Deal. In what has been described as "the hundred days' war," Roosevelt immediately began his campaign against the ravages of the depression. Spurred on by his "firm belief that the only thing we have to fear is fear itself," Americans gave their support to Roosevelt's declaration that the nation must move "as a trained and loyal army willing to sacrifice for the good of a common discipline." As the acts and programs of "the hundred days" emerged in "staccato rhythm" from the chambers of Congress, the hopes of Lexington residents were raised. The passage of such measures as the banking bill and the "beer bill" had an immediate effect on the city. On 7 April 1933, thirty-eight thousand bottles of beer at $.15 a bottle or $2.50 a case went on sale legally in Lexington for the first time since the advent of Prohibition in 1920.[2]

These measures, along with the National Industrial Recovery Act (NIRA), were designed to put business on a sound footing. Signed into law by the president in June 1933, the National Recovery Administration (NRA) attempted to revive business by eliminating unfair competitive practices and by promoting "the fullest possible utilization of the present productive capacity of industries." Businesses were to abide by NRA codes voluntarily, committing themselves to the hiring of more employees, who would be worked fewer hours and paid higher wages. Participating businesses were also bound by the provisions of Section 7a, which guaranteed employees the right to a union and to bargain collectively.[3]

In September 1933, a National Recovery Administration speaking campaign, with programs in the city's theaters, was begun by fourteen Lexington business and professional men. A canvass of the city's businesses was conducted in an attempt to persuade Lexington employers to sign NRA agreements. Women workers canvassed the city and county in an effort to get every housewife to sign a consumer's agreement requiring trade with NRA stores only. By 3 September, 682 out of 984 firms in the city and county visited by the canvassing teams had signed up under the "Blue Eagle," 446 Lexingtonians were employed by Lexington and Fayette County firms "as a result of their having signed the NRA agreement," and the payrolls of participating businesses had increased by $24,306.94 per month.[4]

On Labor Day 1933, what was described as the largest crowd ever gathered in Lexington viewed the NRA Labor Day parade sponsored by the Man O'War Post of the American Legion. More than thirty thousand Lexingtonians lined Main Street, standing for over forty minutes as the two-mile column of marchers, floats, and decorated motor cars filed past. The parade was capped with a speech at Cheapside by Mary E. Hughes, a Lexington native described by the *Herald* as the "militant woman leader of the NRA."[5]

In her speech, Hughes lectured that the "Blue Eagle is different from the old American Eagle; that grim, scraggly bird was a bird of conquest and avarice." America's new eagle, the Blue Eagle, is "a symbol of eternity and hope and happiness," a bird who "looks out with impartial and omniscient eye." Driving her point home, Hughes concluded that the "Blue Eagle knows when the man who has signed the NRA pledge is living up to that pledge and when he is not."[6]

Despite such admonitions, employment increases in Lexington as a result of the NRA codes were slight. Lexington employers, disregarding the omniscient eye of the Blue Eagle, simply "staggered" the hours of their old employees and failed to "put on new ones." Although Lexington's business payrolls increased, especially in the early months, and minimum wage and maximum hour regulations were followed generally, Robert M. Odear, the secretary of the Lexington NRA headquarters, expressed dismay that the city's businessmen violated "the spirit" of the NRA codes. As early as 7 September 1933, numerous violations of NRA agreements in Lexington were reported to Odear's 127 West Main Street office.[7]

The scant significance of the NRA in Lexington was undoubtedly owing in part to the organization's brevity. The haste of administrative decisions and the confusing bureaucratic complexity of the NRA made for an impossible system of codes that proved unenforceable. The Supreme Court's ruling on the unconstitutionality of the NRA in May 1935 ended the Blue Eagle's brief period of "orchestrated ballyhoo" and ineffectiveness. On 1 June 1935 the *Herald* reported that "all questions of relations with employes, competitors and customers now return to each individual merchant for decision."[8]

While the life of the Blue Eagle was brief, the NRA had an indirect effect on the city's business life by promoting a receptive attitude toward labor in later years. Ironically, however, major changes and more long-lasting effects came to the city's economy not from the New Deal's programs for business recovery but from the president's farm policies. In *Hard Times and New Deal in Kentucky, 1929–1939*, George T. Blakey surmised that "if a case can be made that the New Deal revolutionized America, the strongest and most obvious evidence would be in the field of agriculture." The rich limestone soil of the Bluegrass had long made the countryside surrounding Lexington a productive farming region. In 1930, 166,722 out of 172,000 acres, almost 93 percent of Fayette County, was farmland. Out of the 1,704 farms in Fayette

County, averaging 97.8 acres in size, 1,529 were operated by white farmers while 175 farms were run by blacks.[9]

While Lexingtonians often cited the city's location in the Bluegrass as a deterrent to the depression ills experienced by industrial, northern cities, the "most notable effect of the depression on Fayette County was a sharp decline in land values and downward fluctuations in the price of tobacco." The value of farms in the county actually dropped rapidly during the 1920s. The value of Fayette County farms, totaling $50,366,732 in 1920, dropped to $27,377,504 in 1930, and in December 1932 hog prices were at their lowest levels in thirty-five years.[10]

Despite these figures, a short tobacco crop in 1932 that brought relatively high prices during the 1932–1933 marketing season prompted one Fayette County farmer to remark, "The light has begun to shine and the clouds have begun to leave. We are going into better times and I think that within six months business will be far better than it is today." The farmer's enthusiasm was short-lived. The annual report of the University of Kentucky's College of Agriculture predicted that the 1933–1934 prices for tobacco would be well below the 1932–1933 levels.[11] The prediction proved accurate.

In these early years of the New Deal, editorials in the *Lexington Herald* lashed out at the farm programs under consideration in the federal congress. Describing such programs as "a grave danger, threatening the farms with something in the nature of socialization," the *Herald* called for less federal intervention in economics, "especially farm economics." These sentiments did not keep Fayette County farmers from looking to Washington for help, and in 1932, 189 farmers in the county applied for aid to the county agent through President Hoover's Federal Seed Loan Program. When the New Deal's Agricultural Adjustment Act was passed on 12 May 1933, Fayette County farm owners lined up in support of the new measure.[12]

With the purpose of giving American farmers a purchasing power in the American economy equal to that of the period from 1909 to 1914, the Agricultural Adjustment Administration (AAA) was implemented in Fayette County through the state extension office, which was actually directed through the University of Kentucky College of Agriculture's dean, Thomas Poe Cooper, and through the county extension agent, J. Ed Parker. The most radical and criticized change initiated by the program was the authority of the AAA to limit crop production through voluntary contracts signed by individual farmers. The AAA made direct cash payments to participating farmers on a scale based on the number of acres of each crop taken out of production.[13]

Soon after President Roosevelt signed the new farm program into law, the once-critical *Herald* revealed in a series of articles entitled "Why I Signed" that 699 Fayette County farmers had signed up for production contracts. The reduction program having the greatest impact on Lexington involved the regulation of the burley tobacco industry.[14] In his study of Fayette County's New Deal farm programs, Terry Birdwhistell concluded that out of "the three major production control programs initiated in Fayette County between 1933 and 1936, the tobacco program far exceeded the other two both in terms of its extensiveness and its effects on the county's economy." After all, nearly every farm in Fayette County raised at least some tobacco and the city's twenty-four tobacco warehouses made Lexington the "world's largest burley market."[15]

More than any other New Deal agency the AAA's burley tobacco program changed the way Lexingtonians felt about government economic intervention. When portions of the AAA were declared unconstitutional in 1936, the *Herald*, making an about-face from editorials written three years earlier, declared the Supreme Court's decision a mistake. Fayette County residents, once hesitant about government interference, were by 1936 concerned about a lack of regulation. Many area farmers were convinced that government regulation not only was beneficial but was a necessity. Continued government regulation of tobacco production years after the depression decade attested to the long-lasting effects of this New Deal program.[16]

The problem of unemployment plagued the city increasingly as the depression deepened. While measures such as the NRA and the AAA attempted to reform business and farming practices, bringing changes to Lexington that affected the city for years to come, these programs failed to address the city's more pressing problems. Other New Deal legislation raised the expectations of the unemployed. The most popular of these acts created the Civilian Conservation Corps (CCC) in late March 1933. Providing for the recruitment of 250,000 young men between the ages of eighteen and twenty-five, the act launched the largest forest conservation project in the nation's history. On 17 April Fayette County's quota of 145 recruits was filled only a few hours after the recruiting station was set up in the local relief commission offices at 521 South Mill Street.[17]

No CCC camp was located near Lexington until one was established in Carlisle in 1936. The Lexington city government—whether under the aegis of Billy Klair or Paul Morton—had nothing to do with corps activities because the CCC was entirely a federal operation. Yet the impact of the CCC on Lexington, however incalculable, was not insignificant, since hundreds of young men unable to find jobs in the city were given work while living in a disciplined environment. At the same time, the money sent back to their families kept hundreds more from starvation. Despite the fact that quotas placed on the recruitment of blacks denied positions to many needy Lexington youths, the CCC must be considered one of the most successful New Deal programs.[18]

Despite its success the CCC alone could not handle Lexington's growing relief needs. Of the 13,708 families in Fayette County, 3,450 or over 25 percent received relief aid in the first five months of 1933. During that time unemployment relief costs totaled $121,113.11. Compared with some areas of the state, Lexington's relief needs were not great. For example, 49 percent of the residents of Bell County received relief, as did 40 percent in the mining county of Harlan. Compared with the 10 percent receiving relief in Louisville, however, Lexington's relief problem was substantial.[19]

Fortunately for Lexington's unemployed, more federal help was on the way. The Federal Emergency Relief Administration (FERA), headed by Harry L. Hopkins, replaced the defunct Reconstruction Finance Corporation. The FERA funneled funds through the state and county relief commissions. Of greater importance to Lexington, however, was the organization of the Civil Works Administration (CWA). When Hopkins explained that the FERA was not meeting unemployment needs, the president authorized him to set up the CWA solely as a federal operation. Under this particular organization, relief went directly from the national government to the localities without being slowed by state and county red tape.[20]

In Lexington, CWA operations did not peak until the spring of 1934. At that time, it was reported that various CWA road projects gave work to more than 1,200 in Fayette County in a single week. Of the $13,067 cash payroll in that week, $7,747 was paid to over 960 men working on various city and county road projects, $1,727 employed 120 on state projects, and $3,593 was given as wages to 143 on federal building projects. In addition to the cash payroll, $5,560 in scrip was issued to be spent in Lexington stores, and 13,400 pounds of smoked pork, along with 3,360 pounds of cereal, were issued directly to Fayette County residents.[21]

The CWA was highly successful in alleviating Lexington's relief problems, but only for a short period. In the first three months of 1934, a total of $713,970.47 was spent for unemployment relief in Fayette County. Of this amount, CWA funds were responsible for $611,901.47, while the city accounted for a little over $81,388. The remainder of the total was provided by the county, the board of education, and the Family Welfare Society. While these figures indicate its importance, the CWA was doomed to a short existence. In mid-March the combined Fayette County Relief and CWA committees received a telegram from Washington stating that further federal relief would not continue unless state and local governments provided 25 percent of the total relief funds in cash. The telegram went on to state that Kentucky's present beer and whiskey taxes were inadequate in meeting the demand. The threat was soon carried out as hundreds of Lexington CWA workers lost their jobs on 1 April.[22]

The death of the CWA was indicative of administrative conflicts among federal, state, and local governments. Gov. Ruby Laffoon, pledging not to raise taxes, was involved in a continuing feud with Roosevelt's relief administrator, Harry Hopkins. Hopkins aimed a sharp press release at Kentucky officials stating, "There are a few recalcitrant states that want to sit down and let the federal government pay 100 percent of the cost of unemployment relief within their borders. . . . Some states are in for a rude shock in the very near future, if they do not come through with action." Although Laffoon did supplement beer and whiskey revenue with a sales tax, he refused to release more funds until he was convinced that they would be used according to his guidelines.[23]

An agreement was not reached until October 1934 when Laffoon agreed to release $250,000 for the month on the condition that abuses in the administration of relief be corrected and excessive overhead costs abolished. Former CWA projects were transferred to the Kentucky Emergency Relief Administration, a division of the FERA. By mid-October 300 to 400 Lexington laborers resumed work on partially completed road projects throughout the county. Because these projects were administered through state and county offices, it appeared that Roosevelt's experiment in "federal to local relief" had failed. At the same time that the CWA was being dismantled under Hopkins, however, Harold Ickes was organizing another attempt to provide relief for the localities while bypassing state and county administrations.[24]

Relationships between cities and the federal government developed as a result of the depression and the failure of the states to handle the relief situation. The complexity of this relationship was evident in the workings of the Public Works Administration (PWA), a federal program begun in 1933 that directly benefitted Lexington through the injection of thousands of dollars for public works projects in the city. Although $3.3 billion was placed under the control of the Department of the Interior in the summer of 1933, funds were not put to use in Lexington until almost a year later.

When plans for this unprecedented work-relief project were announced, excitement over its potential for Lexington was overwhelming. Editorials in the Lexington newspapers emphasized the importance of taking full advantage of federal funding. John G. Stoll, the editor and publisher of the conservative *Lexington Leader*, did not believe that a huge public works program was based on sound economic principles, yet he pragmatically stated that Lexington "would be foolish not to take advantage of this opportunity."[25]

Stoll identified the need for a storm water sewer system to control the nagging problem of the flooding of Town Branch, the enlargement of the sewage disposal plant, the development of a first-rate airport, the building of a municipal auditorium, and the building of a new jail to replace the one-hundred-year-old structure then in use as a few of the glaring public works needs in Lexington. Maintaining that federal taxes would be increased to fund the program, Stoll stated that "it is hoped that the present administration will lose no time in preparing the necessary application" for its full share of PWA allotments. While the *Leader* emphasized public building, the *Lexington Herald* stressed the large number of jobs that would be made available for local labor.[26]

As the days passed, Lexington residents became concerned that the city administration under city manager Paul Morton was moving too slowly in securing PWA funds. Lexingtonians recalled Billy Klair's ability to "get things done." Henry K. Milward, a local insurance man, stated, "It's a wonderful opportunity. If we don't take advantage of it, we are standing in our own light." Lexington's board of commerce, which included the University of Kentucky's progressive president, Frank L. McVey, wished to "urge upon the present city administration of Lexington that it take immediate steps to prepare an application for as much money as may advantageously be used here." When it was revealed that Louisville, Covington, and Newport had already applied for substantial allotments, a Lexington realtor mirrored the views of many Lexington residents when he stated, "It certainly is good business. Cities all over the United States are realizing this and are getting ahead of Lexington in pushing their applications. I think speed is imperative." Apparently the only opponents of PWA funds that could be found in the city were the members of the Farmers Union, an organization that had "an almost unbroken record of opposition to every progressive measure proposed in Lexington."[27]

In response to mounting criticism, Paul Morton began an aggressive campaign to secure the federal PWA funds. Morton's efforts were rewarded, and on 29 December 1933 Lexingtonians were informed that $1,382,000 had been allotted for "the construction of a comprehensive system of storm water sewers to serve the business district and other developed areas." Additional PWA funds followed, and by 7 July 1934, 1,492 men were employed on PWA projects. When the initial PWA projects were completed in May 1935, hundreds of additional workers had been employed, and the results of their work was indeed impressive.[28]

Disregarding the federal government's role, Morton and the city manager administration took credit for a new storm sewer, a sanitary sewage plant, two community centers, a public health center, and other projects still underway. But even with all these accomplishments, neither Morton nor Roosevelt's New Deal was successful in winning the allegiance of Lexingtonians.[29]

E. Reed Wilson, the "Home Town Ticket's" candidate for mayor in 1935, blamed Morton and his administration for providing inadequate funds for the Family Welfare Society, the local relief agency of which Wilson was president. When a campaign was launched by Wilson to replenish the depleted funds, individuals in surrounding counties gave donations, prompting Wilson to state that "Lexington should bow its head in shame when citizens of outside counties have to come to its aid in helping the needy."[30]

Wilson's criticisms revealed the ambivalence felt by many Lexingtonians toward the federal programs. Grateful for any relief from depression ills, whether from neighboring counties or from the federal government, Lexingtonians were nonetheless slow to greet the coming of outside aid with a warm embrace. In November 1935 the Home Town Ticket—Billy Klair's ticket—easily defeated Charter League candidates by a plurality of 63 percent. The victory of the Home Town Ticket in 1935 was more than a vindication for the machine of Billy Klair; it was also an indication of the reluctance of Lexingtonians to march boldly into the arms of the "welfare state."[31]

Despite the fact that thousands of jobs, provided by federal programs and administered by local officials, were made available to Lexington job seekers, unemployment problems continued to grow. Were such problems the result of deficiencies in local administration of funds now that the "old gang" was back in control, or were they indicative of the inadequacy of a higher power? Was the experiment of federal intervention a failure, or had Roosevelt's New Deal simply failed to go far enough?

As if to answer his critics, on 8 April 1935 President Roosevelt signed into law a measure that appropriated more than $4.8 billion for relief through the Works Progress Administration (WPA). Four federal agencies (RFC, FERA, CWA, and PWA) had provided at least some relief for Lexington's unemployment problems in the early years of the depression before the WPA was organized. Compared with other counties in the state, Fayette County had received a substantial share of the federal allotments. With 13,708 families in 1933, Fayette County represented Kentucky's third largest county. The Reconstruction Finance Corporation (RFC), a New Deal holdover from the Hoover administration, spent $1,538,965 in Fayette County, the fourth largest disbursement in the state. When the RFC suspended its relief program owing to lack of funds in June 1933, more help for Lexington's unemployed was on the way.[32]

The Federal Emergency Relief Administration (FERA) replaced the RFC and eventually spent $742,847 in Fayette County, the sixth largest total in the state. In addition, the short-lived Civil Works Administration (CWA) spent $280,265, Kentucky's third largest allotment, between 16 November 1933 and 14 July 1934 on various city and county road projects. Whereas RFC and FERA funds were funneled through state and county relief offices, the CWA had experimented with direct "federal to local" funding.[33] In Lexington in 1933 and 1934 that meant that CWA projects were administered by Paul Morton and his antimachine city manager administration.

Another attempt to provide relief for the localities while bypassing state and county administrations—yet another plum for Paul Morton—was made in 1933 under the supervision of Harold Ickes. Lexington's allotment from the Public Works Administration on 19 December 1933 of $1,443,000 represented the largest single relief allotment in the city until the WPA began its work in 1935, but when the initial phase of the PWA program was reported complete in May 1935, thousands of Lexington laborers were again without work. Despite the massive PWA building program, the depression continued to be felt in Lexington.[34]

While the storm sewer and various municipal buildings improved the lives of the residents of Lexington, suitable housing for Lexington's growing population was not provided in the early years of the depression. Within blocks of the new public buildings stood what a Lexington clergyman called "the slummiest slums" he had ever seen. Bishop H.P. Almon Abbott of the Episcopal Diocese of Lexington stated in a sermon at the Church of the Good Shepherd that there were dwellings in the city "where it is possible to study astronomy through the roof and geology through the floor and to view the landscape through the walls."[35]

In September 1934 the Family Welfare Society reported that Lexington faced serious housing problems for the coming winter. E. Reed Wilson, the future mayor, asserted that it was almost impossible to find a house to rent for less than $20 a month while the need was for houses renting at $12 to $15 a month. Families on direct or work relief were having difficulty in the payment of rents, while others could not secure housing at all.[36]

New Deal measures to handle the nation's housing problems began in June 1933 when the Home Owners Loan Corporation (HOLC) was created to prevent the loss of property to home owners unable to make mortgage payments. Through a branch office in Lexington, the HOLC purchased delinquent or endangered mortgages from Lexington banks, then rewrote them at reduced interest rates and longer terms. A year later the National Housing Act created the Federal Housing Administration (FHA), which attempted to promote "home ownership, construction, and repair as catalysts for economic recovery and expansion."[37]

Although the FHA made it easier to obtain loans for home building, slum clearance and low-rent public housing that would benefit Lexington's poorer residents were not provided through federal allotments until later in the decade, when Bluegrass Park and Aspendale Apartments were constructed as the city's first public housing projects. Such meager attempts were inadequate in dealing with Lexington's housing problems. Men, women, and children, forced to leave their small farms in the county or already living in dilapidated shacks in the city, found little relief from their housing woes. Bluegrass Park and Aspendale, "segregated by race and income, sequestered in blighted areas, stigmatized by purpose and appearance," offered immediate though insufficient relief for only a few of Lexington's needy residents.[38]

In 1935 the Family Welfare Society's executive secretary, Mary B. Buckingham, identified more than six hundred Lexington residents not only without adequate housing but on the verge of starvation. While the building projects employed thousands, hundreds more suffered because they were unable to work. The combined efforts of the eleven local agencies making up the Community Chest helped to alleviate the problem somewhat. Still, it was necessary to start a drive to solicit funds from private sources. It was estimated that $20,000 was necessary to meet immediate needs. When the solicitation campaign came up approximately $8,000 short, a burgoo picnic was planned to raise more funds.[39] The picnic was a gala affair, complete with James T. Looney, "Kentucky's Burgoo King," serving as chef. Although the feast procured another $1,000 for the "starvation fund," the absurdity of the event was indicative of the inadequacy of relief efforts in Lexington during the early years of the New Deal.

Both federal programs and local relief efforts fell short in their treatment of depression problems in Lexington, a city usually thought to be immune from the ills of the Great Depression. While the visible accomplishments of the massive public works programs were evident, and many Lexington men were given work, other relief needs were neglected. In his campaign for mayor on the Home Town Ticket in 1935, E. Reed Wilson criticized the Charter League administration for being concerned more with the "physical rather than the human side of the community's needs."[40]

Other than a few sewing projects and library work, Lexington women were left out of the employment process. Lexington blacks were also discriminated against, although they comprised more than 25 percent of the city's population. While the city's business interests were not devastated as in larger cities, hundreds of needy residents suffered as the depression wore on. Would the WPA and other federal programs correct these glaring omissions? How would the return of the "old gang" in city politics affect the handling of lingering depression problems?

When asked what the greatest achievement of the New Deal in Lexington was, one man who had firsthand experience of the depression in the city replied, "the storm sewer system." His answer illustrated the neglect of "the human side" in Lexington during the early years of the Great Depression. Despite all of the early ballyhoo over the Charter League administration, Lexingtonians missed the personal touch of Billy Klair. Lexingtonians felt that in the hard times of the Great Depression Klair's expertise was needed more than ever. And with the coming of new WPA projects coinciding with the election of the Home Town Ticket in 1935, Klair had a viable opportunity to reestablish his local power and control.

Like Klair himself, the Works Progress Administration from its inception in 1935 until its demise in 1943 was steeped in controversy. And the projects and politics of the WPA—described as "essentially an urban program"—in Lexington demonstrated the extension of controversy and corruption from the local political machine to an agency of the federal government.[41]

While some heaped praise on the WPA for its efficiency, accusations of scandalous political activity also abounded. At the same time that some hailed the agency as the savior of the nation's unemployed, others, criticizing its "boondoggling, make-work" programs, claimed that the initials WPA should stand for "we piddle around." Despite such contrasting opinions, the many accomplishments of the WPA stand as lasting memorials to the work that was done. "The WPA built or improved more than 2,500 hospitals, 5,900 school buildings, 1,000 airport landing fields, and nearly 13,000 playgrounds." The wide-ranging WPA program was responsible for thousands of service, domestic, and white-collar jobs as well.[42]

As the first central organ of control for the nation's entire relief program, the WPA has usually been treated as a national phenomenon. As Charles S. Ascher of the Social Science Research Council pointed out, however, "It was early recognized that a study [of the WPA] at the national level, capturing chiefly the words and actions of federal administrators, should be supplemented, if possible, by complementary case studies of the actual operation of the program in the field."[43]

A study of the implementation of WPA programs in Lexington provides an excellent view of the response of a small city to a federal program. The funneling of WPA funds through the federal, state, district, and local hierarchy provides a valuable lesson in bureaucratic functioning. At the same time, relationships between federal, state, and local politics are revealed most clearly, perhaps, from the ground level. Controversies in the 1930s surrounding Lexington's local politicians and WPA officials, and involving state and national leaders, certainly did nothing to diminish the truth of James Mulligan's verse assertion that "politics [are] the damnedest in Kentucky."[44] The implementation of Works Progress Administration programs in Lexington revealed the ongoing struggle of a southern city seeking to retain its small-town rural heritage, even as it became one of Kentucky's leading urban centers.

With continuing unemployment problems in 1935, Lexington's tobacco auctions, billed as "the largest loose leaf burley market in the world" and employing more than two thousand persons annually during the sales season, could no longer meet unemployment needs. Doubtless unsettled industrial conditions elsewhere caused many to drift toward the more favored economic areas, of which Lexington was one. The practice of "employment by day rather than the monthly or seasonal employment of farm labor" tended to lure others to the city. Although the New Deal's "alphabet soup" formula for unemployment relief—the RFC, CCC, FERA, CWA, and PWA—had helped deal with the problem in the early years of the depression crisis, the continuing rise in unemployment statistics indicated that more help was needed.[45]

Despite the boastings of the Charter League's administration under Paul Morton, statistics showed that relief efforts in Lexington and Fayette County, as well as in the rest of the state, were deficient. Not only did the unemployment count rise to an unprecedented high with the completion of PWA projects in 1935, but those fortunate enough to be on the work-relief rolls were hardly relieved. *United States News* reported that during 1933, 1934, and 1935, families on relief in Kentucky received the smallest allotment from the federal government of any state in the nation. While Nevada received the highest amount—$3,077 per family on relief—Kentucky received only $370 per family. Not only was Kentucky last in federal allotments, but it ranked eleventh from the bottom in state and local contributions to families on relief. In the total amount spent for relief, including federal, state, and local spending, Kentucky again ranked last.[46] Clearly Morton's city manager regime and the Laffoon administration in Frankfort proved inadequate in securing needed federal dollars.

Lexingtonians, along with other Kentuckians, voiced their concern over the unemployment problem. The *Lexington Herald*, a newspaper that eventually backed New Deal policies wholeheartedly, offered several explanations for the low relief figures. Referring to the recalcitrant state administration under Gov. Ruby Laffoon, a *Herald* editorialist argued that in the early days of relief Washington reduced sharply its contributions to states failing to match federal funds. Many Kentuckians, especially in the Bluegrass region, practiced subsistence gardening, and it must always be remembered, argued the *Herald* writer, that "living costs are lower in Kentucky."[47]

Although it was true that the depression did not devastate the Bluegrass region as it did other areas of the state and nation, this assurance was not enough for those going hungry in Lexington. With the coming of new and innovative relief measures in 1935, however, many Lexingtonians looked expectantly for the end of their plight. When the WPA was finally put in operation, the Lexington working community emitted a collective sigh of relief. Many believed that Kentucky's ignominious "cellar position" as the state receiving the least amount of federal relief aid per family would soon be a thing of the past. The new WPA plan gave "the average Kentucky family on relief, in return for 16 eight-hour days of work per month, more than double the amount paid to relief clients under the old KERA set-up."[48]

While help for Lexington's workers was on the way, others were not able to share in the mood of optimism. On 15 August 1935, the same day that the Social Security Act became law, the *Lexington Herald* reported that "540 families [were] in dire need" in Lexington, a figure that included 119 helpless children. Renewed efforts by private agencies and concerned individuals, including the "burgoo relief picnic," failed to provide an adequate response.[49]

Of the $1,041,699 allotted by the WPA to the state on 4 August 1935, $5,844 was to be spent in Lexington. The allotment allowed fifteen men to begin work on a storm water sewer on North Broadway at a cost of $1,854. In addition, twenty-two men were employed for the same task at $2,570 on Walton Avenue, and eighteen men graded and drained the University of Kentucky's practice field at a cost of $1,420.[50] Significantly, the federal government through the WPA would provide funding for numerous university projects, usurping the role of the state and Billy Klair, once described as "the best friend the University ever had."

Despite such meager beginnings, some twelve hundred workers were employed on various building projects, road improvement and sewer repair projects, painting projects, and the setting up of a county rock quarry by 1 March 1936. Women, although not as fortunate, were given some work on sewing projects, public health projects, school lunch programs, and in various clerical occupations. A work training center for women was also set up to prepare women for other types of work.[51]

It seemed that almost every conceivable type of work was given to WPA workers, from "the elimination of unsanitary devices" to the painting of street names and house numbers on street curbs. The cumulative total of federal funds spent in Fayette County from the WPA's beginning through 31 December 1937 was $672,772 out of the state's allotment of $51,289,798, a figure that ranked Fayette thirteenth among Kentucky counties.[52]

As more projects were begun, WPA workers became increasingly visible throughout the city. Probably the same criticism of the "make-work, ditch-digging and leaf-raking" projects heard elsewhere was evident on the streets of Lexington. Yet while WPA workers were undoubtedly looked down upon by some middle- and upper-class Lexingtonians, most city residents applauded the agency's work. A Transylvania professor, wishing to find out if WPA laborers actually worked, coaxed a star football player into taking work on one of the projects. Returning to class one day with blistered hands and aching muscles, the young man assured his professor that at least one WPA employee had been forced to work.[53]

The great diversity of WPA occupations render generalizations of job value and employee status impractical. At the same time, by 1937 WPA workers had acquired an identity of their own, whether that identity was positive or negative. While women of WPA toy mending or school lunch projects were extolled for their beneficial work, the heading of a newspaper article reporting a Lexington man's chaining of two young boys in a basement read, "WPA Worker Is Jailed for Mistreating Sons." In both instances, the workers were described as WPA employees, much as other workers were identified with the names of their companies or as political hacks associated with the patronage of the boss.[54] As a federal agency, the WPA subverted the role formerly played by Billy Klair.

If WPA employees acquired their own identity, by 1937 they had also developed an active if not always successful organ for articulating their views to federal relief officials. Again, in earlier years disenchanted government workers would have voiced concerns directly to Billy Klair. In the private sector, Lexington had experienced "virtually no labor unrest" in the early years of the twentieth century with local "skilled-trade unions . . . prominent only during the yearly Labor Day parade and picnic."[55] In the early 1930s the only unions functioning in Lexington organized as part of the Lexington Building Trades Council. This organization, composed of eleven building-craft unions, represented employees of private businesses. In 1937 John L. Lewis, the head of the Congress of Industrial Organizations (CIO), launched an ambitious plan to organize the "more than 3 million workers laboring on WPA and other federal emergency relief projects." Presenting the scheme to Harry Hopkins and Aubrey Williams, Lewis bluntly stated, "It's the least that the Administration can do for the C.I.O." Rejecting Lewis's proposal, Hopkins "refused to consider the notion that the government should actively recruit members for CIO."[56]

Although Lewis's plan failed, another more radical group acted as a union for the WPA workers and the unemployed in Lexington. According to one of its organizers, the Kentucky Workers Alliance (KWA), a division of the socialist Workers Alliance of America, was recognized in 1937 as "the official union for WPA and unemployed workers." In the summer of that year the KWA organized a mass demonstration in Lexington to protest WPA Administrative Order No. 44. Described as "a millstone round the necks of WPA workers," the order provided that workers be docked for any time lost though such loss was through no fault of the worker. An eyewitness recalled that "almost a thousand workers paraded from the Short Street hall"—located just down the street from the residence of Billy Klair—to Broadway, thence up Main to Mill Street, and out Mill Street to Dudley School. The writer remembered that "marchers carried banners and signs" and "good order was maintained."[57]

Upon arriving at Dudley School, the marchers' committee approached Ernest Rowe, the local WPA administrator, with the complaint. Although Rowe "was not at all sympathetic to the organization or its aims . . . he evinced no overt hostility." He did, however, "manifest a mammouth [sic] ignorance."

Denying any knowledge of Order No. 44, Rowe promised "to do what he could about it."[58] While the order was never changed, the KWA continued to articulate the growing demands of WPA employees. Because several officers of the KWA were also bosses on WPA projects, some critics accused the WPA of being inspired by communists. John M. Robsion, Kentucky's lone Republican in the U.S. House of Representatives, went so far as to express his fear of the "wide control and influence that Communism has exercised in WPA in many sections of the country."[59]

Clearly, the depression experience in Lexington redefined the old, traditional distinctions between political bossism and progressive reform. Although Klair himself had blurred the lines between bossism and reform, especially during his early years in Frankfort, the aging boss like everyone else was unprepared for the economic crisis of the 1930s. While Klair recognized the necessity of work programs like the WPA, the baffling array of federal relief programs surely perplexed him. A Thanksgiving turkey was simply no longer adequate to appease Lexington's dispossessed, and as the radical reformers of the KWA made clear, the more extensive New Deal programs were often inadequate as well.

As with other New Deal programs, the WPA received criticism from radicals to the left as well as from conservatives to the right. The controversial nature of the WPA was intensified in Kentucky during the 1938 senatorial primary campaigns of Alben Barkley, the U.S. Senate majority leader, and A.B. "Happy" Chandler, Kentucky's governor. In this campaign, which drew national attention, the WPA was involved in what was later described by Harry Hopkins as "about as hot a political campaign as I have ever seen in America, and it was a hot one, and they threw everything at each other but the kitchen stove."[60]

Kentucky had not been the only state to develop political controversies involving the WPA, and southern states proved to be particularly fertile ground for controversy. Problems with Gov. Eugene Talmadge in Georgia (Hopkins removed the handling of relief from his hands) and with Huey Long in Louisiana prompted President Roosevelt to state as early as April 1935 that "politics must be kept out of relief." In Tennessee there were frequent charges that the WPA and other federal agencies were being employed politically "in behalf of the Cooper-Stewart coalition." Charges were made that the Tennessee WPA administrator was "practically the manager of the coalition ticket."[61]

These political improprieties in other southern states were not as damaging to the national WPA administrator as were those in Kentucky, however. When being interrogated by a Senate committee for his nomination as secretary of commerce in 1939, Hopkins revealed that "Kentucky politics had been a headache to him for six years and that, while he had done his best to combat the 'strange ways' of Kentucky politicians, he had been unable to change them." The "strange ways" of two of Kentucky's more prominent politicians became evident soon after Barkley and Chandler opened their campaign drives in the summer of 1938.[62]

Chandler had entertained high ambitions since his gubernatorial victory in 1935. In fact, he confided to "high members of the national administration" that a seat in the Senate was necessary for him to gain a national reputation in preparation for the presidential nomination in 1940. In the early spring of 1938, Chandler became increasingly critical of New Deal policies. In three successive speeches, he stated that the federal budget should be balanced, that farm labor wages were too high because WPA workers were paid too much, and then, contradicting himself, that Kentucky's WPA labor was being paid too little in comparison with other states.[63]

Chandler was unable to lean on Billy Klair's support in 1938 as he had in 1935. Klair had died on 29 October 1937. With Billy Klair's death, Chandler, no longer able to call on the Lexington boss, instead asked Charles W. Fithian to be his campaign chairman for Fayette County. Fithian had taken over Lexington's city manager post after the resignation of Paul Morton. Fithian and others urged Chandler to lessen his emphasis on balancing the budget, and listening to the urgent cries of his friends, Chandler did change his tactics. Instead of criticizing Roosevelt's policies, he "claimed to be an advocate of the New Deal who, because of his youthful vigor, was in a better position to give energetic support to it than the aging Senator Barkley." Chandler continued to criticize Barkley for not using his influence to raise the WPA wage scales to the levels of states north of the Ohio River.[64]

For his part, Barkley of course aligned himself closely with the New Deal and significantly with the lingering machine of Billy Klair. As if to answer Chandler's criticism of the low WPA wages in Kentucky, the Kentucky relief administrator, George Goodman, announced in June 1938 that Kentucky had recently been moved from the number three wage classification to the number two category. For the state, the new scale would boost the wages of sixty-two thousand WPA employees some $700,000 a month, and for Lexington the old scale of $31.20 per month was raised to $39.90.[65]

After officially opening his campaign in Lexington, Barkley's charges matched those of Chandler in originality, if not in intensity. He "contrasted in each county the number of roads built by WPA and those built by the state highway department. As if by magic all over the state rose little red and white signs announcing that this road had been built by WPA and not far from it were to be found other signs announcing that that road was built by the state rural highway department."[66]

Much more important in Barkley's campaign effort was the support of the United Mine Workers, the American Federation of Labor, the railroad brotherhoods, and the Farm Bureau, all of which gave enthusiastic endorsements to the senator, and Barkley's greatest support was probably among Kentucky's tobacco growers. Furthermore, the Kentucky whiskey distillers, so vital to the economy of the Bluegrass, felt "that it would be unwise to oppose [the federal] administration, a branch of the Treasury."[67]

Also significant was the fact that a considerable portion of the remains of the Billy Klair machine in Lexington supported Barkley. Lexingtonians had not forgotten the legendary Klair. Before his death, Klair often made use of the local press to make known his preference for a political office. A typical advertisement would read simply, "I want all my friends to know that it is my intention to vote for. . . ." The backing of Barkley by some of Klair's confidants continued to show the boss's lingering shadow over Lexington politics, although the direction in which the shadow was cast in the 1938 elections added an interesting and ironic twist to the Klair legacy.[68]

Besides the support of the Klair machine, Barkley could also count on the votes of the majority of Lexington's workers. On 7 June 1938, a large labor rally, sponsored by the Lexington branch of the Workers Alliance, was held at the courthouse. Speakers included Lexington attorney John Y. Brown, WPA district administrator Ernest Rowe, and the vice president of the Workers Alliance of America. Brown, a former congressman, warned the Lexington voters not to believe Chandler's claim that he was seeking the Democratic nomination as a friend of the New Deal. Brown declared that "the governor is not, nor has he ever been, a supporter of the President. He knows better, his backers know better, the Republicans who are singing his praise on every street-corner and the American Liberty League know better, and the President knows better or he wouldn't be coming to Kentucky next month."[69]

Chandler's claim of reducing the state debt was accomplished, according to Brown, "at the expense of the aged people of Kentucky, of the blind, and of the dependent children of the state." Echoing Brown's sentiments, the vice president of the Workers Alliance of America refuted Chandler's claims that the WPA had entered politics. The socialist leader remarked, "Certainly there can be nothing political about giving jobs to people who are unemployed."[70]

Because of the growing intensity of the campaign, the Senate's committee on campaign funds began to scrutinize the activities of the candidates closely.[71] This was especially true after Brady M. Stewart, Chandler's state campaign manager, issued several bold charges against Barkley and the WPA in May. Stating that "every federal agency in Kentucky is frankly and brazenly operating upon a political basis," Stewart charged that "it has become common talk among our people that the state administrator of the Works Progress Administration in Kentucky has openly and boldly stated that he and his organization will leave nothing undone to achieve the re-election of Sen. Barkley."[72]

Harry Hopkins and George Goodman did not issue immediate replies to the Stewart charges. Goodman wrote Hopkins's assistant Aubrey Williams that "it is obvious that the Stewart letter was prepared to meet and forestall anticipated charges from the Barkley committee of unfair political activity." Goodman seemed to be more concerned with the WPA projects than with the outcome of the election. While relating to Williams that Chandler was "cramping some of our road projects by withdrawing equipment which they allot to the Fiscal Court, who in turn place it at our disposal," he assured the deputy administrator that he should "not worry about Barkley in this race. He is a certain winner."[73]

Goodman's confidence was well founded. Although the state administrator constantly denied that the WPA was involved in political activities, he had conducted a thorough political canvass to determine the extent of Barkley support throughout the state. The study showed clearly that Barkley would win the primary. Fayette County's entry in the canvass is typical of the county-by-county survey: "Fayette County is a well-known anti-Chandler county. It went against him strong in the general election when he was running for Governor. Since that time he has arranged to move the Eastern State Hospital from this county, although the chamber of commerce and other civic organizations fought hard to keep it here. It will go for Barkley by a big majority."[74]

While the survey made it clear that Barkley "was safe" in the upcoming election, the Stewart charge had placed the reputation of the WPA in jeopardy. In May, Hopkins had sent a letter to all WPA employees assuring them, "No one will lose his WPA job because of his vote in any election or his failure to contribute to any campaign fund." After the Stewart allegations were published, Hopkins sent three of his assistants to Kentucky to investigate the extent of political corruption within the state WPA. Following the two-day investigation, one of the assistants, Howard O. Hunter, released to the press on 13 June a denial of the Stewart charges. He stated that the WPA had not discharged workers "on account of their political faith or votes," the WPA had not employed ineligible people in order "to pad the rolls in favor of some political candidate," nor had the WPA forced employees to contribute to a political campaign. Defending the WPA administrators, Hunter asserted, "It does not seem to me to be reasonable to require that administrative officials of the WPA be intellectual or political eunuchs, or to be placed in a position where they are not entitled to opinions which opinions frankly may be often and freely expressed."[75]

Although Hunter concluded that WPA workers had no reason to fear that their jobs were in danger because of their political affiliation, others were not so thoroughly convinced. Senator Rush Holt, a Democrat from West Virginia, ridiculed Hunter's assertion that there was "no politics in the WPA in Kentucky" and stated that the report would "deserve a hearty horse laugh if it were not such a tragedy for the hungry." To Holt and others, Hunter's report was "the same old story of the WPA investigating itself; never finding a thing."[76] Just as the administration of relief was transferred from the local boss to the federal government during the 1930s, federal relief and reform agencies faced charges of corruption once leveled by reformers themselves against local political machines.

Despite Hunter's findings, instances of political corruption in the senatorial campaign continued to surface in Lexington and throughout the state. On 21 June a Fayette County grand jury reported to circuit judge King Swope that contributions for the campaigns of both candidates had been solicited illegally. The grand jury found that contributions for Chandler's campaign had been collected from the employees of Lexington's Eastern State Hospital and the Greendale Reform School. Dr. J.L. Vallandingham, the hospital's superintendent, dismissed a dietician, Nora Lee Taylor, for "insubordination" because she had collected "for the Chandler-for-Senator campaign." At the same time, the clinical director of the hospital resigned his post, declaring that "medicine and politics don't mix any better than oil and water." Although "severely condemning" the activities of the state employees, the grand jury's report showed no evidence of coercion or of threats to discharge workers who did not contribute. Also lacking was any evidence that the workers had been assessed specific amounts for campaign funding. The jurors were content in simply condemning the questionable practices.[77]

The same report also condemned the practice of soliciting campaign funds from WPA employees for Barkley. Requests for contributions had been received by Lexington's WPA employees from Charles Tachau, a Louisville insurance salesman. Receiving one of the letters, Lexington's district WPA administrator Ernest Rowe stated that he "knew Tachau was not connected with the WPA, and supposed the letter he received was similar to those received by many other persons, whether employed by the government or not."[78]

Following these vague and largely innocuous accusations concerning WPA operations in the state, Ernest Rowe was later forced to respond to more serious and damning accusations aimed toward the actions of Lexington's WPA. The controversy was rekindled when Thomas L. Stokes of the *Knoxville News-Sentinel* published a series of articles in which the WPA was again accused of using its influence to support Barkley. Making his own survey of the state, Stokes concluded that district WPA supervisors were intimidating workers to vote for Barkley and to contribute to his campaign fund. Of the many charges made by Stokes, one directly concerned WPA operations in Lexington.[79]

On 7 June 1938 Stokes wrote, "It was in March also that B.C. Collis, director of operations for District No. 3, with headquarters in Lexington, called in his engineer staff and announced that he expected them to be 100 per cent for Senator Barkley, adding that they would be called on later for 'something else,' according to those who attended the meeting. The 'something else' was presumed to refer to a contribution." After an investigation, Harry Hopkins dismissed the charge. Basing his remarks on an affidavit signed by Collis, Hopkins stated that although the subject of politics did come up in the meeting, it was mentioned only as a warning to the employees "that they would be subjected to pressure from both sides." Included in the affidavit, however, was a statement in which Collis "expressed himself to the effect that he expected every supervisory person under his control to be 100% in accord with the policies of the Works Progress Administration and the President."[80]

Just when Hopkins and Rowe thought they had answered the various allegations satisfactorily, they were forced to deal with an earlier charge made by Brady Stewart, Chandler's campaign manager. Stewart had charged that "relief donations are distributed in paper bags on which are printed 'Paper bags donated by friends of Sen. Barkley.'" In a letter to Senator Arthur Vandenburg, a Republican from Michigan, Hopkins denied that the WPA had distributed commodities to relief clients in bags bearing that description. Explaining the practice in a letter to state administrator George Goodman, Rowe stated that a merchant in his district whose grocery was located across the street from the WPA Commodity Project often provided relief clients with bags to carry WPA commodities. Seeing nothing wrong with the practice, Rowe reiterated that "WPA people had nothing to do with the bags."[81]

Barkley's wide margin of victory over Chandler in the 1938 primary ended one of the most hotly contested campaigns in the history of Kentucky politics. While Chandler claimed that he was defeated by the WPA, a detailed study of the election revealed that "the organized farmer-laborer combine and especially urban voters . . . turned the trick." All of the major urban centers of the state—Covington, Ashland, Paducah, Owensboro, Louisville, and Lexington—were carried by Barkley. In Lexington and Fayette County, support from the remnants of the Klair machine, the Barkley appeal to tobacco farmers and the labor force, and the area's traditional anti-Chandler bias made Barkley an easy winner. The fact that Lexington was especially favored by New Deal programs undoubtedly added to the Senator's plurality in the city, but clandestine political maneuvering by the WPA was certainly not the reason for his victory. As George Blakey concluded in *Hard Times and New Deal in Kentucky, 1929–1939*, "The Roosevelt coalition defeated Chandler. Laborers, farmers, and relief recipients owed too much to the New Deal to abandon it for a singing, smiling governor who promised them less of what they were enjoying."[82] The New Deal proved powerful indeed, and although remnants of the Klair machine backed Barkley, the New Deal seemingly worked against the old Klair machine as well.

Ironically, New Deal agencies such as the WPA sometimes used tried and true machine tactics. Revelations coming to light the year following the election indicated that the WPA in Lexington was far from innocent of political involvement. During interrogation sessions with a Senate committee after his appointment by Roosevelt to the secretary of commerce post, Hopkins was questioned heavily about the activities of the WPA, whose operations in Kentucky were central in the discussions. Replying to questions concerning Kentucky's state administrator, Hopkins stated, "I had numerous complaints against Mr. Goodman . . . because they said he was always hiring Republicans and wouldn't fire them. Goodman would come back and say he wanted to hire good men."[83]

One of the "good men" hired by Goodman was Lexington's WPA district administrator, Ernest Rowe. Throughout the Barkley-Chandler election campaigns, Rowe had feigned complete disinterest in the primary's outcome. He once remarked, "To begin with, I am a Republican and am not interested in a Democratic primary election. I am not aware of any attempts to corner the WPA for any particular candidate. There is no way of my learning the political affiliation, or religion, of those in the employ or on the rolls of the WPA in my district."[84]

Despite his stated unconcern with the political or religious affiliation of his WPA workers, Rowe had found a way to discover the political leanings of the voters in the Lexington district. In a letter written to Goodman on 16 June 1938, Rowe revealed, "This week I asked Messrs. Hugh Crozer and R.C. Page to get together a detailed report about the political situation in each of the 38 counties in the Third District." Showing more than a little interest in the election's outcome, Rowe continued, "I hope these boys are not too optimistic. If their judgement about these counties is correct Senator Barkley will have a landslide in his favor in this jurisdiction." Displaying great adaptability, the "Republican" Rowe stated with zest that "we have a splendid organization in this county and the WPA is giving 100% cooperation."[85]

Further revelations of Rowe's involvement in politics came after Goodman relieved him of his duties on 1 March 1939. On 19 June the central topic of discussion in the House debates concerning the passage of a new relief bill was the deposed WPA administrator from the Lexington district in Kentucky. The reason for Rowe's dismissal was described colorfully by Beverly M. Vincent, a Democratic representative from Kentucky. Addressing Kentucky's lone Republican representative, John M. Robsion, Vincent asked, "Did the gentleman [Robsion] know that [Rowe] was fined in Kentucky for operating a motor vehicle while drunk, and that when he was arrested and they took him to jail, he thought they were putting him in a hotel. . . . And he pleaded guilty and gave the judge a cold check, and they had an awful time collecting that check."[86]

Replying to Vincent's remarks about Rowe's insobriety, Robsion stated, "That is bad, but it is not nearly so bad as Mr. Goodman and others trying to coerce WPA workers and take the few dollars that they get with which to buy something to eat and wear to finance one faction of the Democratic Party." Most of the representatives were much more concerned with two letters that the former "erstwhile prohibition agent" had presented exclusively to the *Lexington Leader* and the *Louisville Times* on 19 May 1939. Both letters, signed by George Goodman, revealed in explicit detail the extent of the WPA's involvement in the politics of the state.[87]

The first letter, dated 23 May 1938, dealt with the assessment of Lexington's WPA employees to support the Barkley campaign. Goodman instructed Rowe to "fund a high grade man who is interested in politics and strong for Senator Barkley to serve as finance chairman for your district and to discuss with employees, either in person or by mail, the matter of assisting financially in the campaign. . . . Lists of administrative and supervisory employees, giving monthly earnings and home addresses will be supplied to you to be given your campaign chairmen. It is suggested that two per cent of annual earnings is a fair contribution."[88]

Then on 27 June 1938 Goodman wrote, "I know you have no correspondence in your files that would violate the WPA regulations and instructions in connection with political matters. However, I suggest that anything you may have that would appear to an uninformed person to involve us in politics be destroyed."[89]

Rowe maintained that he disregarded Goodman's instructions, and in fact refused to receive contributions that WPA employees offered him. Members of the House, however, were so disturbed by the implications of the two letters that they overwhelmingly passed "an act that [made] it possible to put behind bars men who are willing to prostitute the administration of WPA in such a dastardly way." The new bill not only replaced the single national administrator with a three-member board, but also allowed the government to prosecute persons who violated the law by intimidating voters. Kentucky's Robsion felt that the Goodman-Rowe letters had a "substantial effect" on the House's action. After a speedy passage by the Senate, the bill, known as Reorganization Plan No. 1, became law on 1 July 1939. The Works Progress Administration was transformed into the Work Projects Administration, a unit of the newly created Federal Works Agency.[90]

Thus the involvement of Lexington's WPA operations in the political sphere had an indirect impact on national policy. But what effect did these activities have on Lexingtonians? The obvious political corruption so incensed one Lexington resident that he wrote, "The time is not far distant when political decency will demand that not only every individual on relief, WPA, etc., be disenfranchised but that each and every individual in the public pay (those under Civil Service excepted), be it municipal, county, State or Federal, be denied the ballot." Despite these sentiments, advocates of such extreme measures were few in Lexington. As with Kentuckians in general, residents of Billy Klair's Lexington were not unfamiliar with political improprieties, and shady WPA activities in the city were simply taken in stride.[91]

The period of uproar over the senatorial primary in the summer months of 1938 was also the time of the greatest activity and employment for the WPA in Lexington. By 1939, however, the peak had been reached and WPA employment was on the decline. A month before his dismissal, Ernest Rowe reported on 1 February 1939 that 163 fewer people were employed on WPA projects in Fayette County than were employed five months earlier. Rowe stated that Lexington's WPA stopped taking on new employment in October 1938 when it became apparent that funds appropriated by Congress would not be sufficient. Since that time several persons were discharged from WPA rolls each week to take private employment.[92]

More employment opportunities became available as America geared up for World War II, especially after 1940. And as newspaper headlines attested, the war was replacing domestic issues and programs as the important topic of the day. By December 1942 President Roosevelt had decided that employment offered by war industries had reached a point "where a national work relief program is no longer necessary." Praising the agency's nearly seven years of service, the president stated, "I am proud of the Work Projects Administration organization. It has displayed courage and determination in the face of uninformed criticism. . . . With the satisfaction of a job well done and with a high sense of integrity, the Work Projects Administration has asked for and earned an honorable discharge."[93]

WPA-sponsored programs made a mark in Lexington. While quota systems and politics sometimes influenced employment on WPA projects, thousands of needy Lexingtonians were put to work, and Lexington's WPA accomplishments were varied and far-reaching. So-called "ditch-digging and leaf-raking projects" were rare. The city's WPA employees left behind lasting examples of their work. In all, $2,325,293.26 in federal WPA funds were spent in Lexington and Fayette County. Only eight out of the state's 120 counties received more federal aid, this despite the fact that the Lexington area was often cited as the region least affected by the Great Depression.[94]

In Fayette County, 33 miles of streets and roads were built, 443 sanitary outhouses were constructed, and Lexington's sewage system was completed and improved. Numerous improvements were made on the campus of the University of Kentucky. Courses in "recreation and group work" were added to the university's physical education and sociology programs to provide for new fields of employment resulting from the WPA's recreation programs. A total of $356,507 was spent on the construction of new campus buildings, and an additional $6,032 went for various indexing projects, surveys, and studies.[95]

A scrapbook collection of photographs of WPA projects in Lexington presents vivid illustrations of the wide-ranging WPA program; photographs of a shorthand class, a Lexington nursery school, a school lunch program at the Abraham Lincoln School, a toy mending project, a county rock quarry, sewer construction, and construction of the Lexington airport and the city armory are pictured. An addition to Bryan Station High School, the building of a slaughterhouse, and numerous photographs of city streets are there. Some pictures of projects at the university showed a greenhouse, a press box and a running track at Stoll Field, and an addition to Barker Hall. Projects involving the city's black population included a photograph of a "Colored Music Festival."[96]

The WPA's extensive assortment of activities overshadowed obvious examples of neglect. While some jobs were provided for African Americans by Lexington's WPA, the number of jobs did not correlate with Lexington's black population. Comprising one-fourth of the city's total population, Lexington's blacks voiced their dissatisfaction with WPA job opportunities through the local chapter of the Kentucky Workers Alliance. Although a member of the Alliance maintained that quotas for blacks were abolished through the efforts of the local organization, the prevailing attitudes of white city officials demonstrated a continued delight in black subservience. In E. Reed Wilson's 1938 historical sketch of Lexington, the city's mayor asserted that the "negro in the Bluegrass is a good citizen. . . . They occupy a definite place in the life of Lexington and their position is fixed and secure." Wilson maintained that for "the most part they are employed as horse-trainers, stable and exercise boys, farm-hands, domestic servants, waiters, physicians, and teachers."[97]

As early as 17 June 1935, President Roosevelt remarked in an address to state WPA administrators that "we have to be extremely careful not to make any kind of discrimination. We cannot discriminate in any of the work we are conducting either because of race or religion or politics." The president's statement was seconded by T. Arnold Hill, the acting executive secretary of the National Urban League. In a letter to George Goodman, Hill urged the Kentucky relief administrator to consider "the appointment of a Negro to your own staff and to that of the District Administrators. Such individuals can assist in seeing that the President's and your own desire for fairness and equality is made realistic and practical." Goodman's opinion of this advice was not uncertain. In the left-hand margin of the letter, Goodman scrawled emphatically, "NO."[98]

While figures are not available to give a clear picture of WPA employment for Lexington's African American population, it is possible to be more exact in the case of women. Although women represented more than half of Lexington's adult population, the federal WPA allotment providing jobs for women was less than one-seventh the amount for male employment. Of the $144,994.26 allotted specifically for women's employment, by far the largest share, $67,306.26, was used for the setting up and maintenance of sewing rooms.[99]

The WPA was not given responsibility for other areas of need in Lexington; the PWA was in charge of public housing, and local agencies gave inadequate support to the city's "unemployables." William Leuchtenburg's description of the dilemma for the nation as a whole is applicable for Kentucky and Lexington as well: "By turning the unemployables back to the states, [Roosevelt] denied to the least fortunate—the aged, the crippled, the sick—a part in the federal program, and placed them at the mercy of state governments, badly equipped to handle them and often indifferent to their plight." In Kentucky, state governments simply passed the burden on to local governments, which in turn dumped the problem on various charitable agencies. In Lexington the agencies making up the Community Chest made inadequate attempts to raise needed funds through charity "drives" and burgoo picnics. The meager funds that were raised were distributed haphazardly and ineffectively.[100]

Lexingtonians seemed to be more concerned with the activities of politicians whose political antics often overshadowed the pressing needs of the community. The findings of several Senate and House committees investigating the 1938 election influenced the passage of a new relief bill in 1939, a bill that drastically curtailed federal expenditures for relief projects. Activities in Lexington, under the direction of Ernest Rowe, played a role in the passage of the new relief legislation.[101]

Various factors, such as the coming of the war and increased employment in private industries, contributed to the demise of the WPA and to the ending of the Great Depression. As with other periods in Lexington's history, the depression years were dominated by political struggles. The important interplay between the projects and politics of the WPA in Lexington in the late 1930s emphasized a continuity with the projects and politics of the Mulligan ring in the 1880s and 1890s and with the projects and politics of the Klair machine during all the years in between.

9

The Last Hurrah?

The Great Depression brought important changes to the city. Could Lexington's political system be included in those changes? Did the depression destroy the Lexington machine, or was the death of the organization's charismatic leader to blame? Was the machine destroyed at all? What leaders filled the void left by Klair's passing? What role did changing demographics play in altering the makeup of the machine? Did the Lexington organization, so long an influential force in state politics, remain so in the post-depression years?

The role played by the depression and Roosevelt's New Deal in the decline of the old boss-oriented machine has been a subject of controversy for historians. According to the "welfare state thesis," the depression and the resulting New Deal federal programs destroyed political machines in cities across the nation.[1] In *The Last Hurrah*, novelist Edwin O'Connor articulated this idea to explain the demise of his fictional "boss," Frank Skeffington. O'Connor had his character proclaim that Roosevelt was "the man, sport, who really put the skids under" Skeffington. According to O'Connor, "If anybody wanted anything—jobs, favors, cash—he could only go to the boss, the local leader. What Roosevelt did was to take the handouts out of the local hands."[2]

"Happy" Chandler believed that in Lexington Billy Klair remained unaware of the consequences of the Roosevelt Revolution. Chandler recalled that Klair was "for Roosevelt in 1932 and again in 1936." The president's program, however, did not elicit an enthusiastic welcome from the Lexington boss. As Chandler remembered it, Klair "wasn't for the New Deal, of course. Hell, he couldn't be for it, you know, but he didn't know anything about what was going on; he was purely a local politician."[3]

In his *Machine Politics: Chicago Model*, Harold F. Gosnell's findings contradicted the "welfare state thesis." Gosnell explained that "jobs and spoils were the currency of Chicago politics in 1936 as well as in 1928." After the New Deal, bosses simply changed their roles and became "brokers for the various governmental services filling the gaps left by the red-tape provisions of the bureaucrats." According to Gosnell, if the depression had an effect on Chicago's urban machine at all, it was the fact that the other major party organization in the city—the Republicans—was rendered impotent. There was only graft enough for one machine during the depression years.[4]

In Chicago, Edward J. Kelly, successor to Anton J. Cermak, made it clear to "needy Chicagoans that public employment and relief checks came to them as a result of the Democratic party's control of city hall." The administration of relief in Chicago was "relatively immune from spoils politics." In the "windy city," according to Roger Biles in *Big City Boss in Depression and War: Mayor Edward J. Kelly of Chicago*, the "real importance" of federal assistance to Kelly's machine "lay not in the manipulation of relief roles nor in the intimidation of voters but in the financial support provided in a time of economic disaster."[5]

Kelly enjoyed an unusual relationship with Roosevelt, a relationship based on "mutual respect and friendship." The president relied on the boss's counsel "but also socialized with him, inviting him to luncheons in Hyde Park and Washington." Along with Ed Flynn of the Bronx, Kelly "was one of the select few" to reach "the inner circle." Roosevelt merely "stayed on the good side" of leaders like Ed Crump of Memphis and Frank Hague of Jersey City whose support he coveted," and the president even funneled federal dollars away from Tom Pendergast in Kansas City and Boston's James Michael Curley, destroying their machines.[6]

The "welfare state thesis" did not hold true for big city machines, but neither is it accurate to say that the Great Depression and New Deal had no impact on politics. In Kentucky, on the state level, the New Deal certainly dealt the bipartisan combine a heavy blow. Political scientists Malcolm Jewell and Everett Cunningham considered that the "New Deal changed not only the bipartisan balance of power but also the nature of interest-group conflict in Kentucky." The decline of the Republican Party made obsolete Klair's old strategy of supporting a Republican gubernatorial candidate when the winner of the Democratic primary was considered unacceptable by the machine.[7]

Kentucky's economy became more diversified in the depression decade, making it more difficult for the railroad, racetrack, or highway building interests to dominate the political system. The agricultural depression and the federal programs that sought to cope with it persuaded many Kentucky farmers that "the solution to most of their problems lay in Washington rather than in Frankfort."[8] In a largely rural state like Kentucky, for example, the price support and crop reduction programs of the AAA proved to be particularly appealing to the state's wheat, corn, and especially tobacco farmers.

In Kentucky's cities the New Deal altered political allegiances as well. In Lexington, the administration of federal monies coming into the city in the early depression years fell to the reformers' city manager rather than Klair's machine. The coincidence of the brief period of city manager government with the coming of New Deal programs to the city, coupled with Klair's death in 1937, prevented the continued stranglehold of the Democratic machine in Lexington.

Lexington's experience coincided with the findings of Lyle Dorsett in *Franklin D. Roosevelt and the City Bosses,* who in refuting the "welfare state thesis" asserted that in the Roosevelt coalition no single group was more important to Roosevelt than the city bosses. Conversely, no other man was to be so vital to the life and death of urban political machines as Roosevelt. While the Pendergast and Curley organizations were destroyed by Roosevelt, their destruction did not come about because welfare programs were eroding the basis of machine politics. Roosevelt went against Pendergast because of the corruption in his machine, and Curley was ruined simply because Roosevelt chose to give money and patronage to his political opponents in Boston. Other urban bosses, such as Crump, Flynn, Hague, and especially Kelly, cooperated with Roosevelt and actually strengthened their political organizations during the New Deal period.[9]

In Lexington, the city manager system of government, adopted a year before Roosevelt took office, eventually took New Deal patronage out of the hands of Klair, placing it instead at the disposal of other local leaders. Some New Deal programs like the FERA funneled relief through state and county governments, governments that Klair continued to influence during the Morton interlude. Still, Morton capitalized on benefits received in Lexington, however the benefits came to the city. Despite his continued statewide power, it remained difficult for Klair to take credit for federal assistance while he was not in control in Lexington. Lexington voters returned control to Klair in 1935.

Although the city manager system was short-lived, and the Home Town Ticket placed city government again under machine control, Klair's death in 1937 effectively put an end to the tightknit machine organization of the Klair years. The passing of other Kentucky bosses—Allie Young, Percy Haly, Maurice

Galvin, and Ben Johnson—prompted political scientist Jasper B. Shannon to argue that "with the disappearance of the old type candidate, death has gradually thinned out many prominent figures in behind-the-scenes politics." Shannon pointed to Ruby Laffoon as an example of "the old type candidate," a variety of leader "characterized as the oratorical school of political leadership, . . . exponents of the eloquent phrase and perfume scented oratory." According to Shannon, politicians like Laffoon, Morrow, Beckham, and Stanley were replaced in the 1930s with candidates like "Happy" Chandler, a "dynamic and vigorous, hard hitting, wise-cracking, non-florid speaking campaigner" whose campaigning technique was "more suited to a machine age." Such politicians "are quick, adroit, staccato, instead of ornate, florid and long winded."[10] It was the phenomenon of the decline of the "behind-the-scenes" boss, though, rather than the "florid and long winded" stump-speaking politician that the "welfare state" thesis addressed.

The death of nationally known bosses, and the downfall of their machines, engendered the "welfare state" explanation, an explanation that Biles and Dorsett believed erroneous. Dorsett concluded that the "mortality rate of bosses was high in the late forties and fifties because the nation's most notorious city moguls were old men, not because the welfare state rendered them obsolete."[11] In Lexington, as in other cities, federal New Deal assistance worked to oil the cogs of the machine, providing financial support that would not otherwise have been available.

Celebrations over the Home Town Ticket's overwhelming victory over the Charter League's candidates in November 1935, tempered two years later by Klair's death, and the continuation of machine administrations in the following years, was evidence that Klair's shadow lingered over the Lexington political scene. But the machine, though remaining in power, was never the same.

Klair's choice for the important city manager position, James J. O'Brien, died within a year of his appointment. Fred Benckhart, a Paul Morton appointee as director of finance, acted as manager until William White, another Klair follower, was appointed on 3 January 1937. The Home Town administration under Mayor E. Reed Wilson attempted to present administration programs as a picture of progress. Shortly following the appointment of White, Wilson described O'Brien's brief tenure as city manager as a period of "substantial progress" and maintained that the city "may now point with pardonable pride and satisfaction to the accomplishments of the past year."[12]

Wilson pointed to the increased activity of the building inspector's office as an indication of "returning prosperity." The total of 1,028 building permits issued in 1935 had increased to 1,285 in 1936, and improvements valued at $462,892 had risen to $763,411.73. Following a common tack of urban machines during the New Deal period, Wilson took credit for programs provided by the federal government. Stating that "the department of public works has cause to feel especially proud of its accomplishments during the past year," the mayor pointed to major improvements to city streets that were accomplished at "very little cost to the city." A reorganization of the health department, the outstanding work of the city's recreation department, and the serving of free lunches to the city's children proved, according to Wilson, that city hall had been active in the interests of Lexingtonians. The city had trained and supervised "52 WPA and NYA recreation workers to assist in all phases of the work."[13]

Despite Wilson's touting of these advances, James J. Mott asserted in "City Manager Government in Lexington, Kentucky, 1947," that "Mayor Wilson's administration had no distinguished accomplishments." William White, described by one Lexingtonian as being "pushed . . . in as city manager just like he was a little child" by Klair and the machine, conducted the office of manager in a way that prompted Mott to conclude that "there is very little management under White." Contemporary critics lambasted the Home Town administration for "disregarding the spirit of the city manager act" by going back to the old method of the commission form of government. Skeptics scoffed at a proposal by the commissioners to enact a civil service ordinance that would place "nearly every non-elective employee of the municipality, department heads included," under the merit system. A provision that incumbent appointees would keep their posts without taking the civil service examination, coupled with a past suspect record regarding the merit system, was more than enough to raise the suspicion that the administration's civil service proposal was "motivated by the desire to keep present office-holders in office, regardless of their qualifications, after the present mayor and commissioners have retired."[14]

Apparently Klair's ability to present a semblance of progress despite the heavy-handed tactics of the machine was not inherited by the Home Town administration. Although Mott stated that "Klair had hardly been buried before the fight began to determine his successor," party hacks, unable to rally around another boss, yearned for a "public-minded Billy Klair" to improve conditions in the city. William White continued as city manager until well into the 1940s, but the question of Klair's successor at the helm of Lexington's Democratic Party continued to be "an important but unanswered political problem." In 1939, T. Ward Havely, another "old gang" businessman-politician who had been associated with Louis des Cognets in the contracting business before establishing a crushed rock and concrete business for himself, won the mayoral election but died in office in 1943.[15]

If Wilson and White and Havely failed to establish themselves as strong party leaders, Jewell and Cunningham maintained that R.P. "Dick" Moloney became the dominant force in Fayette County within a few years of Klair's death. As a state legislator, Moloney served the Clements, Wetherby, and Combs administrations as "a highly effective legislative leader" until his death in 1963. By the mid-1960s, however, no dominant Democratic leader or strong party organization existed in Lexington or Fayette County.[16]

In the years following the passing of Klair, conflicting political interests were never reconciled, and a striking redistribution of Lexington's population from the lower income precincts in the center of the city to the rapidly growing suburban periphery increased the futility of politicians in maintaining a strong and durable organization along the lines of the Klair machine.

The suburbanization of Lexington began with the first streetcar lines in the 1880s and continued into the 1920s and with the federal policies of the New Deal's FHA in the depression years.[17] It was World War II, however, that really brought down the curtain on the bosses' act. By "greatly increasing the complexity of cities and by developing new interest groups inimical to machine government," the war, not the Great Depression and New Deal, ended the old-time boss-dominated machine rule of cities. Historian Roger W. Lotchin has argued effectively that the "tremendous post-1945 demand for things like automobiles and housing created by war prosperity and scarcities substantially speeded up the process of urbanization and therefore the process of decentralization, accelerating the loss of machine assets to the suburbs." Lotchin found that the war "also generated considerable prosperity, weakening the hold of the boss over the poor." Finally, veterans returning from the European and Pacific theaters to active participation in city politics "tended to regard the old-line bosses as the American equivalents of Hitler, Tojo, and Mussolini. To the veterans it did not seem logical to have fought against authoritarian governments abroad and then come home to tolerate their continued existence."[18]

Lotchin's "authoritarian" argument did not extend through to Lexington; Klair, the son of German immigrants, died in 1937. Lotchin's other arguments, however, are held up by Lexington's experience. Lexington chronicler John D. Wright Jr. stated that "few could have predicted the tremendous changes [that] would transform this community into one of the fastest growing cities in the United States."[19] For Lexington, Lotchin's "World War II" thesis for the decline of Klair-type bossism is more compelling than the "welfare state" thesis of Edwin O'Connor.

The fact that remnants of the Lexington machine continued to linger in local affairs throughout the depression years and into the post-World War II period despite the lack of a clear-cut individual leader was testimony to Klair's lifelong work. While the local machine's power in the 1940s was a mere shadow of the earlier period, it was the Klair legacy that continued to dominate Lexington politics for years after the boss's death. And it was the inability of anyone to fill the void created by Klair's death, coupled with the dramatic changes brought on by the war, that led to the demise of an effective party organization by the 1960s.[20]

For Lexington, there was no single cause for the gradual decline of Billy Klair's machine. The changing role of the federal government and the changing demographics brought on by the depression and especially by World War II all played a part. But more important in the experience of this small, southern city was a simple fact that politically astute Lexingtonians clearly understood. The boss was dead.

Epilogue

Kentucky has been called more than once a land of paradox, and Lexington's story is a story of paradox as well.[1] Both Lexington's saga and the story of Billy Klair, replete with his seemingly contradictory abandonment of a reform agenda in his early years for dependence on the "interests" in his middle and later years, certainly present a study in paradox.

With Klair's return to power in Lexington after the short duration of the Charter League's reform administration from 1932 to 1935 came declining health for the boss. Klair still enjoyed—or tried to enjoy—diversions that he had cultivated throughout his adult life. Thomas Scott's daughter-in-law remembered that "they told him he should stop drinking, but Mr. Scott took him whiskey to his house on Short Street." And in January 1936, the combination of poor health and his particular affinity for the racetrack took Klair to Dania, Florida, where he could enjoy the races at Hialeah and miss the bitter weather of a Lexington winter.[2]

On 24 January, Thomas Underwood wrote to Klair in Florida after his own return to Lexington from a winter vacation: "I hated to leave Florida without seeing you again. . . . It was a great pleasure to see you even for so short a time and to see you in such fine health and spirits. We got back to eight inches of snow and last night it was fifteen below zero, the coldest since 1899." The editor of the *Herald* was unable to write the boss without a mention of politics, informing him, "I got back and found I had been elected president of the board of commerce so I hope you will not be able to say some of the things that you have previously said about that organization." Underwood assured Klair that "between the snow and the job hunters, who are as awful as ever, you are mighty lucky to be there and I certainly hope you will stay. You don't know how wonderful it is down there until you come back into this snow."[3]

Despite his friend's advice, Klair did not remain long at his Florida re-
treat. In 1936 he was appointed postmaster of Lexington, succeeding the retiring I. Newton Combs. After a few months, however, poor health confined
the ailing boss to his bed, although Klair continued to perform his duties as
postmaster until his official resignation on 8 October 1937. Calling his "personal and political friend," Congressman Virgil M. Chapman, to his bedside,
Klair related his desire to resign and his choice of assistant postmaster Roy F.
Williams as his successor.[4]

The *Leader* reported that Klair "was a power to be reckoned with even
after his last illness had confined him to his room." Despite his being bedrid-
den from March 1936 until his death, Klair's devoted wife and friends submitted to his insistence on voting in the August 1936 primary, taking him to
the polls where he cast what proved to be his last vote. His death in October
1937, coming only a few hours after his associates had carried out his plan to
insure strong precinct organization for the following Tuesday's election, sig-
naled the beginning of the end of the boss-oriented machine rule in Lexington that had endured from the days of the Mulligan ring in the city's
Reconstruction past.[5]

Klair's death at the age of sixty-two at 8:30 on the evening of 29 October
1937, from what was described as "hypertensive heart disease," removed from
the scene "one of the leading figures in city and state politics." When informed of Klair's death, Governor Chandler sent a telegram to Mayme, Klair's
widow, assuring her that along with her personal sorrow the "passing of Billy
Klair is a great loss to the Democratic party and to his host of friends."[6]

In the *Lexington Herald,* Underwood, a veteran of many political battles
himself, emphasized Klair's statewide influence, noting that the "proverbial
remarks he made, quoted from Pikeville to Paducah, are in no printed form."[7]
Yet the boss's words and deeds had made a difference: "Across the entire state
of Kentucky wherever democracy is known, wherever live those who came in
contact with the inspiring and friendly figure who numbered all as friends and
gave them the right to call him 'Billy,' wherever youth looks forward with
hope at the chance that freedom gives, a heavy shadow has fallen. The voice of
the 'little statesman' is silenced."[8] The *Herald,* devoting an editorial to the
Lexington political leader, recalled Klair's personal style: "Some called him a
party 'boss,' but he was far from that. He was a matchless leader through the
accumulated gifts and experience and friendships of many years. He had served
his party in many capacities, never failing. Big-hearted, trusting all, with dynamic personality he endeared himself to those who were associated with him

until they followed him. He controlled state conventions, one after another, yet remained in the background leaving to others the limelight and public offices."[9]

Even Klair's long-standing critic, the *Lexington Leader*, while asserting that the paper was often opposed to Klair's program, conceded that Klair was a "man of integrity":

The death of Mr. William F. Klair removes a colorful and magnetic figure from the life of this community and the state. He was a man who, because of his political leadership and astuteness, was often criticized. Most of the criticisms were undeserved. It is the testimony of those who knew him best that he was one of the kindest of men, charitable, generous, and sympathetic. He had many fine qualities in addition. His word was his bond. He carried out his pledges and met his obligations. His years of political leadership demonstrated his great ability to understand human nature and to bind men to him. He acted from motives which seemed to him to be good and for the public welfare.[10]

Forgotten or ignored were Klair's intense political battles with reformers, his suspect loyalty to the Democratic Party, his ties to the "interests"—liquor and the Jockey Club—the "honest" graft of his political machinations, and his racism.

Dignitaries from throughout the state, including Governor Chandler, attended Klair's funeral on Monday, 1 November. Congressman Chapman, Judge Thomas J. Ready, and Klair's business partner, Thomas Scott, were among the active pallbearers. Honorary bearers included Lt. Gov. Keen Johnson, Lexington's mayor, E. Reed Wilson, former mayor Col. John Skain, *Lexington Leader* editor and publisher John G. Stoll, and the Covington Republican politico, Maurice Galvin. State Democratic headquarters, offices in the Fayette County courthouse, and offices at city hall were all closed from 10:00 to 11:00 that morning in honor of Klair.[11]

The Reverend Father Joseph McKenna, in charge of the services, remarked to a "packed" St. Paul's Catholic Church audience that the Lexington political leader "always remained simple, unaffected Billy Klair" and that "God alone knows his many acts of charity to his less fortunate fellow men." As celebrant, Father McKenna sang Requiem high mass at 10:30. Klair was buried at Calvary Cemetery, not far from the grave of Dennis Mulligan.[12]

Lexington old-timers could not help but make the connection with Mulligan. In his 1 November 1937 editorial, Editor Underwood of the *Herald* mistakenly noted that at the beginning of his involvement in politics, Klair had once served as the personal page of the Speaker of the House, James H. Mulligan, the son of Dennis Mulligan.[13] Many of Lexington's older residents undoubtedly viewed the Klair machine as a continuation of the organization begun by Dennis Mulligan. While Mulligan familiarized the city with machine tactics, Billy Klair perfected the art of boss politics.[14] And just as the birth of Lexington's machine came in the wake of the crisis of the Civil War, the death of the city's most capable machine politician, and the death throes of his machine, occurred in the midst of the upheavals of the Great Depression and World War II.

But Lexington emerged from depression and war poised for a new era—an unprecedented era—of growth and prosperity. No longer the sleepy town of Billy Klair's youth, the city at the time of Klair's death was a bustling, urban center. Underwood wrote that the "work that he did lives wherever the accomplishments of Lexington's municipal government, of Kentucky's legislatures and state administrations and those others he assisted in many walks of life, high and low, have succeeded in adding to the sum total of human happiness." Underwood concluded that it "is doubtful if any man nominated and elected to public office within a quarter of a century has been so large a factor in shaping the turn of events."[15]

So what should we make of Billy Klair? As with other businessmen-politicians in turn-of-the-century Lexington, and for that matter in turn-of-the-century America, Klair was an entrepreneur. As a businessman—saloon keeper, bank director, amusement park operator, road constructor, textbook publisher, racetrack supporter, insurance provider, the list goes on and on—Klair involved himself in an astonishing array of activities.[16]

As a businessman, Klair was, in essence, a conservative. When other urban bosses occasionally went to Congress, they invariably voted with the most conservative wing of the party.[17] This was not true with Klair, but then Klair's tenure in the legislature came at the very beginning of his political career when he was determined to make a name for himself as a protector of children and as a supporter of the state university in his hometown. Ever the entrepreneur, Klair worked to establish a reform reputation before his long years in defense of the status quo.

More important to Klair than his private business interests was the business of politics.[18] Along with Plunkitt of Tammany Hall, Klair was a political entrepreneur, a practitioner of "honest" graft. The political boss and his machine followers, "like the businessmen whom they emulated, shared in the largesse of an industrializing society and took advantage of the opportunities presented by expanding urban America." For Klair, the son of German immigrants, as with other "new urbanites," it was politics, "more than the factory or pushcart," and more than any of his other business pursuits, that served as the avenue for economic reward.[19]

Klair's life and career illustrated yet another reward, more important to the boss than economic gain. Making money was certainly important for him, much more so than adherence to any ideological agenda save one. As Klair's will attests, the boss made money just to give it away.[20] Ultimately, the reward sought by the entrepreneur was not a monetary one. The ultimate reward was power. Billy Klair was an entrepreneurial power broker.

As the son of immigrants, yet at the same time a son of the South—born to immigrant parents in a southern city—Klair lacked the Puritan insistence on public service "as a duty undertaken for the good of the community."[21] Instead, Klair expected a reward for his services. Of course, Klair's immersion in the Bluegrass South helped determine the means by which he sought his "reward": bourbon and the Jockey Club. Still, the reward of power was consistently sought and consistently gained.

After his death, Mayme Klair moved to 398 Linden Walk, leaving the downtown home on the corner of Georgetown and Short Streets for a comfortable suburban residence. Ironically, it was the dispersal of hundreds of Lexingtonians—in the 1930s and especially in the post-World War II 1940s—from the inner core of the city to outlying suburbs that helped wreck the organization of the machine that Klair had worked so hard to build.

The life of Billy Klair in many ways mirrored the story of Lexington. His story, and the confusing interplay of bossism and reform in Lexington, tells us much about the transformation of cities in the South in the late nineteenth and early twentieth centuries. Politics in Lexington played a significant role in the development of the city and in the history of the Commonwealth. Lexington's experience also illustrated the prominent, if neglected, role of urban political machines in the turn-of-the-century South.

Traces of Billy Klair's Lexington still remain. St. Paul's Church still dominates a section of Short Street. The Security Trust Building that housed Klair's sixth-story office still stands across from Cheapside. And a street marker identifies Klair Alley running behind Klair's former residence on the corner of Short and Georgetown. The alley runs the length of a block between Georgetown and Jefferson Streets. At the Jefferson Street end, the marker for Klair Alley is juxtaposed—paradoxically—to a similar marker for Jefferson Street. The irony of a street named for the third president—who from his garden house at Monticello envisioned a rural, agrarian America—intersecting with an alley named for the Lexington boss is at first glance striking. Yet it was Billy Klair who witnessed the transformation of Lexington from its pastoral, nineteenth-century, small-town past to its urban present as a twentieth-century southern city.

Notes

Prologue

1. Interview with Joe Scott, Lexington, Kentucky, 16 September 1995.
2. See William L. Riordan, *Honest Graft: The World of George Washington Plunkitt: Plunkitt of Tammany Hall* (St. James, New York: Brandywine Press, 1993).
3. John E. Kleber, ed., *The Kentucky Encyclopedia* (Lexington, Ky.: Univ. Press of Kentucky, 1992), 946, 123, 363, 399.
4. George T. Blakey, *Hard Times and New Deal in Kentucky, 1929–1939* (Lexington, Ky.: Univ. Press of Kentucky, 1986), 168.
5. Histories of Lexington are limited to *Lexington and the Bluegrass Country*, American Guide Series (Lexington, Ky.: Commercial Printing, 1938), and to pictorials such as Bettie L. Kerr and John D. Wright Jr., *Lexington: A Century in Photographs* (Lexington, Ky.: Lexington-Fayette County Historic Commission, 1984), and John D. Wright Jr., *Lexington: Heart of the Bluegrass* (Lexington, Ky.: Lexington-Fayette County Historic Commission, 1982). Wright's discussion of Lexington's experience with political machines is limited to a few paragraphs. See Wright, *Lexington: Heart of the Bluegrass*, 97, 129–130.
6. Thomas D. Clark described Kentucky in this way throughout his *Kentucky: Land of Contrast* (New York: Harper and Row, 1968).
7. Interview with Thomas D. Clark, Lexington, Kentucky, 15 February 1983.
8. *Lexington Herald*, 1 November 1937; Clark interview.
9. *Lexington Herald-Leader*, 19 May 1963; *Herald*, 1 November 1937; interview with John Y. Brown Sr., Lexington, Kentucky, 13 April 1983.
10. Blakey, *Hard Times and New Deal*, 168; Thomas D. Clark, *A History of Kentucky* (Lexington, Ky.: John Bradford Press, 1960), 449.

1. It Is a New Lexington!

1. Charles N. Glaab and A. Theodore Brown, *A History of Urban America* (New York: Macmillan, 1976), 26.

2. Ibid., 26, 27.

3. Ibid., 27.

4. Information on the 1833 cholera epidemic is found in Wright, *Lexington: Heart of the Bluegrass*, 43–45; Henry Clay quoted on page 45.

5. Wright, *Lexington: Heart of the Bluegrass*, 45.

6. Ibid., 72–73.

7. Ibid., 74.

8. Written in 1852, Foster's "My Old Kentucky Home" describes the devastating effects of the institution of slavery on slave families.

9. See Wright, *Lexington: Heart of the Bluegrass*, 77, 78.

10. Ibid., 95.

11. Herbert A. Thomas Jr., "Victims of Circumstance: Negroes in a Southern Town, 1865–1880," *Register of the Kentucky Historical Society* (July 1973): 256.

12. Thomas, "Victims of Circumstance," 255; Wright, *Lexington: Heart of the Bluegrass*, 97, 98.

13. Wright, *Lexington: Heart of the Bluegrass*, 98, 139.

14. Thomas, "Victims of Circumstance," 266.

15. *Lexington and the Bluegrass Country*, 12; as quoted in the *Lexington Leader*, 20 April 1938.

16. *Lexington Leader*, 20 April 1938. My emphasis.

17. Wright, *Lexington: Heart of the Bluegrass*, 123.

18. Ibid., 125, 107.

19. G.W. Ranck, *Guide to Lexington, Kentucky* (Lexington, Ky.: Transylvania Printing Co., 1884), 5.

20. Population data is taken from the 8th (1860) through the 16th (1940) U.S. Censuses. Bureau of the Census (Washington, D.C.: Department of Commerce); John Ed Pearce, *Divide and Dissent: Kentucky Politics, 1930–1963* (Lexington, Ky.: Univ. Press of Kentucky, 1987), 24.

21. Wright, *Lexington: Heart of the Bluegrass*, 107.

22. The prevalence of "factional" and "dominant" political machines is discussed in M. Craig Brown and Charles N. Halaby, "Functional Sociology, Urban History, and the Urban Political Machine: The Outlines and Foundations of Machine Politics, 1870–1945," 3–8 (unpublished conference paper in author's possession).

23. Roger Biles, *Memphis in the Great Depression* (Knoxville, Tenn.: Univ. of Tennessee Press, 1986), 29; on Nashville see Don H. Doyle, *Nashville in the New South, 1880–1930* (Knoxville, Tenn.: Univ. of Tennessee Press, 1985).

24. Terrence J. McDonald, ed., *Plunkitt of Tammany Hall: A Series of Very Plain Talks on Very Practical Politics* (Boston: Bedford Books of St. Martin's Press, 1994), 64.

25. Samuel M. Wilson, "Historical Lexington," *The Louisville & Nashville Employes' Magazine* (May 1927), 7; Wright, *Lexington: Heart of the Bluegrass,* 6.

26. Wright, *Lexington: Heart of the Bluegrass,* 52, 53, 108; Wilson, "Historical Lexington," 7, 8.

27. Brown and Halaby, "Functional Sociology, Urban History, and the Urban Political Machine," 27.

2. The Mulligan Ring

1. *The Biographical Encyclopedia of Kentucky* (Cincinnati, Ohio: J.M. Armstrong, 1878), 582, 585.

2. Ibid., 585.

3. Ibid.

4. J.D. Kuykendall, publisher, *Lexington, As It Was: A Memento* (Lexington, Ky.: Paddock Publishing, 1981), 5; Maxwell Place now serves as the home of the president of the University of Kentucky.

5. Kuykendall, *Lexington, As It Was,* 7; *Biographical Encyclopedia of Kentucky,* 585; Wright, *Lexington: Heart of the Bluegrass,* 97.

6. Wright, *Lexington: Heart of the Bluegrass,* 97.

7. Terrence J. McDonald, *Parameters of Urban Fiscal Policy: Socioeconomic Change and Political Culture in San Francisco, 1860–1901* (Berkeley: Univ. of California Press, 1986), 273.

8. Ibid., 274.

9. Miller is quoted in McDonald, *Parameters of Urban Fiscal Policy,* 85. See also page 94.

10. Wright, *Lexington: Heart of the Bluegrass,* 107.

11. See *Biographical Encyclopedia of Kentucky,* 585; Wright, *Lexington: Heart of the Bluegrass,* 107, 108.

12. Wright, *Lexington: Heart of the Bluegrass,* 108; *A Review of Lexington, Kentucky: As She Is* (New York: John Latham, 1886), 26.

13. Moses Kaufman Papers, Scrapbook No. 3, 1879–1881, Folder No. 3, 7 August 1879, Special Collections, M.I. King Library, University of Kentucky, Lexington, Kentucky.

14. Ibid.

15. Ibid.

16. Moses Kaufman Papers, Scrapbook No. 4, 1883–1904, scattered dates, Folder No. 1.

17. Moses Kaufman Papers, Scrapbook No. 1, 1873 (1881)-1883, Folder No. 1.

18. Ibid.

19. Ibid.; Wright, *Lexington: Heart of the Bluegrass,* 108.

20. Moses Kaufman Papers, Scrapbook No. 1, 1873 (1881)-1883, Folder No. 1.

21. Ibid.

22. Ibid.

23. Ibid.

24. Wright, *Lexington: Heart of the Bluegrass,* 108.

25. Ibid.

26. Moses Kaufman Papers, Scrapbook No. 1, 1873 (1881)-1883, Folder No. 1.

27. Ibid.

28. Wright, *Lexington: Heart of the Bluegrass,* 139.

29. Moses Kaufman Papers, Scrapbook No. 1, 1873 (1881)-1883, Folder No. 1.

30. Wright, *Lexington: Heart of the Bluegrass,* 97, 98.

31. Ibid., 99, 139.

32. For a discussion of the "socioeconomic structural theory," see McDonald, *Parameters of Urban Fiscal Policy,* chapter 3.

33. *Lexington Leader,* 20 April 1938.

34. *Lexington, As She Is,* 26, 27.

35. Wright, *Lexington: Heart of the Bluegrass,* 108, 109.

36. Henry T. Duncan, "Mayor's Message," 3–7, Official Reports, City of Lexington, 1900–1901, Pamphlet, Special Collections, M.I. King Library, University of Kentucky, Lexington, Kentucky; Wright, *Lexington: Heart of the Bluegrass,* 129.

37. Tindall quoted in Don H. Doyle, *Nashville in the New South, 1880–1930* (Knoxville, Tenn.: Univ. of Tennessee Press, 1985), 156.

38. Doyle, *Nashville in the New South, 1880–1930,* 156.

39. John Ed Pearce, *Divide and Dissent: Kentucky Politics, 1930–1963* (Lexington, Ky.: Univ. Press of Kentucky, 1987), 24.

40. *Biographical Encyclopedia of Kentucky,* 585; Kenneth T. Jackson and Stanley K. Schultz, editors, *Cities in American History* (New York: Knopf, 1972), 366; See the section on the Irish in New York City in Nathan Glazer and Daniel Patrick Moynihan, *Beyond the Melting Pot: The Negroes, Puerto Ricans, Jews, Italians, and Irish of New York City* (Cambridge, Mass.: MIT Press, 1963), 217–87.

41. Moses Kaufman Papers, Scrapbook No. 1, 1873 (1881)-1883, Folder No. 1.

42. Glazer and Moynihan are discussed in Jackson and Schultz, *Cities in American History,* 366.

43. Jackson and Schultz, *Cities in American History,* 366.

44. *Lexington Daily Leader,* 1 January 1900; 30 January 1900; 3 February 1900; Pearce, *Divide and Dissent,* 16.

45. James C. Klotter, *William Goebel: The Politics of Wrath* (Lexington, Ky.: Univ. Press of Kentucky, 1977), 129; Malcolm E. Jewell and Everett W. Cunningham, *Kentucky Politics* (Lexington, Ky.: Univ. of Kentucky Press, 1968), 12, 13.

46. Klotter, *William Goebel*, 129.

47. Klotter, *William Goebel*, 127, 36, 15, 28; See Steven A. Channing, *Kentucky: A Bicentennial History* (New York: Norton, 1977), 160; See Urey Woodson, *The First New Dealer, William Goebel: His Origin, Ambitions, Achievements, His Assassination. Loss to the State and Nation: The Story of a Great Crime* (Louisville, Ky.: Standard Press, 1939).

48. Channing, *Kentucky*, 168; Klotter, *William Goebel*, 128.

49. Klotter, *William Goebel*, 127, 128.

3. The Rise of Billy Klair

1. Nancy C. Graves, "William Frederick Klair" (unpublished manuscript, Political Science Seminar, Transylvania College, Lexington, Kentucky, December 1953), 4; E. Polk Johnson, *A History of Kentucky and Kentuckians: The Leaders and Representative Men in Commerce, Industry and Modern Activities*, vol. 2 (Chicago: Lewis Publishing, 1912), 789; Charles Kerr, *History of Kentucky*, vol. 4 (New York: American Historical Society, 1922), 171.

2. Kerr, *History of Kentucky*, 171.

3. *Herald*, 19 April 1908.

4. Graves, "William Frederick Klair," 4.

5. *Herald*, 3 January 1904.

6. Ibid., 19 April 1908.

7. Ibid.

8. Ibid.; Kerr noted that Klair was appointed a page in the state legislature in 1889, was reappointed in 1891–1892, in 1894 was appointed page to the Speaker of the House, and from 1896 to 1898 was assistant sergeant-at-arms of the Senate. See Kerr, *History of Kentucky*, 171.

9. Graves, "William Frederick Klair," 4, 7, 8; Johnson, *A History of Kentucky and Kentuckians*, 789; *Lexington Herald-Leader*, 19 May 1963; *Herald*, 19 April 1908.

10. Graves, "William Frederick Klair," 8, 9; Enacted as law over Gov. William O'Connell Bradley's veto on 11 March 1898, the board of commissioners was abolished by the legislature in 1900. See "Goebel Election Law," in *The Kentucky Encyclopedia*, 378.

11. Graves, "William Frederick Klair," 8, 9.

12. Ibid., 10; Johnson, *A History of Kentucky and Kentuckians*, 789.

13. John D. Buenker, *Urban Liberalism and Progressive Reform* (New York: Charles Scribner's Sons, 1973), 26; William A. Link, *The Paradox of Southern Progressivism, 1880–1930* (Chapel Hill: Univ. of North Carolina Press, 1992), xii.

14. See Link, *The Paradox of Southern Progressivism*; Author's interview with Monsignor Leonard Nienaber, 5 January 1990, quoted in "The Human Side: Politics, the Great Depression, and the New Deal in Lexington, Kentucky, 1929–35," *Register*

of the Kentucky Historical Society (summer 1992), 259; Interview with Sonny Cloud, Lexington, Kentucky, 24 July 1999; Telephone interview with Cordia Jones, Lexington, Kentucky, 30 July 1999.

15. *Herald,* 5 January 1902.

16. *Herald,* 18 January 1903; Graves, "William Frederick Klair," 11; Urey Woodson, *The First New Dealer, William Goebel,* 26, 27.

17. *Louisville Courier-Journal,* 30 October 1937.

18. Graves, "William Frederick Klair," 11, 12, 13, 18; *Herald,* 18 January 1903, 1 November 1937; Carl B. Cone, *The University of Kentucky: A Pictorial History* (Lexington, Ky.: Univ. Press of Kentucky, 1989), 75, 76.

19. *Lexington Club,* Wilson Pamphlets, Special Collections, M.I. King Library, University of Kentucky, Lexington, Kentucky.

20. Mrs. William Preston Drake, *Kentucky in Retrospect: Noteworthy Personages and Events in Kentucky History, 1792–1942* (Frankfort, Ky.: Sesquicentennial Commission Commonwealth of Kentucky, 1942), 113; Johnson, *A History of Kentucky and Kentuckians,* 789; Graves, "William Frederick Klair," 16–18; Paul E. Fuller, *Laura Clay and the Woman's Rights Movement* (Lexington, Ky.: Univ. Press of Kentucky, 1975), 131; The handwritten letter from Laura Clay to Klair is found in Laura Clay Papers, Box 6, 1 March 1910–9 December 1910, Special Collections, M.I. King Library, University of Kentucky, Lexington, Kentucky.

21. Graves, "William Frederick Klair," 14, 15, 16; One bill provided for $150,000 for new buildings at the university; another bill would retire the existing debt; See *Herald,* 28 January 1900.

22. Zane L. Miller, *Boss Cox's Cincinnati: Urban Politics in the Progressive Era* (Chicago: Univ. of Chicago Press, 1968), 93, and Zane L. Miller, "Boss Cox's Cincinnati: A Study in Urbanization and Politics, 1880–1914," *Journal of American History* (March 1968), included in Jackson and Schultz, *Cities in American History,* 387, 388, 382.

4. Honest Graft and the Craft of Bossism

1. Interview with A.B. "Happy" Chandler, Versailles, Kentucky, 13 April 1983.

2. *Lexington Herald-Leader,* 19 May 1963.

3. Quoted in James Joshua Mott, "City Manager Government in Lexington, Kentucky, 1947," (Master's thesis, Univ. of Kentucky, Lexington, Kentucky, 1947), 23.

4. Chandler interview; Clark interview; *Lexington Herald-Leader,* 19 May 1963.

5. Telephone interview with Harry Miller Jr., Lexington, Kentucky, 13 April 1983.

6. Jewell and Cunningham, *Kentucky Politics,* 76; Chandler interview; McDonald, ed., *Plunkitt of Tammany Hall,* 52.

7. Chandler interview.

8. *Lexington Herald,* 30 October 1937; Klair's position on the state central ex-

ecutive committee was important in his acquisition of power. According to Malcolm E. Jewell and Everett W. Cunningham, the state central executive committee "shall constitute the supreme governing authority of the Democratic Party in Kentucky, and shall have control and supervision over all matters relating to or affecting party organization, and management of campaigns, unless otherwise provided by law." The state central executive committee consisted of two men and two women from each congressional district and seven members from the state at large. The committee usually included the governor, several of the most important leaders of the governor's faction, and a sample of local leaders who had been loyal and valuable to that faction of the party. See Jewell and Cunningham, *Kentucky Politics,* 27, 36, 38.

9. Kerr, *History of Kentucky,* 171; Clark interview; Chandler interview. See Mott, "City Manager Government in Lexington, Kentucky, 1947," 118.

10. Chandler interview.

11. Ibid.

12. Chandler interview; Mott, "City Manager Government in Lexington, Kentucky, 1947," 24; Jewell and Cunningham, *Kentucky Politics,* 76; Clark interview.

13. Kerr, *History of Kentucky,* 171; Seymour J. Mandelbaum, *Boss Tweed's New York* (New York: John Wiley & Sons, 1965), 58; For the Vare machine in Philadelphia, see Sam Bass Warner Jr., *The Private City: Philadelphia in Three Periods of Its Growth* (Philadelphia: Univ. of Pennsylvania Press, 1968), 216; *Lexington Herald,* 10 September 1899.

14. E.J. Flynn, "Bosses and Machines," *Atlantic Monthly* 179 (May 1947): 39, 40; *Cincinnati Enquirer,* 30 October 1937.

15. Jewell and Cunningham, *Kentucky Politics,* 67, 76.

16. *Louisville Courier-Journal,* 30 October 1937; See Frank J. Sorauf, *Party and Representation* (New York: Atherton Press, 1963).

17. Jewell and Cunningham, *Kentucky Politics,* 70; *Cincinnati Enquirer,* 30 October 1937.

18. Gregory A. Waller, *Main Street Amusements: Movies and Commercial Entertainment in a Southern City, 1896–1930* (Washington, D.C.: Smithsonian Institution Press, 1995), 13; Census statistics from *Population, Twelfth Census of the United States, 1900* (Washington, D.C.: U.S. Census Office, 1902), vol. 1, table 22, lxx, quoted in Waller, *Main Street Amusements,* 13–14.

19. Waller, *Main Street Amusements,* xiii-xiv.

20. Ibid., 16–17.

21. Ibid., 14.

22. Ibid., 15.

23. Ibid., 281, note 37. The German page was printed in the *Lexington Herald,* 21 October 1900, 3.

24. *Lexington Herald,* 21 January 1896, quoted in Waller, *Main Street Amusements,* 15–16.

25. *Lexington Herald,* 30 October 1937; *Lexington Herald-Leader,* 19 May 1963.

26. Nicholas C. Burckel, "A.O. Stanley and Progressive Reform, 1902–1919," *Register of the Kentucky Historical Society* (spring 1981): 155; See also Thomas W. Ramage, "Augustus Owsley Stanley: Early Twentieth Century Kentucky Democrat," (Ph.D. diss., Univ. of Kentucky, Lexington, Kentucky, 1968), 203, and "Scrapbook, Governor, 1915–1919, Clippings," A.O. Stanley Papers, Special Collections, M.I. King Library, University of Kentucky, Lexington, Kentucky.

27. "Scrapbook, Governor, 1915–1919, Clippings," A.O. Stanley Papers.

28. Ibid.

29. See "Politics, Klair, William F., 1927–1939," Thomas Rust Underwood Papers, Special Collections, M.I. King Library, University of Kentucky, Lexington, Kentucky.

30. *Louisville Courier-Journal,* 30 October 1937.

31. Information on the office setup of the Klair & Scott firm and on Bessie Birch is derived from a letter from Marjorie R. Scott to James Duane Bolin, 6 November 1995, in possession of author.

32. Nancy C. Graves, "William Frederick Klair," 25; *Lexington Herald,* 1 November 1937.

33. Mott, "City Manager Government in Lexington, Kentucky, 1947," 26; Humbert S. Nelli, *The Business of Crime: Italians and Syndicate Crime in the United States* (Chicago: Univ. of Chicago Press, 1976), 120; Clark interview.

34. Interview with Joe Scott, Lexington, Kentucky, 16 September 1995.

35. See McDonald, ed., *Plunkitt of Tammany Hall;* Clark interview; Chandler interview; *Cincinnati Enquirer,* 30 October 1937, as quoted in Graves, "William Frederick Klair," 21.

36. Interview with Charlie Wiley, Lexington, Kentucky, 12 June 1991.

37. Frank L. McVey to Henry K. Milward, 9 May 1925; Frank L. McVey to Johnston Miller, 23 February 1932; Klair and Scott to Executive Committee, Board of Trustees, University of Kentucky, 23 February 1931, Frank McVey Papers, Box 24, Folder, "Insurance, University Buildings, Etc.," Special Collections, M.I. King Library, University of Kentucky, Lexington, Kentucky.

38. Chandler interview; *Louisville Courier-Journal,* 30 October 1937.

39. Henry T. Duncan, *The Fusion Movement,* 14 October 1909, 1–4; This publication was found in the stacks at the M.I. King Library, University of Kentucky, Lexington, Kentucky. No publication information was evident, but it is assumed that it was published by Duncan; Mott, "City Manager Government in Lexington, Kentucky, 1947," 23, 12.

40. *Lexington Leader,* 7 September 1911; *Lexington Herald,* 15 June 1911.

41. Duncan, *The Fusion Movement,* 4; Klair served on the board of the Home Construction Company. See Home Construction Company, *Some Roads in the Blue–*

grass (Lexington, Ky.: Transylvania Press, n. d.), Special Collections, M.I. King Library, University of Kentucky, Lexington, Kentucky.

42. *Lexington Herald,* 18 June 1911.

43. Joe N. Strader, *Lexington, Kentucky* (Lexington, Ky., 1906), quoted in James Duane Bolin, "From Mules to Motors: The Street Railway System in Lexington, Kentucky, 1882–1938," *Register of the Kentucky Historical Society* (spring 1989): 142.

44. 12th (1900) through the 15th (1930) U. S. Censuses, Bureau of the Census, Washington, D.C.

5. The Age of Progressivism and Beyond

1. Henry T. Duncan, *The Fusion Movement,* 1, 3; Graves, "William Frederick Klair," 19; *Lexington Herald,* 26 September 1909.

2. Duncan, *The Fusion Movement,* 5, 6.

3. Graves, "William Frederick Klair," 19; *Lexington Herald,* 4 November 1909.

4. *Lexington Leader,* 1 November 1910.

5. Ibid., 5 November 1911; 24 October 1911; 2 October 1911; 23 October 1911.

6. Chandler interview; *Lexington Leader,* 8 October 1911; 1 October 1911; 10 September 1911.

7. *Lexington Leader,* 30 October 1911; 2 November 1911; 31 October 1911; 1 November 1911.

8. Ibid., 31 October 1911; 1 October 1911.

9. Frank K. Kavanaugh, *Official Manual for the Use of Courts, State and County Officials and General Assembly of the State of Kentucky* (Frankfort, Ky.: Frankfort Printing Company, n.d.), 103; See Nancy C. Graves interview with Thomas Scott, Klair's insurance partner, in Graves, "William Frederick Klair," 26, iii; *Louisville Courier-Journal,* 30 October 1937.

10. E. Merton Coulter, *The Civil War and Readjustment in Kentucky* (Chapel Hill: Univ. of North Carolina Press, 1926), 243.

11. *Arkansas Evangel,* 26 November 1885.

12. Duncan, *The Fusion Movement,* 5, 10.

13. *Lexington Leader,* 1 November 1917; 2 November 1917; "Lincoln Institute," in Kleber, editor, *The Kentucky Encyclopedia,* 558.

14. *Lexington Leader,* 23 October 1911; *Lexington Herald,* 3 October 1911.

15. For Cox see Miller, *Boss Cox's Cincinnati,* 86; For Howse see Don H. Doyle, *Nashville Since the 1920s,* 64.

16. Biles, *Memphis in the Great Depression,* 34, 40, 41.

17. George C. Wright, *Life Behind a Veil: Blacks in Louisville, Kentucky, 1865–1930* (Baton Rouge: Louisiana State Univ. Press, 1985), 186, 190.

18. *Lexington Herald,* 4 November 1909; *Lexington Leader,* 31 October 1911.

19. Gerald L. Smith, *A Black Educator in the Segregated South: Kentucky's Rufus B. Atwood* (Lexington, Ky.: Univ. Press of Kentucky, 1994), 64, 192 note 18. The Klair & Scott contract with Kentucky State, then called the Kentucky Normal and Industrial Institute, was made when Klair's ally, Thomas Combs, served on that institution's board of trustees. See "Politics, Klair, William F., 1927–1939," Thomas Rust Underwood Papers, Special Collections, M.I. King Library, University of Kentucky, Lexington, Kentucky.

20. Lowell H. Harrison and James C. Klotter, *A New History of Kentucky* (Lexington, Ky.: Univ. Press of Kentucky, 1997), 287, 288.

21. Paul E. Fuller, *Laura Clay and the Woman's Rights Movement* (Lexington, Ky.: Univ. Press of Kentucky, 1975), 90; *Lexington Herald,* 6 November 1901, as quoted in Fuller, *Laura Clay,* 90.

22. Fuller, *Laura Clay,* 90, 187.

23. Ibid., 89, 90, 91.

24. Ibid., 92.

25. Ibid., 93.

26. *Lexington Herald,* 17 June 1911.

27. *Lexington Leader,* 3 September 1911.

28. Fuller, *Laura Clay,* 131; See Laura Clay to William F. Klair, 16 March 1910, Laura Clay Papers, Box 6, 1 March 1910–9 December 1910, Special Collections, M.I. King Library, University of Kentucky, Lexington, Kentucky.

29. *Lexington Herald,* 23 December 1909; 26 December 1909.

30. *Lexington Leader,* 1 November 1910; 7 November 1910.

31. Ibid., 6 November 1910.

32. Ibid.

33. Ibid., 4 November 1910; 9 November 1910.

34. *Lexington Leader,* 15 October 1911; 11 September 1911; 8 November 1911; "Commission Government in Brief," Pamphlet, Wilson Collection, compiled by campaign committee, 1911, Special Collections, M.I. King Library, University of Kentucky, Lexington, Kentucky.

35. See Alan DiGaetano, "The Rise and Development of Urban Political Machines: An Alternative to Merton's Functional Analysis," *Urban Affairs Quarterly* (1 December 1988): 245, and Brown and Halaby, "Functional Sociology, Urban History, and the Urban Political Machine," 15.

36. Mott, "City Manager Government in Lexington, Kentucky, 1947," 10.

37. *Lexington Leader,* 9 November 1910.

38. See series of editorials against Klair in the October 1917 issues of the *Lexington Leader; Lexington Herald,* 9 October 1917.

39. Thomas H. Appleton Jr., "Prohibition and Politics in Kentucky: The Guber-

natorial Campaign and Election of 1915," *Register of the Kentucky Historical Society* (January 1977): 28.

40. Ibid.

41. Harrison and Klotter, *A New History of Kentucky*, 279; see also James C. Klotter, *Kentucky: Portrait in Paradox, 1900–1950* (Frankfort, Ky.: Kentucky Historical Society, 1996), 199.

42. *Lexington Herald*, 9 October 1917.

43. Ibid.

44. Ibid., 3 November 1917; Graves, "William Frederick Klair," 22.

45. *Lexington Leader*, 2 November 1917; *Lexington Herald*, 7 November 1917.

46. *Lexington Leader*, 6 November 1917.

47. Ibid., 4 November 1917.

48. Ibid., 7 November 1917.

49. Wright, *Lexington: Heart of the Bluegrass*, 162.

50. Ibid., 163; J. Winston Coleman Jr., *The Squire's Sketches of Lexington* (Lexington, Ky.: Henry Clay Press, 1972), 80.

51. Coleman, *Squire's Sketches*, 81.

52. *Lexington Herald*, 15 April 1917; Coleman, *Squire's Sketches*, 80.

53. Wright, *Lexington: Heart of the Bluegrass*, 133.

54. John Alexander, *Miss Belle: Lexington's Famous Madam, Who Ran the "Most Orderly of Disorderly Houses"* (Lexington, Ky.: Coleman Publications, 1983), 27; J. Winston Coleman Jr., "Belle Breezing: A Famous Lexington Bawd," *Kentucky Images Magazine* 5 (November 1986): 34, 36.

55. Wright, *Lexington: Heart of the Bluegrass*, 133.

56. *Report of the Vice Commission of Lexington, Kentucky* (Lexington, Ky.: Press of J.L. Richardson, 1915), Special Collections, M.I. King Library, University of Kentucky, Lexington, Kentucky, 9; Alexander, *Miss Belle*, 24; Serving on the committee was machine member George S. Shanklin, whom Klair later dubbed "the proponent of civic righteousness." See Alexander, *Miss Belle*, 30.

57. *Report of the Vice Commission*, 13.

58. Ibid., 15.

59. Ibid., 25, 16.

60. Ibid., 8, 17.

61. Ibid., 26.

62. Ibid., 29, 30.

63. Ibid., 31.

64. *Lexington Herald*, 23 October 1917; Alexander, *Miss Belle*, 30.

65. *Lexington Herald*, 23 October 1917.

66. "City of Lexington Invites the Central USA to Locate in Fayette County, Kentucky, The Concentration Camp," Pamphlet, Wilson Collection, 18, 19, 20.

67. Wright, *Lexington: Heart of the Bluegrass,* 164; Harrison and Klotter, *A New History of Kentucky,* 289. Klair's loyalty was obviously not questioned widely, as he won another term in the General Assembly in November 1917.

68. Wright, *Lexington: Heart of the Bluegrass,* 165.

69. 14th Census (1920); Wright, *Lexington: Heart of the Bluegrass,* 146.

70. L. Segoe, *Comprehensive Plan of Lexington and Environs, 1931* (Lexington, Ky.: City Planning and Zoning Commission, 1931), 22; Wright, *Lexington: Heart of the Bluegrass,* 146; "Housing Survey of Lexington, Kentucky," January to April 1924, Pamphlet, Wilson Collection, 37.

71. Segoe, *Comprehensive Plan,* 22, 23.

72. Ibid., 37.

73. Ibid., 23.

74. Ibid., 38.

75. Ibid., 7.

76. Ibid.

77. Wright, *Lexington: Heart of the Bluegrass,* 139.

78. Ibid., 3.

79. Brown interview.

80. *Official Souvenir Program of Sesqui-Centennial Jubilee Celebration of Lexington, Kentucky, May 31–June 6, 1925* (Lexington, Ky.: Citizen's General Committee, 1925), 82, Special Collections, M.I. King Library, University of Kentucky, Lexington, Kentucky.

6. King Klair and the Bipartisan Combine

1. *Lexington Herald,* 17 June 1911; Klair apparently had a hand in various endeavors around the state. For example, as early as 1912, he wrote to Cassius Marcellus Clay asking for his support for William F. Warren for treasurer of the state university: "Mr. Warren is a gentleman in every sense of the word and his election to succeed Major Bullock would be most gratifying to me." William F. Klair to Cassius Marcellus Clay, 19 March 1912, Cassius Marcellus Clay Papers (56 M315), 1896–1913, Special Collections, M.I. King Library, University of Kentucky, Lexington, Kentucky.

2. See the photograph in Wright, *Lexington: Heart of the Bluegrass,* 170, 171.

3. John W. Manning, *The Government of Kentucky* (Lexington, Ky.: Univ. of Kentucky, 1940), 67, 68.

4. Harrison and Klotter, *A New History of Kentucky,* 289; "Florence McDowell (Shelby) Cantrill," in Kleber, ed., *The Kentucky Encyclopedia,* 160; Wright, *Lexington: Heart of the Bluegrass,* 170.

5. Wright, *Lexington: Heart of the Bluegrass,* 170.

6. Klotter, *Kentucky: Portrait in Paradox, 1900–1950,* 244.

7. Hambleton Tapp and James C. Klotter, *Kentucky: Decades of Discord, 1865–1900* (Frankfort, Ky.: Kentucky Historical Society, 1977), 366.

8. Robert F. Sexton, "Kentucky Politics and Society, 1919–1932" (Ph.D. diss., Univ. of Washington, 1970), 239.

9. Smith, *A Black Educator in the Segregated South*, 65.

10. James C. Klotter and John W. Muir, "Boss Ben Johnson, the Highway Commission, and Kentucky Politics," *Register of the Kentucky Historical Society* (winter 1986): 33.

11. Haly had been appointed adjutant general by Beckham and "relished using the title 'General' throughout his life." See Thomas H. Appleton Jr., "William Purcell Dennis Haly," *The Kentucky Encyclopedia*, 399.

12. Ibid., 400.

13. James C. Klotter, "Ben Johnson," *The Kentucky Encyclopedia*, 472–73.

14. "Michael Joseph Brennan," *The Kentucky Encyclopedia*, 122.

15. Albert B. Chandler with Vance H. Trimble, *Heroes, Plain Folks, and Skunks: The Life and Times of Happy Chandler* (Chicago: Bonus Books, 1989), 95.

16. *Lexington Herald*, 16 June 1911.

17. Ibid., 20 February 1916.

18. Ibid., 20 October 1937.

19. Harrison and Klotter, *A New History of Kentucky*, 286.

20. "James Buckner Brown," *The Kentucky Encyclopedia*, 127, 128.

21. Harrison and Klotter, *A New History of Kentucky*, 350.

22. See James Philip Fadely, *Thomas Taggart: Public Servant, Political Boss, 1856–1929* (Indianapolis, Ind.: Indiana Historical Society, 1997), 59–82.

23. Harry M. Caudill, "Johnson Newlon Camden Jr.," *The Kentucky Encyclopedia*, 153.

24. Tracy A. Campbell, "James Campbell Cantrill," *The Kentucky Encyclopedia*, 160.

25. Sexton, "Kentucky Politics and Society, 1919–1932," 47.

26. See Alex Gottfried, *Boss Cermak of Chicago: A Study of Political Leadership* (Seattle: Univ. of Washington Press, 1962), 313. Chapter 13 of Gottfried's work is entitled "Boss of Illinois."

27. No attempt is made here to outline Kentucky statewide politics in the 1920s and early 1930s. My purpose is to illustrate Klair's significance by pointing to several specific examples. For a more thorough overview of state politics in this period, see Harrison and Klotter, *A New History of Kentucky;* Klotter, *Kentucky: Portrait in Paradox, 1900–1950;* Sexton, "Kentucky Politics and Society, 1919–1932."

28. Sexton, "Kentucky Politics and Society, 1919–1932," 40.

29. Klotter, *Kentucky: Portrait in Paradox*, 267.

30. Harrison and Klotter, *A New History of Kentucky*, 352; Klotter, *Kentucky: Portrait in Paradox*, 268; Sexton, "Kentucky Politics and Society, 1919–1932," 46.

31. Harrison and Klotter, *A New History of Kentucky*, 352.

32. "Politics, Primary Organization Lists," Alben W. Barkley Papers, M.I. King Library, University of Kentucky, Lexington, Kentucky.

33. Sexton, "Kentucky Politics and Society, 1919–1932," 67.

34. Ibid., 69.

35. Ibid., 68, 69.

36. Ibid., 62; For Bingham's life and career see William E. Ellis, *Robert Worth Bingham and the Southern Mystique: From the Old South to the New South and Beyond* (Kent, Ohio: Kent State Univ. Press, 1997).

37. Klotter, *Kentucky: Portrait in Paradox*, 266.

38. Elwood Hamilton to Alben W. Barkley, 25 January 1924, "Politics, 1924," Alben W. Barkley Papers.

39. Donald McWain to Alben W. Barkley, 4 February 1924, "Politics, 1924," Alben W. Barkley Papers.

40. Sexton, "Kentucky Politics and Society, 1919–1932," 86.

41. *Louisville Courier-Journal*, 13 May 1924.

42. Ibid., 13 May 1924.

43. Ibid., 14 May 1924; 15 May 1924.

44. Ibid., 15 May 1924.

45. Ibid.

46. Harrison and Klotter, *A New History of Kentucky*, 355.

47. Klotter, *Kentucky: Portrait in Paradox*, 276.

48. Henry A. Pulliam to Alben W. Barkley, 5 December 1925, "Politics, Campaign, Senate, 1926, A-C," Alben W. Barkley Papers.

49. *Louisville Courier-Journal*, 13 March 1926; Henry B. Simpson, "General Assembly of 1926" (Master's thesis, Univ. of Kentucky, Lexington, Kentucky, 1926), 21–22.

50. Sexton, "Kentucky Politics and Society, 1919–1932," 66, 67.

51. Ibid., 138, 139.

52. Hunt's argument in *The Anti-Race Track Gambler* is quoted in Sexton, "Kentucky Politics and Society, 1919–1932," 139.

53. J.L. Vallandingham to Alben W. Barkley, 19 April 1926, "Politics, Campaign, Senate, 1926, M-Z, Jan.-April 23," Alben W. Barkley Papers.

54. Sexton, "Kentucky Politics and Society, 1919–1932," 129; W.J. Fields to Alben W. Barkley, 3 April 1926, Alben W. Barkley Papers, quoted in Sexton, "Kentucky Politics and Society, 1919-1932," 130.

55. Sexton, "Kentucky Politics and Society, 1919–1932," 132; See also Harrison and Klotter, *A New History of Kentucky*, 355.

56. Harrison and Klotter, *A New History of Kentucky*, 356.

57. Ibid.

58. Sexton, "Kentucky Politics and Society, 1919–1932," 149, 150; John H. Fenton, *Politics in the Border States* (New Orleans: Hauser Press, 1957), 54–55.

59. Sexton, "Kentucky Politics and Society, 1919–1932," 149, 145, 150, 153.

60. Election results are recorded in Harrison and Klotter, *A New History of Kentucky*, 356; Sexton, "Kentucky Politics and Society, 1919–1932," 155, 156; and "Politics, Election Results, 1914–1929," Thomas Rust Underwood Papers, Special Collections, M.I. King Library, University of Kentucky, Lexington, Kentucky.

61. "Politics, Klair, William F. Klair, 1927–1939," Thomas Rust Underwood Papers, Special Collections, M.I. King Library, University of Kentucky, Lexington, Kentucky.

62. "Politics, Klair, William F., 1927–1939," Underwood Papers; Sexton, "Kentucky Politics and Society, 1919–1932," 159.

63. Sexton, "Kentucky Politics and Society, 1919–1932," 159.

64. Ibid., 160; "Politics, Hardin, Charles A., 1928–1931," Underwood Papers.

65. "Politics, Hardin, Charles A., 1928–1931," Underwood Papers.

66. Sexton, "Kentucky Politics and Society, 1919–1932," 160–62.

67. Ibid., 162; "Politics, Hardin, Charles A., 1928–1931," Underwood Papers.

68. *Western Recorder*, 13 September 1928, page 13 quoted in Sexton, "Kentucky Politics and Society, 1919–1932," 174. For a treatment of the use of writings of a Lexington Baptist minister to sway votes away from Smith in the 1928 election, see Grace Anderson Cruickshank, "The Political Parson of 1928" (Master's thesis, Univ. of Kentucky, Lexington, Kentucky, 1929).

69. The Breathitt letter quoted in Sexton, "Kentucky Politics and Society, 1919–1932," 178.

70. In *A New History of Kentucky*, James C. Klotter wrote that with the election, "the state Democratic Party was in tatters." See Harrison and Klotter, *A New History of Kentucky*, 356.

7. Bossism and Reform in the Great Depression

The author thanks Dr. Thomas H. Appleton Jr. and *The Register of the Kentucky Historical Society*. Portions of chapters 7 and 8 were published in James Duane Bolin, "The Human Side: Politics, the Great Depression, and the New Deal in Lexington, Kentucky, 1929–35," *Register of the Kentucky Historical Society* (summer 1992): 256–83.

1. *Lexington Herald*, 28 October 1979; Cone, *The University of Kentucky: A Pictorial History*, 105.

2. *Lexington Herald*, 28 October 1979; 27 November 1930.

3. Ibid., 28 October 1979.

4. Ibid.; For the advantages of Lexington as compared to northern cities see *Lexington Herald,* 9 January 1938.

5. Statistics included in this paragraph can be found in *Fifteenth Census of the United States, 1930: Population,* vol. 3, part 1 (Washington, D.C.: U.S. Government Printing Office, 1932), 912, and vol. 4, page 593.

6. *Lexington and the Bluegrass Country,* 2, 3.

7. Ibid., 3, 4.

8. Donald W. Whisenhunt, "The Great Depression in Kentucky: The Early Years," *Register of the Kentucky Historical Society* (January 1969): 56; *Lexington Herald,* 27 November 1930.

9. Lawrence W. Levine, *The Unpredictable Past: Explanations in American Cultural History* (New York: Oxford Univ. Press, 1993), 265.

10. *Lexington Herald,* 20 January 1930; 28 November 1930; 29 November 1930.

11. *Fifteenth Census of the United States, 1930: Unemployment,* vol. 1 (Washington, D.C.: U.S. Government Printing Office, 1931), 405.

12. Interview with Allen McElfresh, Lexington, Kentucky, 11 November 1981.

13. *Lexington Herald,* 8 December 1930; 7 April 1930.

14. Ibid., 17 April 1931; 30 January 1931.

15. Ibid., 24 September 1931.

16. Ibid., 9 October 1931; 14 October 1931.

17. McElfresh interview.

18. George Brown Tindall and David E. Shi, *America: A Narrative History,* vol. 2 (New York: Norton, 1996), 1009.

19. *Lexington Herald,* 23 January 1930; 3 August 1930; James Joshua Mott, "City Manager Government in Lexington, Kentucky, 1947" (Master's thesis, Univ. of Kentucky, Lexington, Kentucky, 1947), 31.

20. Mott, "City Manager Government in Lexington, Kentucky," 30.

21. Ibid., 131.

22. *Lexington Herald,* 7 November 1931; 22 November 1931.

23. John W. Manning, *Government in Kentucky Cities: Local Government Study No. 3* (Lexington: Bureau of Government Research, 1937), 11.

24. *Lexington Herald,* 22 November 1931.

25. Ibid., 1 December 1931.

26. Mott, "City Manager Government in Lexington, Kentucky," 56; *Lexington Leader,* 2 July 1933; *Louisville Courier-Journal* clipping found in Thomas Rust Underwood Papers, "Politics, Klair, William F., 1927–1939," Special Collections, M.I. King Library, University of Kentucky, Lexington, Kentucky.

27. Thomas Rust Underwood Papers, "Politics, Klair, William F., 1927–1939"; *Courier-Journal* editorial quoted in *Lexington Herald,* 28 October 1933.

28. *Lexington Herald,* 1 July 1934; 7 July 1934; 11 May 1935; The campaign booklet, *Two Short Years: The Story of a Change,* is cited in Mott, "City Manager Government in Lexington, Kentucky, 1947," 40.

29. These publications are cited in Mott, "City Manager Government in Lexington, Kentucky," 61, 62.

30. Ibid., 55, 54.

31. See Ibid., 52.

32. Ibid., 57.

33. Ibid., 42, 43, 66; Among the "old gang politicians" on the Home Town Ticket were E. Reed Wilson running for mayor, and Florence Shelby Cantrill, James P. Keller, and R. Mack Oldham running for positions on the commission.

34. Sexton, "Kentucky Politics and Society, 1919–1932," 211, 212. For a discussion of the fall of the National Bank of Kentucky, see *Lexington Herald,* 5 May 1931.

35. Sexton, "Kentucky Politics and Society, 1919–1932," 220.

36. Graves, "William Frederick Klair," 24.

37. Klotter and Muir, "Boss Ben Johnson," 23, 25, 31.

38. Ibid., 35.

39. Orval W. Baylor, *J. Dan Talbott: Champion of Good Government: A Saga of Kentucky Politics from 1900 to 1942* (Louisville, Ky.: Press of Kentucky Printing Corporation, 1942), 99–101; Klotter and Muir, "Boss Ben Johnson," 24–26.

40. Baylor, *J. Dan Talbott,* 99–101; Klotter and Muir, "Boss Ben Johnson," 27, 28.

41. Klotter and Muir, "Boss Ben Johnson," 29.

42. *Mt. Sterling Gazette and Kentucky Courier,* 26 June 1931, in Thomas Rust Underwood Papers, "Politics, Fennell, Charles, 1930–1944"; Klotter, *Kentucky: Portrait in Paradox, 1900–1950,* 285.

43. *Mt. Sterling Gazette and Kentucky Courier,* 26 June 1931, in Thomas Rust Underwood Papers, "Politics, Fennell, Charles, 1930–1944."

44. Graves, "William Frederick Klair," 32.

45. *Louisville Times,* 30 October 1937; Klotter and Muir, "Boss Ben Johnson," 23, 25. For a letter in which Laffoon implored then-congressman Vinson not to "forget that I am depending on you to nominate me in the Convention," see Ruby Laffoon to Frederick Vinson, n.d., Frederick Vinson Papers, "Political File, 1931, H-L," Special Collections, M.I. King Library, University of Kentucky, Lexington, Kentucky.

46. Ruby Laffoon to Fred M. Vinson, 29 May 1931, Frederick Vinson Papers, "Political File, 1931, H-L."

47. Baylor, *J. Dan Talbott,* 170–71.

48. Klotter and Muir, "Boss Ben Johnson," 38; Graves, "William Frederick Klair," 33; *Lexington Herald* newspaper clipping in Thomas Rust Underwood Papers, "Politics, Fennell, Charles, 1930–1944."

49. Channing, *Kentucky: A Bicentennial History,* 195, 196.

50. Chandler with Trimble, *Heroes, Plain Folks, and Skunks,* 101, 102.

51. *Lexington Herald-Leader,* 19 May 1963; See *Lexington Herald,* 30 October 1937, and *Louisville Times,* 30 October 1937; Clark, *A History of Kentucky,* 446.

52. Thomas Rust Underwood Papers, "Politics, Chronological File."

53. Chandler interview.

54. Baylor, *J. Dan Talbott,* 166. Chandler recalled that Klair helped elect Brown in 1929, the same year he helped elect Chandler to the Kentucky Senate. Chandler interview.

55. Baylor, *J. Dan Talbott,* 166.

56. *Lexington Herald,* 4 April 1932, and Graves, "William Frederick Klair," 33.

57. Chandler interview.

58. Thomas Rust Underwood Papers, "Politics, Klair, William F., 1927–1939"; *Lexington Herald,* 5 April 1932.

59. *Lexington Herald,* 9 April 1932; 10 April 1932.

60. Jewell and Cunningham, *Kentucky Politics,* 32, 28; *Lexington Herald,* 9 April 1932; 10 April 1932.

61. *Lexington Herald,* 9 April 1932; 10 April 1932.

62. Ibid., 10 April 1932.

63. Chandler interview; *Lexington Herald,* 1 November 1937.

64. Letters in the files of the Thomas Rust Underwood Papers and the Frederick Vinson Papers contain repeated admonitions from various leaders to consult Klair on matters—large and small—in party politics: "I am writing Billy about it," or from Allie W. Young to Fred Vinson, "get in touch with Billy Klair, Dan Talbott, and Glenn and any other of our friends you may desire, and put the matter over." See Thomas Rust Underwood Papers, "Politics, Charles Fennell, 1930–1944"; Frederick Vinson Papers, "Political File, 1931, Underwood-Young."

8. Lexington's New Deal

1. Jasper Shannon and Ruth McQuown, *Presidential Politics in Kentucky, 1824–1939* (Lexington, Ky.: Bureau of Government Research, 1950), 107, 112; for the Klair quote see Thomas Rust Underwood Papers, "Political, Keen Johnson, 1932–1943," Special Collections, M.I. King Library, University of Kentucky, Lexington, Kentucky.

2. William E. Leuchtenburg, *Franklin D. Roosevelt and the New Deal, 1932–1940* (New York: Harper and Row, 1963), 41, 46; *Lexington Herald,* 7 April 1933.

3. Blakey, *Hard Times,* 149, 157.

4. *Lexington Herald,* 1 September 1933; 3 September 1933.

5. Ibid., 5 September 1933.

6. Ibid.

7. Ibid., 6 September 1933; 7 September 1933.

8. Blakey, *Hard Times,* 153, 148; *Lexington Herald,* 1 June 1935.

9. Blakey, *Hard Times*, 166, 104; Terry Birdwhistell, "New Deal Farm Programs in Fayette County, Kentucky, 1933–1936" (unpublished manuscript, Univ. of Kentucky, Lexington, Kentucky, 1977), 1.

10. Birdwhistell, "New Deal Farm Programs," 3.

11. *Lexington Herald*, 9 January 1933, as quoted in Birdwhistell, "New Deal Farm Programs," 2; See also Birdwhistell, "New Deal Farm Programs," 3.

12. Ibid., 3, 4.

13. Ibid., 4, 5, 6.

14. Ibid., 7, 8.

15. Ibid., 10; *Lexington Herald*, 21 December 1933. The basic plan of the AAA's tobacco reduction program was to reduce acreage in 1935 by one-half. Participating farmers would receive twenty dollars for each acre taken out of production, plus two additional payments based on factors such as the market price. By 30 June 1937, Fayette County had received $620,794.69 in rental and benefit payments for tobacco from the AAA, the largest share of any county in the state. See Blakey, *Hard Times*, 114; *Lexington Herald*, 18 November 1933, as quoted in Birdwhistell, "New Deal Farm Programs," 11; *Lexington Herald*, 12 December 1933; 11 December 1933; Alben W. Barkley Papers, "Politics-Primary, Senate; Barkley-Chandler-Federal Projects in Kentucky, 1938," Special Collections, M.I. King Library, University of Kentucky, Lexington, Kentucky.

16. See *Lexington Herald*, 9 January 1936; Birdwhistell, "New Deal Farm Programs," 16, 17.

17. *Lexington Herald*, 3 April 1933; 18 April 1933.

18. Interview with Jasper Shannon, Paris, Kentucky, 11 November 1981. Dr. Shannon revealed that Judge Fred Vinson was instrumental in establishing the camp at Carlisle. For the type of work done on the projects, consult Leuchtenburg, *Franklin D. Roosevelt*, 174.

19. *Lexington Leader*, 2 June 1933; 20 June 1933.

20. Leuchtenburg, *Franklin D. Roosevelt*, 121.

21. *Lexington Leader*, 11 March 1934.

22. *Lexington Herald*, 6 April 1934; 8 March 1934; These figures illustrate how state and local funding was inadequate in meeting the 25 percent share.

23. Quoted in James T. Patterson, *The New Deal and the States: Federalism in Transition* (Princeton: Princeton Univ. Press, 1969), 67.

24. *Lexington Herald*, 3 October 1934. Laffoon was especially critical of Thornton Wilcox, the state administrator of relief funds. *Lexington Herald*, 11 October 1934.

25. *Lexington Leader*, 23 June 1933.

26. Ibid., 19 June 1933; *Lexington Herald*, 23 June 1933.

27. *Lexington Leader*, 23 June 1933; 26 June 1933; 27 June 1933.

28. *Lexington Herald*, 29 December 1933; 16 June 1934.

29. Ibid., 1 July 1934; 7 July 1934; 11 May 1934. Morton outlined the accom-

plishments of his administration in *Two Short Years: The Story of a Change,* cited in Mott, "City Manager Government in Lexington, Kentucky," 40.

30. *Lexington Herald,* 2 October 1935; Mott, "City Manager Government in Lexington, Kentucky," 42.

31. Mott, "City Manager Government in Lexington, Kentucky," 42, 43, 66.

32. As so many of the relief statistics are given by counties, Fayette County statistics must be given to represent Lexington's share. The major portion of Fayette County's population of 68,543 (1930 census) resided, of course, in Lexington (population—45,736); *Lexington Leader,* 20 June 1938. These statistics were taken from charts in the Alben W. Barkley Papers, "Politics-Primary, Senate; Barkley-Chandler, Federal Projects in Kentucky, 1938."

33. Alben W. Barkley Papers, "Politics-Primary, Senate; Barkley-Chandler, Federal Projects in Kentucky, 1938."

34. *Lexington Herald,* 29 December 1933.

35. Ibid., 5 August 1935.

36. Ibid., 2 September 1934.

37. Blakey, *Hard Times,* 30, 33.

38. Alben W. Barkley Papers, "Politics-Primary, Senate; Barkley-Chandler, Federal Projects in Kentucky, 1938"; Blakey, *Hard Times,* 36.

39. *Lexington Herald,* 19 July 1935; 1 September 1935.

40. Ibid., 2 October 1935.

41. John D. Millet, *The Works Progress Administration in New York City* (Chicago: Public Administration Service, 1938), vii.

42. Leuchtenburg, *Franklin D. Roosevelt,* 125–126.

43. Millet, *The Works Progress Administration in New York City,* vii.

44. From the poem "In Kentucky," written by James Mulligan, the son of Dennis Mulligan and the editor of the *Lexington Morning-Transcript,* as quoted in *Lexington and the Bluegrass Country,* 48.

45. *Lexington Herald,* 27 November 1930; 8 December 1930; *Lexington and the Bluegrass Country,* 1–2.

46. Although unemployment statistics are not available for 1935, a growing discontent among Lexington residents was evident in the year. In 1937, after WPA projects were well underway, there were still 4,225 people in Lexington needing full- or part-time work, and only 848 were employed on federal projects. See Alben W. Barkley Papers, "Politics-Primary, Senate; Barkley-Chandler, Federal Projects in Kentucky, 1938." While 25 percent of Fayette County's residents received relief in the first five months of 1933, only 10 percent received relief in May 1935. While more people needed relief, less relief was provided. See "Records of the Office of the State Administrator of the WPA in Kentucky," WPA Papers, Kentucky State Archives, Frankfort, Kentucky; From article in *U.S. News* in Goodman-Paxton Papers, WPA Scrapbook,

Special Collections, M.I. King Library, University of Kentucky, Lexington, Kentucky; *Lexington Herald,* 16 May 1936.

47. *Lexington Herald,* 16 May 1936.

48. Ibid., 16 May 1936.

49. Ibid., 15 August 1935; 9 August 1935; *U.S. News,* in Goodman-Paxton Papers, WPA Scrapbook; *Louisville Courier-Journal,* 1 December 1935.

50. *Lexington Herald,* 5 August 1935.

51. Ibid., 1 March 1936.

52. Alben W. Barkley Papers, "Politics-Primary, Senate; Barkley-Chandler, Federal Projects in Kentucky, 1938."

53. For example, many WPA workers were admired for their work in relief efforts in the 1937 flood, while it was more difficult to look up to someone who painted numbers on street curbs. Four classes of WPA workers—unskilled, intermediate, skilled, and professional—were described in Millet, *Works Progress Administration,* 145; Interview with Jasper Shannon, Paris, Kentucky, 11 November 1981.

54. See Goodman-Paxton Papers, WPA Scrapbook. For the complimentary pictorial of women's toy mending and school lunch projects, see *Lexington Herald,* 30 July 1936.

55. Waller, *Main Street Amusements,* 18.

56. *Lexington Leader,* 4 July 1933; Melvyn Dubofsky and Warren Van Tyne, *John L. Lewis: A Biography* (New York: Quadrangle/The New York Times, 1977), 316.

57. Glenna Graves, "Working-Class Radicalism in Lexington in the 1930s" (unpublished paper in possession of author), 34; Allen McElfresh and Giles Cooper, "They Fought Hunger!: The Story of the Kentucky Workers Alliance During the 1930's," 1973, Special Collections, M.I. King Library, University of Kentucky, Lexington, Kentucky, 146, 154.

58. McElfresh and Cooper, "They Fought Hunger," 155; Graves, "Working-Class Radicalism," 36.

59. *Lexington Leader,* 16 June 1935.

60. Jasper B. Shannon, "Presidential Politics in the South: 1938, I," *Journal of Politics* 1 (1939): 166.

61. *Lexington Herald,* 20 April 1935; Shannon, "Presidential Politics," 156.

62. *Louisville Courier-Journal,* 12 January 1939.

63. Shannon, "Presidential Politics," 159, 161.

64. *Lexington Herald,* 10 June 1938; Shannon, "Presidential Politics," 162; *Louisville Courier-Journal,* 26 June 1938.

65. Shannon, "Presidential Politics," 164; *Louisville Courier-Journal,* 26 June 1938; 27 June 1938.

66. Shannon, "Presidential Politics," 164.

67. Ibid., 165; "WPA and the Politicos," *New Republic* 95 (6 July 1938): 250.

68. Shannon, "Presidential Politics," 165; *Lexington Herald*, 6 August 1937.

69. *Lexington Herald*, 7 June 1938; 8 June 1938.

70. Ibid.

71. Shannon, "Presidential Politics," 166.

72. *Cincinnati Post*, 25 May 1938.

73. George Goodman to Aubrey Williams, 26 May 1938, Goodman-Paxton Papers, Box 2.

74. Goodman-Paxton Papers, Box 2, Folder January-April, 1938, Political Analysis of Kentucky Counties.

75. Harry L. Hopkins, "Letter to All Project Workers, Foremen, Supervisors, and the Administrative Staff of the Works Progress Administration," 5 May 1938, Goodman-Paxton Papers, Box 2; *Lexington Herald*, 13 June 1938.

76. *Louisville Courier-Journal*, 13 June 1938; *Lexington Herald*, 14 June 1938.

77. *Cincinnati Enquirer*, 21 June 1938; *Lexington Herald*, 14 June 1938.

78. *Lexington Herald*, 20 June 1938.

79. The grand jury also found evidence that inmates of the county infirmary had received $2 each for their votes in recent elections. "The source of the fund was not learned." See *Cincinnati Enquirer*, 21 June 1938; Shannon, "Presidential Politics," 166. Stokes later won a Pulitzer Prize for his series of articles; Charles, *Minister of Relief*, 196.

80. *Louisville Times*, 1 July 1938; Goodman-Paxton Papers, Box 3, Folder 16 June-30 June, 1938.

81. *Louisville Courier-Journal*, 10 July 1938; Goodman-Paxton Papers, Box 3, Folder 16 June-30 June, 1938.

82. Shannon, "Presidential Politics," 169–70; Blakey, *Hard Times*, 188.

83. *Lexington Leader*, 12 January 1939.

84. *Kentucky Post*, 25 May 1938.

85. Ernest Rowe to George Goodman, 16 June 1938, Alben W. Barkley Papers, "Politics-Primary, Senate; Barkley-Chandler, A-2, 1938"; Leuchtenburg, *Franklin D. Roosevelt*, 270.

86. *Lexington Leader*, 20 June 1939. The new relief bill, passed overwhelmingly by the House, would set up a three-member board to replace a single administrator; *Louisville Times*, 20 June 1939.

87. *Louisville Times*, 20 June 1939; For the text of the letters see *Lexington Leader*, 19 May 1939.

88. *Lexington Leader*, 19 May 1939.

89. Ibid. In the Goodman-Paxton Papers, materials for the 1935–1937 folder in Box 2 are missing. Whether these materials were destroyed in Goodman's cover-up is unknown.

90. *Lexington Leader*, 19 May 1939; 16 June 1939; 20 June 1939; WPA Papers, Microfilm #1641, Administrative Washington Correspondence.

91. *Louisville Times*, 12 September 1938.

92. *Lexington Herald,* 1 February 1939; 779 persons were employed on WPA projects in Fayette County.

93. *Lexington Herald,* 5 December 1942; Franklin D. Roosevelt to General Fleming, 4 December 1942, WPA Papers, Microfilm #1641, Administrative Washington Correspondence.

94. See WPA Papers, Microfilm #1641, Administrative Washington Correspondence. This total is out of $163,659,000 spent in the state.

95. *Louisville Courier-Journal,* 5 April 1942.

96. Goodman-Paxton Papers, WPA Scrapbook.

97. Lexington did not have a local chapter of the NAACP until 1946 or 1947. See McElfresh and Cooper, "They Fought Hunger." E. Reed Wilson, "History of Lexington, Kentucky" (unpublished manuscript), E. Reed Wilson Papers, Special Collections, M.I. King Library, University of Kentucky, Lexington, Kentucky.

98. T. Arnold Hill to George Goodman, 26 June 1935, Goodman-Paxton Papers, Box 2.

99. Figures are taken from WPA Papers. This figure is perhaps highly inflated. A total of $305,871.26 was allotted for jobs that might possibly have been performed by women. Only $144,994.26 was designated specifically for women. The one-seventh ratio was arrived at by dividing $305,871.26 into the total amount allotted, $2,325,293.26.

100. Leuchtenburg, *Franklin D. Roosevelt,* 130.

101. See Shannon, "Presidential Politics," 146–70.

9. The Last Hurrah?

1. See Lyle W. Dorsett, *Franklin D. Roosevelt and the City Bosses* (Port Washington, New York: Kennikat Press, 1977), 3.

2. Edwin O'Connor, *The Last Hurrah* (New York: Bantam Books, 1956), 330.

3. Chandler interview.

4. Harold F. Gosnell, *Machine Politics: Chicago Model* (Chicago: Univ. of Chicago Press, 1937), 25, 74, 183, 184.

5. Roger Biles, *Big City Boss in Depression and War: Mayor Edward J. Kelly of Chicago* (DeKalb: Northern Illinois Univ. Press, 1984), 76, 78.

6. Ibid., 83.

7. Jewell and Cunningham, *Kentucky Politics,* 13.

8. Ibid.

9. Dorsett, *Franklin D. Roosevelt and the City Bosses,* 3, 6, 114.

10. Jasper B. Shannon et al., *A Decade of Change in Kentucky Government and Politics* (Lexington, Ky.: Bureau of Government Research, 1943), 7.

11. Ibid., 116.

12. See James Joshua Mott, "City Manager Government in Lexington, Ken-

tucky, 1947" (Master's thesis, Univ. of Kentucky, Lexington, Kentucky, 1947), 44; *Lexington Leader,* 17 January 1937.

13. See *Lexington Leader,* 17 January 1937.

14. Mott, "City Manager Government in Lexington, Kentucky, 1947," 44, 69, 70; *Lexington Herald,* 7 October 1937; *Lexington Leader,* 9 December 1938.

15. Mott, "City Manager Government in Lexington, Kentucky, 1947," 128, 134, 44, 26, 45.

16. Jewell and Cunningham, *Kentucky Politics,* 76.

17. See Roger W. Lotchin, "Power and Policy: American City Politics Between the Two Wars," in Scott Greer, ed., *Ethnics, Machines, and the American Urban Future* (Cambridge, Mass.: Schenkman Publishing, 1981), 16.

18. Ibid., 20.

19. Wright, *Lexington: Heart of the Bluegrass,* 193.

20. Mott, "City Manager Government in Lexington, Kentucky, 1947," 128; Jewell and Cunningham, *Kentucky Politics,* 76. For an argument that machines in other cities continued on after World War II, see Raymond E. Wolfinger, "Why Political Machines Have Not Withered Away and Other Revisionist Thoughts," *Journal of Politics* (1972): 365–98; and Bruce M. Stave, *The New Deal and the Last Hurrah: Pittsburgh Machine Politics* (Pittsburgh: Univ. of Pittsburgh Press, 1970).

Epilogue

1. See for example Klotter, *Kentucky: Portrait in Paradox, 1900–1950.*

2. Scott interview.

3. Thomas Underwood to W.F. Klair, 24 January 1936, Thomas Rust Underwood Papers, "Politics, Klair, William F., 1927–1939," Special Collections, M.I. King Library, University of Kentucky, Lexington, Kentucky.

4. Graves, "William Frederick Klair," 34; *Lexington Herald,* 9 October 1937.

5. *Lexington Leader,* 30 October 1937.

6. Ibid.

7. Ibid., 1 November 1937.

8. Ibid.

9. Ibid.

10. Ibid., 30 October 1937.

11. *Lexington Herald,* 31 October 1937; 1 November 1937.

12. Ibid., 2 November 1937; 31 October 1937.

13. See ibid., 1 November 1937.

14. The careers of Mulligan and Klair in Lexington supported the arguments of Brown and Halaby in "Functional Sociology, Urban History, and the Urban Political Machine: The Outlines and Foundations of Machine Politics, 1870–1945." Brown and Halaby's assertion that "machine *contenders* for power emerged earlier and more

often than did dominant machines," and that the "decentralized nature of representation and power in the city was congenial to the emergence and prosperity of these neighborhood organizations, and equally uncongenial to the consolidation of city-wide control," described the "factional" machine of Dennis Mulligan. Brown and Halaby's argument that "to succeed, dominant machines had to institutionalize, render stable, a broad pattern of loyalties by forming durable coalitions and organizing to control, as much as represent, their diverse "supporters" is an apt description of the "dominant" machine of Billy Klair. See Brown and Halaby, "Functional Sociology, Urban History, and the Urban Political Machine," 27.

15. *Lexington Herald,* 1 November 1937.

16. Joel A. Tarr, "The Urban Politician as Entrepreneur," *Mid-America* (January 1967): 62–63.

17. Ibid., 57.

18. I use the phrase "the business of politics" much like Humbert S. Nelli used the phrase "the business of crime" in his *The Business of Crime: Italians and Syndicate Crime in the United States* (New York: Oxford Univ. Press, 1976). Both politicians and syndicate criminals provided services in return for votes or payment.

19. Tarr, "The Urban Politician as Entrepreneur," 62, 67, 55.

20. Ibid., 55.

21. Ibid., 56.

Bibliographical Essay

Since the days of the Tweed ring in New York City, the city boss has been vilified by reformers and castigated by journalists and historians. More recently historians, sociologists, political scientists, and even novelists and motion picture producers have viewed bosses and their machines with increasing objectivity, if not sympathy. In spite of claims that machine politics died with the coming of the New Deal, the city boss continues to interest scholars.

In order to understand the development of urban America, the boss and the political machine must be understood. And according to Alexander Callow, the editor of *The City Boss in America: An Interpretive Reader* (New York, 1976), understanding would come only through scholarly studies of the political machine as an institution: "The city boss is seen no longer as a snarling Satan or as an amusing swashbuckler, but as an integral figure in the history of American urban politics, often a dynamic one performing a role vital to the growth of both the city and its citizens." Callow's view differed markedly from older approaches to bossism and machines.

In *The American Commonwealth* (New York, 1888), James Bryce, British ambassador and honorary member of the American Historical Association, referred to urban government as "one of the conspicuous failures of the United States." Josiah Strong echoed the prevalent pessimism of the period in *The Twentieth Century City* and asserted in *Our Country* that "our largest cities are the worst governed." Strong saw little hope that the trend of misgovernment would be altered, emphasizing only that "the government will become more corrupt, and control will pass more completely into the hands of those who themselves most need to be controlled." This "patrician elitist" interpretation of urban power posed a conflict between the "rich, well-educated, and good on the one side and the corrupt and ignorant on the other." For a useful discussion of varying historical views of bosses and machines see David C. Hammack, "Problems in the Historical Study of Power in the Cities and Towns of the United States, 1800–1960," *American Historical Review* 83 (1978): 323–349. See also Terrence J. McDonald, *Parameters of Urban Fiscal Policy: Socioeconomic Change and Political Culture in San Francisco, 1860–1901* (Berkeley, 1986).

In *The Unheralded Triumph: City Government in America, 1870–1900* (Baltimore, 1984), Jon C. Teaford disagreed with the "patrician elitist" condemnation of urban government. As Teaford's title suggested, cities were generally successful in meeting the needs of residents in the face of drastic industrial changes. Earlier, in 1902, however, Lincoln Steffens confirmed the suspicions of Bryce and Strong and the "patrician elitist" interpretation: "All our municipal governments are more or less bad." Calling this misrule the "shame of the cities," Steffens criticized the bosses, but placed the bulk of the blame for urban corruption on the apathy of America's citizens: "The misgovernment of the American people is misgovernment by the American people." It was this idea that set Steffens's interpretation apart from the "patrician elitist" framework. For Steffens, "the shame of the cities" resulted from reformers, businessmen, and a public that allowed and supported urban misrule. Steffens sought "to demolish the moralistic pretensions of middle-class reform and [exalted] in its stead the pragmatic, pluralistic, humanitarianism of machine politicians." See Lincoln Steffens, *The Shame of the Cities* (New York, originally published in 1902).

Both Richard Hofstadter in *The Age of Reform* (New York, 1955) and Oscar Handlin in *The Uprooted* (New York, 1951) relied on Steffens in their development of what Terrence McDonald called the "political cultural theory" of urban politics, a theory used to legitimate, more than anything else, "the political economy characteristic of the New Deal-Fair Deal tradition." McDonald argued that this "presentist attempt to read the New Deal back into the political machine and to portray the bosses as Franklin Delano Roosevelt 'writ small'" represented a fundamental error in the "political cultural theory."

Since the turn of the century, when Steffens's *The Shame of the Cities* was published, other assessments of the political life of the city with differing explanations of the appearance and longevity of political machines in urban America have appeared. Ironically, it was Steffens himself who suggested alternative interpretations of the role of political machines. Despite his criticism of bossism, Steffens implied that the boss performed a function and a service that was "dictated by the nature of political life in the city."

Sam Bass Warner asserted that "the nature of political life in the city" was centered around a tradition of privatism, a tradition that emphasized the private ambitions of businessmen and politicians alike. In Sam Bass Warner Jr., *The Private City: Philadelphia in Three Periods of Its Growth* (Philadelphia, 1968), Warner maintained that for cities to function properly they "require habits of community life, and attention to sharing scarce resources, and a willingness to care for all men." He concluded that urban America had failed to create such a humane environment, primarily because of "an enduring tradition of privatism in a changing world."

According to Warner, the tradition of privatism abetted a "system of politics which was so weak it could not deal effectively with the economic, physical, and social events that determined the quality of life within the city." Because of this weakness, local, state, and national political bosses emerged in order to control the city and county offices and to benefit from the private business conducted with these governments. The private ambitions held by businessmen and politicians doomed Philadelphia to inefficient government. Warner concluded that except for "the brief and creative union of equalitarian goals and business leadership in the early nineteenth century" the tradition of privatism had kept any one group from understanding the city as a whole and dealing effectively with its problems.

Historian Seymour Mandelbaum agreed with Warner that the American city had been cursed with a lack of cohesion. In *Boss Tweed's New York* (New York, 1965), he described New York City before 1870 as "a fragmented mass, only loosely held together by its internal street car lines, newspapers, mail routes and associations." Mandelbaum argued that Tweed provided the function of interpersonal communication and that Tweed became a symbol for a society with a primitive communications network. As the city grew, Tweed united the elements of a divided society in the only manner that they could be united—"by paying them off."

Some scholars have maintained that Tweed and other bosses were merely reflections of "the growing pains of the American city." For example, in *Boss Cox's Cincinnati: Urban Politics in the Progressive Era* (Chicago, 1968), Zane Miller concentrated on the alterations and tensions experienced in Cincinnati at the turn of the century. According to Miller, conflict between the city's core (the Circle), the periphery (the Zone), and the area of residence of the city's elite (the Hilltop) was eased by George Cox, the city's Republican boss. No graft monger like Tweed, Cox soothed cultural and racial antagonisms, eased the growing pains of the city, and even instituted needed reforms. In short, Cox brought order out of chaos.

In his introduction to an edition of William L. Riordan's *Plunkitt of Tammany Hall* (New York, 1963), Arthur Mann suggested—in another example of the "political cultural theory"—that the machine acted as a social welfare agency and familiarized millions of immigrants with representative government. Other more recent editions of Plunkitt are William L. Riordan, *Honest Graft: The World of George Washington Plunkitt* (St. James, 1993), and Terrence J. McDonald, ed., *Plunkitt of Tammany Hall* (Boston, 1994). Sociologist Robert Merton reinforced this view by arguing that the machine developed as an alternative to a confused and impersonal formal government structure; the machine personalized politics for the "deprived" classes. In his *Social Theory and Social Structure* (New York, 1968), Merton argued that the "key structural function of the Boss is to organize, centralize and maintain in good working condition 'the scattered fragments of power' which are at present dispersed through our political organization."

Merton reinforced the view of Lincoln Steffens and of historians like Hofstadter and Handlin by his "codification" of the "political culture theory" in sociological terms. According to Terrence McDonald, Merton's "structural/functional theory" replaced the "patrician elitist" approach of earlier writers: "Under the aegis of the patrician elitist theory, historians denounced the corruption of the machines and praised the virtue of reformers, whereas those writing within the functional framework praised the pragmatism of the machine and denounced the moralism of the reformers."

Merton maintained that bosses and machines satisfied "the needs of diverse subgroups in the larger community." These subgroups included "deprived" immigrant classes. In his autobiography, Lincoln Steffens recorded his conversation with the Boston ward leader Martin Lomasny, a conversation that Merton included in *Social Theory and Social Structure*. Lomasny related his understanding of the essential function of the boss: "I think that there's got to be in every ward somebody that any bloke can come to—no matter what he's done—and get help. *Help, you understand; none of your law and justice, but help.*"

Under "constitutional restraints" in America the "legal possibility of highly centralized power" was precluded. The system of checks and balances established by Madison and the framers indicated their distrust of power, and the dispersion of power provided by the framers for the national level was also evident, according to Merton, on the local level. Merton cited Herbert Croly's

186 Bibliographical Essay

contention in *Progressive Democracy* that because the dispersion of power made "decision and action" difficult, "a much more human system of partisan government, whose chief object soon became the circumvention of government by law" was necessary. Under the constitution, action was "hemmed in by legal considerations." A "lawlessness of the extra-official democracy was merely the counterpoise of the legalism of the official democracy." Croly argued that because the "lawyer [was] permitted to subordinate democracy to the Law, the Boss had to be called to extricate the victim, which he did after a fashion, and for a consideration." Merton paraphrased Croly's conclusions in sociological terms: "the functional deficiencies of the official structure generate an alternative (unofficial) structure to fulfill existing needs somewhat more effectively."

The "latent" functions of political machines included not only help for the "deprived classes" but also for the business classes—big and small—providing "political privileges which entail immediate economic gains." At the same time, bosses and machines fulfilled the function of "humanizing and personalizing all manner of assistance to those in need." Bosses rendered services as did conventional welfare agencies and settlement houses, but, Merton argued, to assess the function of the political machine adequately "it is important to note not only that aid is provided but the manner in which it is provided." In contrast to the "cold, bureaucratic dispensation of limited aid" given by conventional agencies, were the "unprofessional techniques of the precinct captain who asks no questions, exacts no compliance with legal rules of eligibility and does not 'snoop' into private affairs."

Merton also argued that machines provided social mobility for "those otherwise excluded from the more conventional avenues for personal 'advancement.'" Finally, Merton likened political machines to "legitimate" businesses, both "concerned with the provision of goods and services for which there is an economic demand." Merton offered a sociological basis for bossism and more than anyone else fostered a more sympathetic view of bosses and political machines.

Although Merton's sociological arguments continue to influence historical interpretations of the rise of bosses and machines, historians and sociologists alike have challenged Merton's views. Roger W. Lotchin, for example, suggested in "Power and Policy: American City Politics Between the Two World Wars," in Scott Greer, *Ethnics, Machines and the American Urban Future* (Cambridge, 1981), that for those following the functionalist approach "the connection between immigrants, especially new immigrants, the poor and machine politics has perhaps been exaggerated." Similarly, in *The Politics of Progress* (Englewood Cliffs, 1974), Raymond E. Wolfinger argued that some machines were not "heavily dependent on the votes of the poor and foreign." In "The Rise and Development of Urban Political Machines: An Alternative to Merton's Functional Analysis," *Urban Affairs Quarterly* (December 1, 1988): 242–67, Alan DiGaetano presented a historical analysis to argue that machines developed because of "extensive state-building activities in the second half of the nineteenth century" in the context of federalism rather than because of the inability of city governments to provide "latent" functions for a city's population. It was the "expansion and institutionalization of local state authority," first in public agencies—police, fire, public works—and then in charter reform, that provided a conducive environment for the rise of machines. Centralization of city government predated machines.

Although Terrence McDonald suggested in *Parameters of Urban Fiscal Policy* that the danger exists that "if we abandon the functional framework, having lived so long in its shadow, we may lack any organizing principle for urban political history," he agreed with DiGaetano that a study of state-building could offer a new framework. After all, McDonald argued, the American state was built from the bottom up, "namely, from the local and state levels to the national level—and many of the political struggles for control of government and debates over the proper role of government were conducted in city halls and state legislatures."

While readily admitting a "Merton consensus" on the "abiding presence" of the urban political machine in city politics, sociologists M. Craig Brown and Charles N. Halaby noted in an unpublished conference paper, "Functional Sociology, Urban History, and the Urban Political Machine: The Outlines and Foundations of Machine Politics, 1870–1945," that "there has been surprisingly little progress in systematically describing or accounting for the historical outlines of machine politics." In the conference paper and in "Machine Politics in America, 1870–1945," *Journal of Interdisciplinary History* (winter, 1987): 587–612, Brown and Halaby argued that "without a firmer notion of the 'typical' machine and the prominent variations among machines, the representativeness of each 'case' (i.e., machine) is unclear." The sociologists made a distinction between machines with limited power—"factional" machines—and "dominant" machines that maintained citywide power, controlling the election of the executive and a majority of the city council for at least three straight elections. Significantly, Brown and Halaby noted that cities like Buffalo in the early 1870s and Kansas City before the rise to power of the Pendergast brothers had no machines. Perhaps machine control, at least in the "dominant" sense, was not as prevalent as historical and popular accounts would suggest.

After placing their definition of machines "on a firmer empirical footing," the sociologists assessed "the adequacy of predictions drawn from Robert Merton's functional conception of machine politics—undoubtedly the most influential bit of theory to date." Brown and Halaby found that "factional" machines were more common than "dominant" machines before the 1930s. In the 1930s, however, "dominant" machines reached their apex, only to decline in the late 1930s, causing the writers to conclude that "it seems clear that national level forces"—the New Deal and World War II—began to undermine machine control.

In contrast to Merton's arguments, Brown and Halaby agreed with DiGaetano; "dominant" machines developed as trends in political fragmentation declined. As "strong mayor charters, smaller unicameral councils, nonpartisan and at-large elections, and reform government structures all provided more centralized mechanisms of government . . . fragmentation was mitigated." Furthermore, over time smaller cities were found to be more apt to have "dominant" machines, a trend "contrary to that expected by the functional view" because smaller cities would necessarily have fewer disparate groups in need of services. The writers concluded that "machines became more common in relatively small cities because . . . they remained of a 'manageable' size."

Along with historians and sociologists, novelists used political bosses as subjects for their works. In *The Last Hurrah* (New York, 1956) Edwin O'Connor's Frank Skeffington was described as a man whose "entire career seemed to have been devoted to the contravention of the law," but even Skeffington's political rivals could not overlook the other side of the boss. A fellow politico remembered "the astonishing good-humored audacity of the man which had so often stunned a roomful of opponents" and "the courage, the generosity, the charm, the sheer ability of the man." Bosses added much more than color to the urban scene, however.

In addition to the inefficiency and graft evidenced in political machines in cities around the country, it is also true that machines rendered valuable services and performed an indispensable function for American cities. Whether that function came before or after the increasing centralization of urban government, bosses "bound the citizen to his neighborhood, the neighborhood to the machine, and the machine to a people's politics, humanizing and personalizing the political system, offering to that always endangered species—the underdog—the chance to survive." (See Callow, *City Boss*, 3) The machine flourished, not because it provided "good government" or programs for the "public interest," but because it satisfied the "craving for the things men crave: for money, power, prestige, respect, security and order."

Works such as Mandelbaum's *Boss Tweed's New York* and Alexander Callow's *The Tweed Ring* (New York, 1966) centered on the most infamous of the urban bosses, William Marcy Tweed. According to Plunkitt of Tammany Hall, however, Tweed should not be considered as the prototype of a city boss: "If he only looks after his own interests or shows no talent for scenting out jobs or ain't got the nerve to demand and get his share of the good things that are goin', his followers may be absolved from their allegiance and they may up and swat him without bein' put down as political ingrates." Concerned only with "the big pay-off," Tweed did not function as a "true" boss. A "true" boss provided services, and except for the few members of his ring who profited from the graft, Tweed was not a provider for his constituents.

More in keeping with the practice of "true" bossism were those who controlled Tammany Hall after Tweed was convicted and imprisoned. Writing about the "reformed" Tammany, Gustavus Myers asserted in *The History of Tammany Hall* (New York, 1917) that John Kelly, and the other bosses following Tweed, realized that "a large part of the voting mass cared nothing for good government but looked upon politics solely as a means of livelihood." Kelly profited from Tweed's mistakes not only because he learned that services must be given, but also because he realized the value of moderation; he limited stealing, or "dishonest graft."

Of course, New York does not offer the lone example of boss politics. In "lusty" Chicago, the vice-ridden activities of "Bathhouse John" Coughlin and Michael "Hinky Dink" Kenna in the first ward illustrated at least one machine's connections with underworld activities. See Lloyd Wendt and Herman Kogan, *Bosses in Lusty Chicago: The Story of Bathhouse John and Hinky Dink* (Bloomington, 1971). Alex Gottfried's *Boss Cermak of Chicago* (Seattle, 1962) chronicled the rise of Anton J. Cermak, the Czechoslovak-born boss who united various ethnic populations in Chicago to supplant the Irish-dominated organization of "Big Bill" Thompson. In his work, Gottfried included a "Leadership and Psychosomatic Analysis," a study of Cermak's rise from obscure origins to citywide and statewide prominence. After Cermak, Democratic boss Edward J. Kelly ruled from 1933 to 1947. Unlike Cermak, Kelly cultivated the black vote and provided services for various segments of Chicago's population. See Roger Biles, *Big City Boss in Depression and War: Mayor Edward J. Kelly of Chicago* (Dekalb, 1984). Other studies of bossism in Chicago include

Joel Tarr, *A Study of Boss Politics: William Lorimar of Chicago* (Urbana, 1971), and John Allswang, *A House For All Peoples: Ethnic Politics in Chicago, 1890–1936* (Lexington, 1971).

In Kansas City, the Pendergast brothers also developed a powerful political machine by providing services, along with controlling patronage and dominating the Democratic Party machinery. The Pendergasts not only gave welfare services to the poor in the city's core, but also gained the support of the middle classes in the city's periphery. Younger brother Tom established control of the suburbs, in part through illegal voting tactics, unlike the Republican George Cox in Cincinnati, who gained middle-class support by providing needed reforms. See Lyle W. Dorsett, *The Pendergast Machine* (New York, 1968), and Zane L. Miller, *Boss Cox's Cincinnati.* For more recent studies of the interplay between bossism and reform see James Philip Fadely, *Thomas Taggart: Public Servant, Political Boss, 1856–1929* (Indianapolis, 1997), and James J. Connolly, *The Triumph of Ethnic Progressivism: Urban Political Culture in Boston, 1900–1925* (Cambridge, 1998). Connolly portrays Boston's James Michael Curley as a leading architect of urban reform. For bossism and reform see also Michael P. McCarthy, "On Bosses, Reformers, and Urban Growth: Some Suggestions for a Political Typology of American Cities," *Journal of Urban History* 4 (November 1977): 29–38, and David P. Thelen, "Urban Politics: Beyond Bosses and Reformers," *Reviews in American History* 7 (September 1979): 406–12.

In the South, bosses were also known for their reform activities. In Memphis, reform was coupled with bossism in the person of Edward Crump. Crump tried to identify the needs of almost every interest group of significant size in Memphis; he then answered those needs with the delivery of specific services. This sometimes meant welfare services in the black community, while in other areas reform measures that presented Memphis as a progressive city on the move were in order. See William Miller, *Mr. Crump of Memphis* (Baton Rouge, 1965), and Roger Biles, *Memphis in the Great Depression* (Knoxville, 1986). Martin Behrman, the outstanding leader of the Choctaw Club, followed a similar line in New Orleans. See George M. Reynolds, *Machine Politics in New Orleans, 1897–1926* (New York, 1936). For discussions of urban politics in other southern cities see Carl V. Harris, *Political Power in Birmingham, 1871–1921* (Knoxville, 1977), James B. Crooks, *Politics and Progress: The Rise of Urban Progressivism in Baltimore, 1895 to 1911* (Baton Rouge, 1968), Don H. Doyle, *Nashville in the New South, 1880–1930* (Knoxville, 1985), and Don H. Doyle, *Nashville Since the 1920s* (Knoxville, 1985).

In the North and South, changes in post–Civil War America provided new voting blocs that were exploited by astute political bosses. Migration from the countryside and increased immigration from abroad created a new electorate that proved more advantageous to the Democratic Party, a party in search of ways to rebound from the Civil War and Reconstruction. And with the increasing urban populations came new opportunities, opportunities relished by urban bosses. New construction, the letting of franchises to favored companies, and countless other opportunities for graft were all relied on by the machines as sources of patronage and profit. In addition, the cities' established elites, crowded or displaced by "men of obscure origins," were replaced in positions of influence by groupings of people more likely to be swayed by machine tactics. Methods—many of them centered around the polls—were perfected to take advantage of these emerging blocs of voters. Machines soon controlled the voting places through the issuance of fraudulent immigration papers, and by making use of multiple voters, or "repeaters."

Changing demographics and voting irregularities were found in northern and southern cities alike, as southern politicians were certainly no more reluctant to take advantage of demographic trends than were their northern counterparts. Southern bosses found no dearth of support for their urban machines. In fact, the southern penchant for deferential politics, dating back to colonial times and continuing into the antebellum period, was resurrected in the post–Civil War South. In a sense, southern bosses were the urban, New South counterparts of the rural, Old South planter elite. Political bosses, whose activities are well-documented in larger urban settings to the North, certainly found fertile soil in smaller southern cities as well. Billy Klair's career in Lexington is a good example, but in light of the historiographical debate, a debate dating back to the nineteenth century, where does Billy Klair fit in?

John D. Buenker, in *Urban Liberalism and Progressive Reform* (New York, 1973), thought that bosses of Klair's ilk were "urban liberals" and that the "difference between machines and reformers was minimal." See also George B. Tindall, "Business Progressivism: Southern Politics in the Twenties," *South Atlantic Quarterly* 62 (winter 1963): 92–106, and J. Joseph Huthmacher, "Urban Liberalism and the Age of Reform," *Journal of American History* 49 (1962): 31–41. Although Klair supported reform measures as a young legislator, and even backed the structural reform of commission government as Lexington's boss, the whole of his career makes Buenker's "urban liberal" thesis untenable for Klair. As Roger W. Lotchin pointed out in "Power and Policy," "it would be more realistic to observe that the bosses were power brokers, interested primarily in maintaining their control over affairs, and that reform sometimes served their purposes." Such was the case with Klair.

Klair used reform when it was convenient. Lotchin contended that a power broker's use of reform was not unusual: "Bismarck initiated social welfare legislation in Germany, and Disraeli accepted a large measure of the same kind of reform in Britain in the nineteenth century." Both Bismarck and Disraeli "considered themselves conservatives and both in fact were power brokers. So were the American city bosses of the period 1920–1945." Klair was no Bismarck and no Disraeli, but he was a city boss. And he was a power broker, a title made all the more appropriate by the New Deal. As Harold G. Gosnell argued for Chicago in *Machine Politics: Chicago Model* (Chicago, 1937), with the coming of the New Deal, bosses simply found more services to broker. Such was the case in Lexington.

As I argued in the epilogue of this work, Klair functioned as an entrepreneur—in business and in politics. In "The Urban Politician as Entrepreneur," *Mid-America* (January 1967): 55–67, Joel A. Tarr suggested this entrepreneurial model by listing the various business activities of Chicago politicians. Billy Klair—singly—was involved in most of the same business activities of Chicago politicians listed—collectively—by Tarr.

Tarr asserted that the "typical urban boss was a man who regarded politics as a business and who used his power for personal and party gain. He was a businessman whose chief stock in trade was the goods of the political world—influence, laws, government grants, and franchises—which he utilized to make a private profit." In short, Tarr concluded, the boss was a "political entrepreneur." I use the term "entrepreneurial power broker"—an amalgam of Tarr's and Lotchin's conclusions to describe Klair's niche in the historiographical debate.

The story of Dennis Mulligan, Billy Klair, and politics in the southern city of Lexington, Kentucky, has been pieced together through research in various manuscript collections and newspapers, and through interviews with contemporary individuals. Please refer to the chapter notes for the specific citations to these primary sources.

Photographic Sources

Kentucky Historical Society

Lexington-Fayette County Public Library

Lexington Herald-Leader

Marjorie R. Scott, Lexington, Kentucky

University of Kentucky Special Collections

Carl B. Cone, *The University of Kentucky: A Pictorial History* (Lexington: University Press of Kentucky, 1989).

Wynelle Deese, *The Postcard History Series: Lexington, Kentucky: Changes in the Early Twentieth Century* (Charleston, S.C.: Arcadia Publishing, 1998).

Thomas M. House and Lisa R. Carter, *Images of America: Lafayette's Lexington, Kentucky* (Charleston, S.C.: Arcadia Publishing, 1998). (The original photographs from this book are all housed in UK Special Collections.)

Bettie L. Kerr and John D. Wright Jr., *Lexington: A Century in Photographs* (Lexington: Lexington-Fayette County Historic Commission, 1984).

Index

Breckinridge, William Campbell
Preston, 57
Breezing, Belle, 65, 68
Brennan, Michael Joseph "Mickey," xiv,
23, 78–79, 80, 110
Brown, Craig, 10, 180 n 14
Brown, James Buckner, 81, 82, 85–86,
90, 92, 94, 108
Brown, John Y., Sr.: and Billy Klair, xvi-
xvii, 113–15, 174 n 54; mentioned,
73, 82, 103, 134
Brown, Tom, 28
Bruce, W.W., 7
Brucetown, 6–7, 70
Bryan Station High School, 141
Buckingham, Mary B., 126
Buckingham Theater (Louisville, Ky.),
xiv, 27
Buckley, Christopher, 13
Buenker, John D., 27
Bullock, Frank A., 45, 46, 57
Burnell, Barb, 65

Calvary Cemetery, 19
Camden, Johnson Newlon, 81, 84
Camp Buell, 64, 69
Camp Stanley, 68–69
Cantrill, Florence Shelby, 76, 173 n 33
Cantrill, James Campbell, 81–82, 83,
85, 86
Carlisle, Ky., 120
Cassidy, J. Ernest, 58, 65, 68
Catt, Carrie Chapman, 55
Cermak, Anton J., 82, 145
chamber of commerce (Lexington), 7,
47
Chandler, A.B. "Happy": assessment of
Billy Klair, 35, 36, 37–38, 44, 45, 113,
114, 115, 144, 152, 153; on Ruby
Laffoon, 112–13; challenges Alben

W. Barkley for U.S. Senate seat, 132–
38; mentioned, 80, 99, 147, 174 n 54
Chapman, Virgil M., 152, 153
Charter League: in municipal elections,
104–6, 113, 124, 127; mentioned,
103, 107, 110, 116, 128, 147, 151
Cheapside, 64, 76, 114, 115
Chesapeake & Ohio Railroad, 42
Chicago Bottom, 70
child labor legislation, 30
Chinn, Joseph, 6
cholera, 4
Churchill Downs, 84
City National Bank, 41
Civilian Conservation Corps (CCC),
120–21, 128
Civil Works Administration (CWA),
121–22, 125
Clark, Thomas D.: on Billy Klair, xvi,
36, 37; mentioned, xv, xvii, 99
Clay, Cassius Marcellus, 5, 6, 30, 55,
168 n 1
Clay, Henry, 4, 6, 12
Clay, Laura, 30, 55–57, 58, 76
Cloud, Elizabeth, 72
Cloud, Sonny, 28
Cobb, Irvin S., 77
Coleman, J. Winston, Jr., 77
Collis, B.C., 137
Combs, I. Newton, 152
Combs, Thomas A.: and Billy Klair, 33,
45, 48, 50, 52, 166 n 19; mentioned,
46, 52, 58–59, 60, 84
Combs Lumber Co., 49
Community Chest, 126, 143
Cone, Carl, 30
Congleton, W.T., 103, 104, 106, 107
Congress of Industrial Organizations
(CIO), 131
Conlon, Paul, 17, 18